Conan Doyle's Wallet:

The Creator of Sherlock Holmes

By Patrick McNamara
Psychic-Medium

ISBN: **978-0957415607**

Ghostcircle Publishing

European address:
36a Elbe Street, Fulham, London, SW6 2QP

Web: www.ghostcircle.com

Cover and typesetting: by Karl Fallon

2

Contents

"This book is dedicated to Tom Fallon, **a great spirit,** and a loving family man"

About the Author

Patrick McNamara

British Psychic-Medium

Patrick McNamara has received spirit contact since he was a small child and has been a psychic medium all his life. He resides in England. Through his physical mediumship abilities, Patrick's aim is to prove to others that we do live on after this life in a spiritual dimension. There is no death.

A long-standing member of The Society for Psychical Research (SPR) in London, Patrick tries to provide objective scientific proof of supernatural phenomena by capturing spirit evidence on camera. The group and website, *ghostcircle.com* was created to distribute his evidence.

Since leaving school, Patrick has been a serial entrepreneur, investing in different business areas. He has also worked in the entertainment industry. Patrick's main interests are history, art, antiques, and reading. But his passion is the paranormal, especially investigating old haunted houses. Today he spends his time as a psychic-medium advisor and consultant.

See Patrick's web site http://www.ghostcircle.com

Foreword

This is a book about Sir Arthur Conan Doyle, his life after death, and the philosophies he imparted to me from the spirit world. I bought his wallet at a public sale. These items and the subsequent events from this purchase compelled me to write about him. Before you learn more about my relationship with Sir Arthur Conan Doyle, I must tell you that I am a psychic-medium. Our relationship is that of the spiritual realm.

Under the guidance of Sir Arthur Conan Doyle, I wrote this book to show that the way we live our lives here on earth can affect our spiritual lives in the afterlife. Its aim is also to enlighten those who have lost their loved ones, and provide encouragement to those who feel that they are lacking direction in their lives. If you like Conan Doyle's books, you will enjoy this one too!

Sir Arthur Conan Doyle died on July 7th 1930, but his spirit is alive. We know his physical body ceased to exist on earth but the essence that made up his body lives on. Sir Arthur crossed to the 'other side' where we all live when we die. What does this mean? It means that we do NOT die. Nobody does. We just change our state of existence; just like ice becomes water when it melts or turns into steam when it is heated. The physical body dies, but the personality or spirit survives.

What are the revelations that Sir Arthur wants to share? Most of it is concerned with knowledge about the afterlife; the new world in which he now lives. Sir Arthur communicated his revelations so that I could write the findings. I have seen Sir Arthur, and we have interacted. Through the items I found in his wallet I will reveal the things that were most meaningful to him: his family, his belief in the afterlife, the search for truth, and the messages he received from the spirit world himself. Having discovered an incongruous item in his wallet I wondered why Sir Arthur had kept it close to the things he cherished. This particular item of interest consisted of two paper picture masks held together. One of the silhouette cut-outs was more important than the other, as I later discovered. He kept it with him at all times. "But why" I asked. The intriguing answer was revealed to me clairvoyantly one night by Sir Arthur Conan Doyle himself.

Although Sir Arthur is no longer living in our physical world he is still transmitting his beliefs today as passionately as he was in life during the 1920's until just before his death. Conan Doyle inspired me to write about the relevant spiritual philosophy that can be applied to your own life, and to encourage you to find the truth for yourself. The message written on these pages will hopefully bring comfort and understanding to those who fear death, or have lost someone dear to them. I can give you my complete assurance that we all survive death. Being a medium has given me the chance to provide proof to others, and in turn received it myself. I have encountered some sceptics who disregard the evidence I have provided, but they represent a minority. Before I explain in more detail look at the magnificence of life, nature, and the 'great plan' in operation. Can you really believe that we have one life, one chance, one existence, and then oblivion? If that is the case, then ask yourself? 'Why be good?', 'Why be moral?', 'Why care about anyone or anything?' It's because the spirit or the soul within us drives our thinking, our feelings, and our consciousness. We distinguish right from wrong.

This book is not about religion but rather the start of a philosophy for a better life. The philosophy is based on the revelations given to me as a medium by Sir Arthur Conan Doyle. This was done to assist people in leading a richer more fulfilling life based on spiritual laws. You will also read the story of how I came into possession of Sir Arthur's wallet and the incredible items within it. The message he conveyed to me about surviving death is the same belief I and many others share. Our personality continues exactly as we were on earth. However race, religion, colour, and sexuality make no difference once we die. What matters most are the thoughts and actions we carry out during our life on earth. This governs the level of existence we'll achieve in the next life - the spirit realm.

I must add a proviso here; that everything in this book was told to me from Sir Arthur Conan Doyle's words and that you should take what "you can understand". Indeed any of the information that I have written I believe it to be accurate from what I have been given.I believe that death is not the end but finding answers to your own questions is far more interesting and you should use the information in this book to help you live your life explore spirituality. The message is simple:

Take what you can understand, leave that which you find difficult to believe, search for your own answers.

Introduction

The material things we possess in this world are unnecessary once we die or cross over to the spirit world as it is frequently referred to. We can't take our possessions or money with us because we actually don't need them. We spend too much energy focusing on the mundane things in life instead of focusing on things that really matter, such as love, helping one another, and growing in spirituality. These are the things which we can take with us to the spirit world. You take all the love you have received in your life, including all the thoughts and memories good, and bad, that you had right up to the moment before you expire.

How can you carry this love into the afterlife? Does it stay in your heart? You probably asked yourself how can this be if the heart stops and decays? Do you believe our soul survives the experience of the physical deterioration to later transcend and reach our final destination which is heaven, Nirvana or the afterlife? This has been a well-kept secret for thousands of years since the beginning of civilisation. The Egyptians, Romans, and Greeks have always believed in the afterlife. They had their prophets and oracles, astrologers and mediums. We, in the 21st century, are close to proving through science that death is not the end. Our body changes into a finer substance when we die. This substance is finer than subatomic particles. These particles allow our spirit to move through people and matter. Although we cannot see an atom with the naked eye we know it exists. We also know through science that atoms are made up of protons, electrons, and neutrons. These atomic particles are made up of subatomic particles called 'quarks'. According to science these fine particles are part of the basic building blocks of the universe. Our world is made up of matter; the world of spirit is made up of 'ether', and even finer particles which are called 'vibrations'. Each of these vibrations is unique and infinite in number. They are so microscopic that matter is no barrier. These vibrations are what we become when we die.

We are made up of vibrations which form subatomic particles, and these in turn, make up atoms, molecules, cells, organs, blood, bones, and so forth. The vibrations pulsate at different frequency levels. When we die our physical body dematerialises, but our spirit (which is made up of these vibrations) survives. The reason we cannot see the spirit is because it vibrates at a speed faster than light. Einstein was mistaken when he said that nothing can travel faster than the speed of light. If these vibrations are traveling faster than the speed of light then those who die cannot be seen by the naked eye except when they materialise as apparitions or ghosts. Therefore they are not detectable (yet) by our current scientific instruments. The 'dead' cannot touch people per se because their chemical constitution passes through physical matter. So how do we know that people are transformed into these finer vibrations if science cannot prove it? This is where mediums come in.

What is a medium? A medium is a person who has developed an attunement to vibrations. They are an interface between this world and the afterlife. There are many different types of mediums. The definition of a [spiritual] medium is 'a person who makes themselves available to the spirit world so that members of the spirit world can communicate with people who are still alive.' What is the spirit world? It's where we come from and where we go back once our spirit is released. I am a spirit in a physical body. You are a spirit in a physical body. Every living thing on earth has the power of spirit within it including all animals, minerals, nature, the earth, and our oceans.

Based on these findings another question arises. Can you be a medium? Yes you can. You are a spirit incarnated in a human body. Unfortunately only a few have managed to develop mediumship. Mediumship is the ability of a person (the medium) to experience and/or to tell others about their experiences of contact with spirits of the dead, spirits of non-corporeal entities, and/or nature spirits. In addition to experiencing these spiritual phenomena directly the medium generally facilitates communication between non-mediumistic people and spirits who may have messages to share.

How does mediumship development begin? Development involves two aspects: first it is your desire to become a medium which is picked up in spirit, and second the spirit world gravitates towards you because of your thoughts. The process begins from there but desire and dedication is required from you to make this really happen. The spirits will always help as long as you have the willingness to expand your mediumship. The spirits will guide you to evolve your abilities and sensitivity.

Learning to develop your mediumship skills can take years to achieve and this was my own experience. Some people are actually already sensitive which means they can develop more quickly. However the overall experience will change your life for the better. I should add that I am also clairvoyant, that is, I am able to see images in my mind in the past, present, or future. I interpret these images and hopefully give an accurate message. I also hear clairaudiently which means the spirits speak to me in my mind. To best depict this imagine the stereo effect with headphones where you have sound in the middle of your head. Clairaudience does not come to me as often as clairvoyance.

Through the spirits I am also a healer. The spirits send healing rays that flow through me to help individuals who are ailing. Thoughts are energy and they go out like radio waves which are made up of electromagnetic energy. This healing energy, or absent healing, as we mediums call it, is sent to a person in the form of a wave and works on them unconsciously to make them feel better or heal an illness. Some healers practice energy channelling through the hands which emanates either a warm or cool flow. I do this occasionally and it is very satisfying.

And finally, I am a physical medium. Physical mediumship is very rare due to the punishment that one's body takes from allowing sprits to materialise from their world into our world. To do this they take substances from my body to form what is called 'ectoplasm'. This substance can also be taken from other physical objects like clothes, carpets, and furniture, in a psychic circle, but it mainly comes from the physical medium's body. Once the ectoplasm is made a spirit can clothe itself in this material to be seen in our world. This is usually done in a séance, or psychic circle as I prefer to call it. It can be physically painful as it leaves the medium depleted and weary for 24 hours or even longer.

If you are looking for the answers to the universe, the afterlife and the spirit world, this book will provide a starting point. I have tried to provide some answers passed on to me from the spirit world by Sir Arthur Conan Doyle. This is the story of Sir Arthur Conan Doyle's' wallet and how he communicated with me through the items in his wallet.

Chapter One

My Early Years

I didn't have the best start in life. Right from the beginning my chances of survival were slim. I was born eight weeks premature; I could have been an Aries instead of the bull Taurus. My premature birth was brought on by my mother straining over a washing mangle (used to squeeze the water out of clothes) which is well before the days of tumble dryers. Considering the conditions I was born into there must have been some divine help to get me through the first few days of my life.

The birth was induced by a midwife in the front room in Tynemouth Street, Fulham. Even though I was premature there was no chance of me being put in a life support machine in my day. No the best my parents could do, and I don't blame them (as I was not expected to survive) was to put me in a shoebox filled with cotton wool. The small box was then placed in an old cupboard with the door closed over to keep the draught away.

I survived those early months but I was never in good health. My body seemed to get everything going, chest infections, whooping cough, mumps, and measles. You name it, I had it. I was always underweight; so much so that I went to a special school where the children were either terminally ill, or not expected to survive. Only two classmates from that school lived to see the end of our school years - myself and another boy who went into the Royal Navy. Even the teachers were terminally ill and they all passed away during school.

So I had death on my door step all through my life. Looking back now I can see that the school was a strange place really. However there were some good points. I met a very wise teacher and mentor called Alex. He was of Indian origin and could do lots of tricks like an Indian fakir. He was terminally ill too although I didn't know it at the time. Alex had a great physical strength while being quite short in stature. Alex could pick me up with ease on one hand. I learnt lots of interesting things from him. His subjects were English and History. He kind of looked out for me and encouraged me to mix with the other children as I was a bit of a loner. I preferred his company to my classmates. The other children used to call me the professor. However I made the best of the situation as I always do. We were allowed to do what we liked to a certain extent. They organised lots of school outings to museums, stately homes, cathedrals, pretty villages, scenic areas and even picnics. I travelled all over and saw the best England has to offer.

I enjoyed school and read lots of books. I was an avid book reader in my younger years, and I am still the same now. By the age of ten I had read all the classics, like Dickens, Robert Louis Stevenson and Jules Verne. By eleven I was delving into Roman, Greek and Egyptian history. Reading in those days helped me step out of the harsh realities of this world. Books are wonderful things and help you escape your problems for a while like the movies.

I grew up in the 1950's which was full of hardship still lingering from the Second World War, people were poor and there was rationing. Our family was large. I grew up with five brothers and two sisters so everything had a competitive edge. Meal times were especially frantic. Feeding time in our house was like when you feed puppies. When food was ready we all descended on the table and only the strongest and biggest seemed to get the most food. There wasn't a lot of food to go round.

In our first house there were six children, but that rose to eight later on with two sisters and six brothers. We all slept in a large double bed. There were four on each side of the bed at the time in one small room. When the two girls grew up they shared a double bed. On top of the bed covering us were two army surplus blankets from the Second World War and the names of the soldiers and their serial numbers painted on them. One of the names was R. Moss.

In winter I can remember waking up because it was so cold and seeing frost on the blanket that had hardened as ice that you could crack. We used to go to jumble sales where we picked up most of our clothes. I was quite a canny buyer and a good haggler when buying my goods. Although we never had a lot Dad and Mum made sure we never went without, and we were always clean. Baths were in tin bath in front of an open fire. Our toilet was outside and you would never take out a newspaper to read, I can tell you, especially in winter.

My Dad worked in a pet shop that specialised in selling tropical fish. He would make extra money collecting fish worms from the mud banks on the river Thames normally when the tide was out in the early morning. Dad sold the worms in plastic bags on to other pet shops; as tropical fish need these worms to give them a good lustre and keep them healthy. Some of these worms were also fed to the fish in his shop.

I can vividly remember getting up at 5:00am or earlier to go down to the Thames near Lots Road, then to the Chelsea Embankment, and up to Vauxhall bridge with Dad. We would crack the Ice near the water's edge as it was so cold. The worms were sifted into buckets and taken home later where we would wash the mud off them. This cleaning could take hours where we wash the worms under a cold tap to clean them. Tubeworms were the best food for tropical fish so we could make a good living from collecting them, but it was hard going.

Another profitable line was collecting water fleas from the local ponds using a net to scoop them off the top of the water. Dad could get three pence a bag. The shop he worked in not only sold tropical fish, but it had monkeys, turtles, dogs, cats, you name it we had them. One of the strangest pets I saw were man eating toads from South America. They looked like little fat middle-aged old men. All they were missing were bowler hats and umbrellas. If you threw meat with a bone into the tank all you would see is mass writhing and frothing as they picked the bone clean.

I can remember when I was in the shop one day and a container full of geckos escaped in the pet shop and we were running around the shop trying to catch them all. We never managed to capture them all as some got into the local buildings nearby and the shop walls. Every now and then one would appear in the shop. I remember for years afterwards there was always a report of geckos being seen in the mansion blocks nearby. One thing is for sure there were no reported problems with cockroaches in the shop, or those buildings.

There was also the story of when I was out with my dad when he went over to a pet shop in the east end of London. He went there because there was a Lion who used to sit in the shop window and he had a contract to look after him as the owner was too nervous to go near him, but he still had him in his shop. Thinking about it now it was pretty cruel to have this scenario and it would not happen these days but in the early 1950's it was still a different world. In the shop windows was this toothless, well virtually toothless, old lion. And he would pace around this cage in the big window. I have a great memory of my Dad, who loves animals, sitting in the cage with this big old lions' mouth open cleaning his teeth. The Lion was very tame and placid but can you imagine seeing something like that today!

Life was very hard, but I always made the best of my situation and was working hard in my early teens bringing in good money. The entrepreneurial spirit was definitely with me and I saw opportunities for making money everywhere. The sixties were good times to start businesses or make money. In my early teens I had a coal bag delivery round bringing these bags to my neighbours. I also sold firewood door to door, and did house clearances. These were the days of the great London smog when everyone had a fire for cooking or heating their house.

I worked for an entrepreneur called Danny Mahoney who had a shop nearby. It used to be an old dairy so he had a big freezer room, and was the first person I know who sold meat pre-packed. He also owned a chicken farm down the country where we travelled to and collected fresh eggs and chickens to sell. Any excess food, or anything near its sell by date he would always give to me for my mum. He was a generous person. This really helped put food on our table with ten hungry mouths to feed. As I said, I also did house clearances and I would buy or take away old furniture which other people would then buy from me.

I always kept an eye on old renovations in my area. These were the days when people threw out antiques into skips. I sold everything and anything. The money came thick and fast, so much so, that when we moved to a big house in Racton Road, Fulham, I managed to get my own room. Sometimes I was earning more than my Dad so I helped stock the house with food and furnish it where needed. I earned about £8 to £12 on a good week when the average wage was £5. If you were in Fulham then you would have seen me smoking a cigar walking down the high street. I liked a drink as well. To relax I would build a nice fire in my room and sit in my Queen Anne armchair, smoking a cigar, and having a brandy. I wouldn't recommend it now to any teenagers; times have changed indeed especially with regard to smoking and drinking.

My brothers and sisters were not always nice to me; I suppose it was jealousy and sibling rivalry. I had to keep my room locked as things would "disappear" otherwise. We moved around a lot as a family mainly because it grew larger. From Tynemouth Street we moved to May Street where we stayed about six to seven years, and finally ended up in Racton Road where the rest of my family lives now.

Racton Road was, and is still today quite haunted. I lived there during my teenage years and was quite sensitive as a teenager, but my psychic abilities were about to take a change of direction around the age of sixteen when I believe a spirit possessed me.

Chapter Two

Psychic Development

I was born with natural psychic abilities. I may have inherited my psychic genes, if there is such a thing, from my grandmother on my Mums side as she was very psychic and could see spirits.

My earliest memories of seeing spirits occurred around the age of four where I used to talk to a young blonde haired boy in the side alley of the house in Tynemouth Street. My Gran used to ask me how my friend was so I used to pop outside and ask him if he was there. We would have conversations and I would tell my grandmother about them. Unfortunately my mother was sceptical, and called it fantasy and rubbish, whereas my grandmother would stick up for me and tell my Mum off. She was the only one who really understood the psychic ability in me. She would always say to my Mum that I would rise to the very top in life.

The little boy I used to talk to faded out of my life as my Mum kept scolding me about talking to him. I used to get so much grief over talking to him that eventually the connection became harder to hold and I lost it, but not my psychic ability. I was extremely sensitive to people criticizing my abilities. My brothers and sisters used to tease me all the time about it so I invariably had some fights with them, as you do when you are young. This teasing actually helped toughen me up as a person; otherwise my sensitivity would have made me miserable.

Many children are aware of the spirit world when they are very young. They lose this ability as they grow up because other people knock their belief in spirit friends out of them. In a way I didn't lose this ability as I grew older, but it was suppressed. The problem for a young psychic child really is the sensitivity to the world around them. This sensitivity can cause them to be incredibly hyperactive. If a young child sees invisible friends then they should be encouraged as a negative reaction can only cause frustration and anger to the child who believes what he is seeing to be true. I was very much attuned to the spirit world when I was three to four years old. I only found peace among nature and animals.

By five or six years of age I could see people walking up and down the street disappearing into buildings, or emerging through doorways, it was strange and normal to me.

When we grow up as children our mental growth needs to be stimulated through our imagination. Our imagination should be encouraged as well as the physical growth combined with a properly balanced food diet. We want children to develop artistically so we get them to paint and play with Lego, or plaster scene.

Being psychic as a child enabled me to see spirits and that way I could live in two worlds, theirs and mine. I could speak to them and ask questions so my mind was stimulated much earlier than other children. My big problem was my mother who told me I was stupid and my brothers called me crazy.

This caused me untold grief but I know I am a better person for it as I have a great imagination which I believe was a result of the early connection to spirit world. Spirit friends should be encouraged, not discouraged, when a child is aware of them. Einstein once said that if he had to start life all over again he would rather have imagination than intellect.

I had those instincts when I knew trouble was near me. It came like a dark cloud moving towards me. I instantly knew there was trouble ahead. It's kind of like knowing when arguments are about to happen. If you have had that experience you will understand. I understand it now as some people think an argument in their mind before they say it. So what actually occurs is that these thoughts start to form a dark cloud around the person in their aura. If you are a sensitive, like myself, then you can pick up on this phenomena.I not only felt people's thoughts, but on occasions I saw spirits as well. My Dad was a Catholic and Mum was born from a non-practicing Jewish mother. We used to go to the Catholic Church on Sundays, and I really didn't like it as the people there were not very nice. You would think people who go to church would be good people wouldn't you, but invariably I found they said the prayers but didn't practice what they preached.

I could read their thoughts sometimes and it was not always pleasant. Some people were dedicated and spiritual, others were bored out of their mind but going out of conscience, and the rest going because of duty. Another reason for not liking Sunday mass was that I would see, and feel, lots of nasty spirits around the door of the church where they would wait for people to latch on to coming out from mass. They can jump into people's aura as the people move near them. It was the people's attitude that kept them in their aura. It was like a pickup joint at the back door. There were good and bad spirits hanging around waiting for victims, or the good ones were there trying to prevent the bad ones attaching to peoples auras. It can be a right old battle ground you know. It is people's attitude that attracts these spirits. How they think, how they feel, whether their mood is up or down. Like likens to like as they say. I will discuss this further.

I remember a frightening waking nightmare when I was living in Tynemouth Street. There were six of us in the bed that night, three up three down, with our army surplus blankets from the First World War, and coats thrown on top to cover us. I was in the middle. I remember hearing horses approaching and the sound of a carriage. The room became bitterly cold - colder than it was earlier. The reason was because I was having a psychic experience, and the temperature in the atmosphere normally drops quite suddenly when this happens, as it was happening now. The hooves became louder as the horses approached from my left where the window on the street was. I knew there couldn't be horses coming through the wall but it was absolutely real at the time. I was awake and I could see my brothers and sisters were fast asleep. I put my head under the covers as it got louder and louder. The hooves of horses could be heard crunching on the sound of gravel. The horse's harnesses were rattling, and I heard the sound of a wooden carriage creaking. It came to a sudden halt in the middle of the bedroom. I was still under the covers and I could feel horses breathing above the blankets and hear their snuffles as they gasped for air. Then I heard the sound of a carriage door opening and two foot falls down some wooden steps from the coach and on to the ground and a door closing behind the individual who had disembarked. Then I heard a horses whip crack and the sound of horses shooting off into the distance. I know it sounds hard to believe but I could hear every sound exactly as I've described, and I could also see these images even though I was still under the covers. I was only six at the time. I was wide-awake and terrified. It was very real and is still clear in my mind even today. Dreams aren't usually vivid afterwards. Incidentally my house at Tynemouth Street is one house away from Townmead Road which was a coaching route in Victorian times, not a major one though, and the road followed the river down to Wandsworth Bridge as it still does today. I guess it could be described as a loop in time. It happened once and may happen again. It could have been a residual haunting. Certain Hauntings can be described as "atmospheric memories" echoing from the past that have put a permanent stain in the building or the atmosphere, hence, they are sometimes called residual memories.

As a small child my mother used to have a nap in the afternoon. She would always take a pile of women's magazines into the back room and pile them on the bed. Invariably she would place me next to her on the bed against the wall. On one particular afternoon I was lying there on the bed and she was engrossed in her magazine reading when at the base of the bed a grey blue mist appeared. The mist started to form the outline of a figure which began to materialize into the form of a very tall skeleton, well very tall compared to me. On his right hand I could see a big ring with a blue stone. I watched the skeleton for about twenty seconds in wonderment. I decided to tell my mum that there was something at the end of the bed. She took no interest and told me to be quiet. I started to tug her arm to make her see this apparition still standing there. Finally she lowered her magazine and saw the skeleton standing there. She started to shake and jumped up, started to scream, and nearly wrenched my arm out of my socket as she flung herself out of the door dragging me like a sack of coal. If that wasn't bad enough the skeleton was starting to move in an animated way towards us as we bolted out of the door. Mum decided to leave the house and head for the neighbours' next door - a lady called Wynn.

Then a haunting story was told to her over a cup of tea. Wynn informed my mum that an old man called Mr Joyce used to live in our house and he wore a large blue stoned ring on his right hand exactly as I saw it. He was very tall and had actually passed away in that room. My mother not being the brave person that I remember immediately swapped rooms with us children and ordered Dad to move the bed within minutes after he arrived home from work. It was a strange incident indeed, and I would add that Mr Joyce must not have liked children, or more likely didn't like my mum, as he never appeared to us again!

We moved to May Street in Fulham when I was about seven. It was like a small cottage. The house was an improvement on the rat-infested Tynemouth Street with its orange box walls and outside toilet. The house had a nice garden with an extra room and a bath. Some parts were dark because the windows were small and I felt depressed in some areas of the house. Of course the place was haunted as well. I had a feeling of being watched by some entity. When this happened I used to get a foul smell around me and I felt the presence of a nasty man with this.

My sister Joan was the eldest girl, and she had her own room. I felt the presence of this nasty man in her room sometimes. He would try and frighten her so that he could draw energy from her aura. I understand this now because this is how some of the nasty spirits work. They use fear to gain their energy just like a drug addict needs drugs. I can remember on a few occasions that the ceiling lampshade would move in circles round and round for sometimes up to an hour. Joan was frightened at first and would shout out for somebody to come and sit with her until it stopped, which it invariably did. In the end she actually got used to it as she is a strong psychic as well. In the downstairs living room I often saw a black mongrel running around the room. On one occasion it jumped into the air at my face and disappeared.

My sister Joan is very psychic herself. When she got married she moved into a rented basement flat near Earls Court. She got a very cheap rent on the place. She soon found out why it was so cheap. It was quite a dark flat as far as I remember - most basement flats are I suppose. Soon after moving in she started to tell me about the servant bells ringing constantly even though they were disconnected.

I used to pop round there from time to time. On one occasion I was sitting in her kitchen. The room has a glass door to allow light in from the yard at the back. I suddenly saw a shadow of what looked like an old man with a cloth cap on his head. It was so solid that the light in the kitchen was blocked out. I said to myself, "who the hell is in the back yard?" I thought it might be a burglar.

I immediately launched myself at the door and within seconds I standing in the back yard and couldn't see anybody. Nobody could have physically disappeared from the yard as there was a high wall at the back that would have been impossible to have jumped over by the time I got there. I checked the outside toilet (still had them in my day) and found no trace of this old man. I later saw him again in the front room of the house as a shadow walking in front of the window. It was getting dark in the late afternoon and although the light was off there was light coming in from the street. This light projected a silhouette and I saw his flat cap with grey hair and a green jacket with a white collared shirt. I immediately reached for the light switch. The light came on and he disappeared with the blink of an eye.

One day I stayed in Joan's overnight and woke up to see a nasty ghost who looked like the picture of Shakespeare. The man was balding on top with grey hair around the sides. He wore a high-necked cape like Dracula would wear in those old movies. I say he was nasty as he looked at me with malevolent eyes and I could feel these horrible vibrations coming off him. My Mum, Joan, and my other sister Sally all saw the same figure from time to time. He was definitely haunting the place.

The most frightening incident in the flat happened to Joan. She always wore a gold chain with a cross around her neck but one day she had a rash on her neck which was irritated by the chain so she took it off and then decided to have a shower to relax as it was quite warm. As she got into the shower she could feel a pair of hands around her neck choking her. The grip became tighter and tighter and nothing she did could shake off the invisible grip. As Joan is psychic herself she briefly saw the face of the entity and it was this evil man who looked like Shakespeare. Scrambling out of the shower covered in soap gasping for air she remembered the gold crucifix was on a bathroom shelf. The moment she grabbed it and prayed the choking grip was released and she could breathe again. Joan phoned my mum who immediately came around as she only lived a few streets away. My mum described seeing Joan incredibly upset as she relayed the story to her. On Joan's neck Mum could clearly see red fingerprint marks left by the ghost who attacked her. They were still there the next day for me to see when I called in. It was a very haunted flat. You felt like you were being watched, it was depressive, there were horrible smells, the lights went on or off, and as I said the servants bells were ringing independently all the time. A baby was heard crying from time to time but there were no children in the flat or next door either side of the house.

We later found out that the row of houses where she lived was built on land that had previously been a mental institution. It had stood there from the 16th century. It was knocked down in the late 19th century to build the same houses on and the spirits that had died there lived on in their reality, hence the haunting. I know for a fact that the flat must still be haunted because it is constantly up for sale whenever I have passed it by from time to time.

Chapter Three

My School Years

The most peaceful times of my early years were when I went to a special open-air school called Charterfield. The reason I went there was because I was ill from an early age and was not expected to live. I always seemed to be ill. You name it I had it, whooping cough, mumps, measles, pneumonia, diphtheria, scarlet fever, and German measles.

I was very skinny then and suffered from a very bad chest. It was a very unusual school - it was called an "open air school" because the children who went there were not expected to live mainly because they were all ill or they had terminal illnesses. Even the teachers who taught us were ill. I was a bit of a loner and did not really partake in lessons but sat at the back and read my books. I was reading the classics books and roman history so the teachers left me to my own devices. My classmates used to call me the professor. There was no pressure on us and we didn't take exams, what was the point as we were not expected to survive. We went on lots of day trips and excursions to places like The Tower of London, Canterbury, and Warwick Castle, anywhere in England really.

As I described earlier, I struck up a friendship with one teacher called Alex Sing. He taught History and was dying from cancer although at the time I didn't know it. He encouraged me to mix with the children, but I just wanted to read and listen to his wisdom. He was very wise and charming in a way. He told me stories about magic and the Indian fakirs.

Alex was short in stature but strong physically, as strong as an ox. Alex took a shine to me and I to him. I could relate more to him than the children around me. He was very well travelled and knew history, geography, languages; you name a topic and he could talk about it. I could ask him questions about philosophy or the different major religions. He opened my mind to lots of things. He always said "Don't take anything on face value; always investigate." So I did. I bought lots of books and basically educated myself. I can give an opinion about most subjects by applying what Alex said to me although I have no educational qualifications.

During school breaks or free time I would head off to the fields around the school and lay down on the grass communing with nature. By this I mean tuning into the nature forces around me, the grass, the trees, the flowers, and of course any spirit guides coming close to me. It was a wonderful time, and it kept me sane from the poor children around me who were often sad, and looking back now I guess it probably helped heal me as I became stronger the more I attuned to the nature around me. Quite often I felt as if I could sense the grass and the trees growing around me. How do I know this? It's so hard to explain. We have so many senses within us that remain dormant right through our life.

Some people manage to open up these senses but they are dulled by distractions of our material world. The quietness of the school environment in the countryside allowed me to expand some of these senses. While I was lying there on the grass I felt a golden light surrounding me. It was a relaxing pulsating energy of supreme peace and stimulation. If there was an animal nearby I could detect their presence before seeing them. Each animal had a different "sense" about it. Rabbits had a different sense to birds for example. I have never been able to recapture this ability mainly because I live in London, but I can meditate and get the gold presence around me. It is quite literally like having sunlight in your room when it is in complete darkness. When you get this presence there is nothing comparable on this planet. The gold light comes from higher spiritual guides who are present with you while you meditate. The light comes from their aura linking with yours. It is a high like no other; you feel great all day, and the next day, smiling from the inside out.

Eventually I was on the move again this time from May Street to Racton Road as our family was bigger then. I had five brothers and two sisters who were all now growing into teenagers, so we needed space. The house in Racton Road only had five bedrooms so we still had to share, but we had more space than May Street. I remember going to see the new house. It was a warm summer afternoon. After having a look round the house which was empty we all trooped out with my sister Joan and I being the last ones out. Just before closing the door we both heard lots of voices, people running around, banging upstairs, and doors slamming. We both looked at each other and Joan ran out white with fear. I didn't have any fear but found it quite interesting. I closed the door with a smile on my face and a comfortable feeling that I would enjoy staying here. I was right because I eventually got my own room.

I was able to stamp my character into my own bedroom. This was very important to me not only for living space, but I needed to be meditating more with my guides who were becoming more familiar to me. I could now start to grow more as a person while expanding my psychic abilities. The room had a fireplace which I liked to sit next to and read my books in a nice Queen Anne chair. Three people haunted the room, a young boy with blonde hair, a policeman and an older lady. We later found out that a policeman lived there during the war and the lady was a teacher who had lived there. The old lady was seen by most of the family. She wore a beret and walked from the Kitchen to the Living room. Her apparitions usually happened during wintertime for some reason.

As I said earlier my room was very active if I use haunting terminology. The opposite of this is residual. At times it was as if there seemed to be a vortex

30

of energy in the room which caused these hauntings. A vortex is like a charged rotating field of energy that acts as a doorway between dimensions which can be sensed but not normally seen. Out of this vortex one day came what can only be described as a master spirit guide because the whole room filled with the gold light of his presence when he appeared. He was transparent in this gold light. His eyes imparted joy, peace and contentment as he smiled at me. The feeling of Love from this spirit was overwhelming. He had a bald head and wore what can only be described as a fur collared sable gown. His hands were crossed in front of him. I have never seen a vision as beautiful as this before, or since this occurred. Meeting with this being of light had such a profound effect on me that my physical body, or spirit, was buzzing for two days afterwards. This was a turning point for me because, just like Saul, I was now about to start my road to Damascus where my life changed in a completely different direction to the one I thought I was going.

Chapter Four

My Road to Damascus

I said earlier that I felt I was possessed in my early teen years. When people talk about possession they usually think of the exorcist or Christ casting out devils from possessed people. The Exorcist is an extreme example of possession, very extreme. For that to happen takes a huge amount of energy (thought energy) and certain conditions. In reality possession can in fact be temporary, and they happen to people more often than they know.

In fact a lot of obsessions can in fact be described as possessions as well. I will explain this more later on, but my road to Damascus began around the age of sixteen when I was playing or mucking about in the church garden next to my house in Racton Road.

The Church that was there has been demolished now but before it was removed there was a small graveyard in the grounds. One day I jumped into the church graveyard to scrump some plums. While there I stepped on something sticking out of the ground. With my shoe heel I managed to dig it out from under the grass. I pulled out what was in fact a hard cardboard box that was thrown there by some parishioner after a funeral I guess. The lid was taped down on so I undid it and put my hand in. I brushed the ashes with my hand. I felt this strange feeling come over me. I suddenly became dizzy with a sick feeling in my stomach. I felt so ill that I went back to the house and fell asleep in my chair. I got into bed later but couldn't read to get to sleep. I could hear this clock ticking all the time like a grandfather clock. I stopped all the clocks in the house hoping that it would remove this sound in my head. I kept asking my dad if he could hear it but of course he couldn't.

From that day on I became a different person. I drank more, smoked cigars, lost my energy and drive for making money. I basically started to lose my way in life. Looking back now I could see that I had a form of possession from a spirit that was attached to the ashes I put my hand into. I have learnt now that even as you die you do not necessarily move on to a better life in spirit world, and that spirits sometimes stay with their bodies, even if they are ashes.

This idea that "you hang around" may be more of a concern to people who have lived a more materialistic or base level existence. Those people who have not necessarily grown spiritually and are materialistic. By this I mean those concerned with money, power, sex, domination, selfishness and so on. The changes that came over me were actually coming from this person who possessed me. He was quite a materialistic person so I was influenced by him to drink, smoke, and I became more obsessive about sex.

On spirit side those spirits who were very earthly in their ways still have those feelings for drink smoking, and sex. You may have died one day but the next day in spirit world you are still the same person. I had unwittingly let a spirit attach itself to my aura by touching his ashes. He was now influencing me in subtle ways that I did not realise. I was of course still sensitive and quite open, but I now became a bit more aggressive and belligerent. I had obsessive thoughts, and depression which made me drink more, and work harder. Sex became more important even beyond the normal teenage feelings. I am not sure how long this possession lasted but it was certainly there for a few years.

From that point on my psychic abilities grew as the years went by. I became increasingly sensitive and hyperactive. I couldn't relax; I had to be doing things. I started to drink more to help me calm down. I understand now that after the possession it was my sensitivity that was causing the imbalances that I felt happening in my body. Just walking down the street I would see people walking down the road and disappearing. I could tell people what was wrong with them if they were ill, or that they were going to be ill. I gave predictions and clairvoyance but I felt out of control most of the time so drink and sex became my release. In a way I became more materialistic and followed a more earthly or base form of life.

The materialistic side of life is really directly counter to a spiritual form of life. Expanding on this point what I really mean is that materialistic, or earthly, people find that when they die they may have achieved a lot of things on the earth but their spiritual growth had been negligible. As a person they probably had little time for anyone and may have treated people harshly. When they die they are confused as they cannot access their material things and may not receive any love from the earth because they did not have time to form a loving relationship with somebody as they concentrated solely on material aspects of life. Those people who have not lived a spiritual life sometimes stay in a sort of purgatory, possibly hanging around close to their body, that's one of the reasons why graveyards are haunted. People are seeing these confused spirits hanging around not believing that they are dead, or maybe if they are very religious waiting for the resurrection. Sometimes these spirits can attach themselves to people and thus move around by jumping from one person's aura to another. In my case the spirit stayed with me. I say he because it felt like a male possession, but it can also be female.

I am not against people making money or enjoying earthly pleasures, the few that are worth anything that is, but I am pointing to those who only think of earthly possessions, money, greed, sex and don't have a care how they get it or who they hurt along the way. We should all have somebody to love or be loved by somebody. Love helps us grow as spirits. If we don't love somebody then we cannot get emotionally hurt, but we lose out on a lot of spiritual growth. Love hurts, but we grow spiritually because we have to think of the other person's feelings, hopefully; and make sacrifices to make a loving relationship work. Relationships should of course be two-way traffic except when we get divorced we want it all!

Anyway, as I said, when you die you still have those earthly feelings from your time on earth. You can satisfy your lust or thirst by what I call partial possession. By this I mean possession from these earthly spirits living in the astral plane. The astral plane is the next level of spirit that we move to when we die and it is the closest spiritual dimension to the earth. These earthly spirits hang around the astral level which is comfortable for them as the conditions closely resemble earth conditions.

I will give you an example, you may have had a drink and felt afterwards that it was a total waste of time especially when you have drink inside you. Drink lowers your resistance, or will power, and it allows these beings to connect with your aura and feel what you feel. You will find that you taste less, and physically feel less. The reason is because these spirits are feeling the taste of drink or food. The astral spirits are able to possess you when your guard is down due to consuming drink and taking drugs. Drink obviously plays a part in your sensitivity to you surroundings. But this astral spirit possession is normally temporary and the spirit detaches itself as you sober up and you regain your will power.

Will power and right thinking is the key to whether you become possessed or not. Strong willed people are able to resist possession. In other words a stronger will power and the ability to control ones emotions and feelings will reduce the chances of being possessed.

In my case because I was psychic I was more open than most to possession. I am very strong willed now, but I live in two worlds. One part of my mind lives in this world; the other part is always linked to the spirit world.

In my teenage years I knew surprisingly little about the spirit world although I saw ghosts and had lots of psychic experiences. As I made my way through my teens, switching jobs, making money, travelling a bit and growing into adulthood. I eventually moved into my own haunted house. There I expanded and experienced more activity than I can remember. The house was a big old Georgian dwelling in St Georges Square, Pimlico, London.

Chapter Five

Moving On

I moved into this massive Victorian house and lived on the second floor of the five-storey mansion. The house was used as a hotel during the war. It was filled with soldiers, mainly US Soldiers, and where there were soldiers there were always prostitutes.

I found out that on one occasion a prostitute fell pregnant to a US Soldier. She wanted to have his baby and waited for him to return from a bombing raid. Unfortunately he was killed in action and she was devastated of course. She couldn't cope, and threw herself out of my bedroom window where she was impaled on the railings below. Every time I went near the window I could feel myself being propelled forward. I had this strong urge to throw myself out of the window. I understand now that people's thoughts can impregnate the atmosphere long after they have gone. This is what we call residual energy. The energy stains the walls and surroundings especially where great emotion has been expressed, as with the case of this poor girl. The emotions were quite powerful and made me feel really uncomfortable. So much that I decided to move down to the basement flat when it became available.

The basement flat was also quite haunted. I used to wake up and see what I can only describe as a man in a butlers' uniform. He was middle aged, average height, with a scowling face. He didn't like me invading his space. Well that's the way he saw it I guess. We call this ghost in the mediumship trade an active spirit. In this case he was bloody furious! When I decided to convert the old pantry into a kitchen, and the kitchen into a bedroom, I would go to bed and wake up to find the wallpaper ripped and the plaster damaged, tools strewn about the place or a pot of paint knocked over. The pantry was "his room" going back to Victorian times. I used to get a strong smell of alcohol in the panty from time to time as well ammonia which I believe he used to clean the silver used by the old residents of the house.

The servants in those days would not be allowed in there except by invitation. At the back of the basement was a big room that used to be the old staff hall where they would all congregate and eat together. The scowling butler was the master of all the servants there. Even in death he felt he could still put his weight about; showing that you don't become angels when you die.

As I said he was not happy to have me there. What happened in this basement flat is what you would call classic poltergeist activity. The difference here was that I knew exactly what was going on whereas others would probably be terrified and move out, as happened on previous occasions. The butler was able to draw the energy from somewhere, more than likely my mediumship energy, which he used to make objects move in the flat. Some poltergeist activity is used to draw attention to something usually the spirit haunting a place that wants to communicate, or impart some information.

The butler in this case was just being malicious as he wanted to upset and frighten me. He didn't succeed as I was determined to stay there. I used to laugh at him and tell him he didn't frighten me. This really upset him but my will was stronger than his so his power over the situation became less and less. These nasty spirits feed on our fears as a source of negative energy. I am sure any normal person would have eventually left and let him have his way. I was having none of his tantrums. This was my place now. I would go to the front door of the flat and see his shadow in the corner of my eye. When I looked round he disappeared.

The Butler was a bully. I knew this because I used to see a little boy, a spirit child, at the back window with his nose pressed against the glass crying on many occasions. I felt he was a boot boy and the Butler treated him badly putting him out in the cold and rain as a punishment. He had died of a cold and he wanted to come back into the warmth. I helped the boy move on into the spirit light as he died while he worked there. He was still being held to the earth so my prayers helped push him into the light. I surrounded him with a gold light and said "great spirit please help this boy into the light". After a few more prayers I could feel the sense of uplift from the boy as he found the light and left his miserable existence.

What we don't realise is that our prayers are like waves of energy or like a strong wind. They encompass and surround spirits like a force of energy. Spirits know straight away if we are thinking about them. They see light if we send good prayers and they feel heavy if we send thoughts of sadness. That is why when people die we should be happy for them. It is understandable that you have grief when you lose somebody. This is part of the cycle of death and rebirth into spirit. Our loved ones who pass on will miss us of course, but they will have entered a new life; they are only a thought away. So I try to be happy for those who have passed into spirit.

I remember a very interesting apparition while I was standing outside the door of my first floor flat. I was chatting to some friends at the top of the wide Victorian stairs. It was wide enough to get a car down. I saw an old woman who lived upstairs called Gladys at the bottom of the stairs on the ground floor. As it was a bit dark I pressed the timer light next to me to give her some light as she walked up. She was an old lady so she took her time, as one does. I continued chatting with my friends and watched her moving up the stairs, eventually passing us, to go onto the second stair level where she had her flat, when the timer light suddenly went out. I shouted out "hold on Gladys" and pushed the button back in. There was no sign of her on the stairs. We all looked at each other and laughed saying "Did you see that?" We had just seen an apparition of Gladys out of her body. She was not dead as I went upstairs to her room straight after to check on her. I spoke to her and she said she had been asleep for a few hours and had not left her room. When I saw her she was as solid as you or me and could not have raced up the stairs without me seeing her. Usain Bolt could not have done it.

Gladys was having an out of body experience where the spirit actually leaves the body and appears in another place or country while the person is still alive. Many of these types of apparitions have occurred throughout history.

On the second floor there was a shared bathroom off the landing. The tenants who used this bathroom had a feeling of depression and sadness. Several people had seen a shadow of a man in the bathroom. I checked out what the reason was for all this activity. I contacted a man who was a previous tenant in his forties who had hung himself, not while I was around! He had been depressed for a while and just gave up. I said some prayers for him and this helped lift the atmosphere. As you can imagine nobody lingered in there for long, I guess, having a shower in there reminded people of the shower scene from psycho. This resulted in a queue for the other bathrooms on the first floor, or the third floor.

The other most active haunting in the house were three women dressed in 1920s clothes. Many residents saw them at the top of the second floor stairs usually on a Friday night. I never used to see them as Friday nights I was always out in the clubs. I hung around one Friday evening because so many people had reported seeing them to me. I managed to pick up on the activity that evening. I found out that they had lived in the 1920s with one of the ladies being the owner. On Friday nights they played cards together while their men were out in the clubs. They enjoyed it so much that they continued the tradition in spirit coming back to their old "haunt", if you excuse the pun. It proves a point that you don't have to change, or give up everything just because you pass over to spirit.

I know from many spirit conversations and books written on the subject that people who were artists still paint on the other side, but can use their mind instead of brushes, writers write with their mind and try to influence writers on earth, musicians still play their instruments or create tunes mentally, inventors and scientists continue to invents things for this world and the next. I have been told that many inventions have been perfected for earth and will be given to certain individuals when they and the earth are ready for them. The spirit inventors will never give a major invention like Nuclear power to one person only, but instead give it to a few individuals at the same time so nobody can monopolise it. If you look at nuclear power, Russia, Germany, America, and Britain were all working on it at the same time.

Chapter Six

When I First Met Arthur Conan Doyle

Sir Arthur Conan Doyle has always been a part of my life. Before he contacted me I knew through his writings that he was a special person. From a very young age I was an avid reader, and became a big fan of Arthur Conan Doyle (ACD) searching for anything related to him, such as books, newspaper clippings, magazine articles, or radio plays. He is mostly famous for the creation of his legendary detective, Sherlock Holmes, but it was his historical novel, *Brigadier Gerard* that introduced me to him.

When I first became aware of spirits around me I would occasionally see the presence of a man with a moustache and a pleasant smiling face. I did not pay much attention to it until many years later when I realised the spirit guide I occasionally saw was ACD. When things were working against me, or I was feeling sad, I could feel this warm glowing presence surrounding me, lifting me up. As you may know everyone has a spirit guide. I am not saying that ACD is my guide. However I would say he has been a frequent presence throughout my life. ACD was always influential in all stages of my life from his books to his spiritual guidance.

As a young boy I was inspired by Sir Arthur's works, especially his historical novels. While reading one of his historical books I imagined myself as a character in the story. His writings were so detailed and vivid they brought life to historical facts. Two examples of these are The *White Company* and *Micah Clarke* which were exceptionally well written. ACD's books were the type that left you wanting to read more and more. I started reading his historical novels when I was about eight, and as I matured this led to the Sherlock Holmes series of books. I found that the books alleviated my distress and confusion at a time when I was becoming more sensitive, and things got more complicated in my life. Sensitivity and mediumship have their own advantages. For instance, as I read Conan Doyle's books, I could sometimes feel his presence around me. His spirit would connect with my aura and absorb my emotions as I read; he gave me rare insights about the characters that the book did not reveal. ACD was able to embed these thoughts into my mind about Sherlock Holmes because I am a medium. It gave me ineffable joy as I read. Long after the book was closed I could still 'feel' the story in my head.

Arthur Conan Doyle has told me how spirits read books in the spirit world. Every material object that is made on earth has an exact etheric copy, or a double, in the spirit side. There is a double of the Mona Lisa, the Crown Jewels, the Vatican, and The Seven Wonders of the World, of everything that is or was a material object. Another example of this is the Great Library of Alexandria which was destroyed by fire over one thousand seven hundred years ago. The Library contained half a million documents and books that reputedly comprised all the collected knowledge of the ancient world. While the earth library was destroyed by fire the etheric, or spirit, copy of this library is still intact in the spirit world. Books are collected and kept in what are called 'halls of learning.' The halls include vast libraries which contain a copy of every book ever published. It includes those long forgotten books that have been destroyed long ago by war, or fire, and time. It also contains copies of unpublished books.

When a spirit reads a book all they have to do is pick it up. They don't even need to open it in order to read it although they can if they choose. Spirits don't have to know languages in which books are written as the thoughts are language independent. Thoughts have no language. The spirit world has no language. Spirits telepathically connect with the book's aura and they instantly know the whole story in a matter of seconds. They not only know the story they are able to understand what authors were thinking as they wrote each page, how the characters or plots developed, and even the thoughts of every person who ever handled and read the books. Spirits can see books from many different angles. Everything related to books can be revealed. It is quite astounding!

Chapter Seven

Arthur Conan Doyle Appears to Me

The first time I saw Sir Arthur Conan Doyle (ACD) was the day he appeared in a white cloud, silhouetted as a person, while I attended a psychic circle. This appearance was the opposite of the usual clairvoyant image. As I sat there his face materialised in a white cloud of ectoplasm that formed above my eye level. Three or four other faces also accompanied him. One of these was Sir William Crookes. Later, in some old psychic books, I saw photographs of ACDs face in ectoplasmic clouds and these pictures were similar to what I had previously seen. The closest description I can provide is that of an early 20th century photograph that actually moves.

ACD is well-known for his creation of Sherlock Holmes. Unfortunately not enough has been said about his interest in the afterlife and spiritualism. On one occasion he told me clairvoyantly that *"although I spent most of my fortune on promoting and investigating spiritualism, I look back now and realise that not one penny of it was wasted."* What else do people know about him?

Arthur Ignatius Conan Doyle was born on Picardy Place in Edinburgh on May 22, 1859. His mother, Mary, was Irish and traced her ancestry back to the famous Percy family of Northumberland and from there to the Plantagenet lineage. This historical blood line probably inspired him in later years to write his famous novels, *The White Company*, *Sir Nigel*, and *Micah Clarke*. It is more than possible that Sir Arthur's writing talent came from his mother's side as she had a passion for books, and was an accomplished storyteller. Later in his schools years he noticed he had a talent for entertaining younger schoolmates with stories that he made up.

The Doyle family was a large one. Arthur was born into a family of ten children, seven of whom survived to maturity. Conan Doyle's mother struggled to bring up the children on the modest income her husband Charles earned as a civil servant. Charles Altamont Doyle was the youngest son of John Doyle, the caricaturist; 'H.B.' Charles also painted and made book illustrations to complement his income. On occasions he also worked as a sketch artist at criminal trials. Charles' brothers were quite talented as well. They all made names for themselves: Charles' brother, James, wrote *The Chronicles of England*, another brother Henry was Manager of the National Gallery in Dublin, and a third brother, Richard, became famous as an artist, best known for his work on the cover design of the satirical British magazine *Punch*. Although Charles Doyle had artistic talents he exercised his skills only intermittently, and this apparent lack of drive led to the loss of his job at the Office of Works in Edinburgh. After losing his job Arthur's father steadily lapsed into alcoholism. He also had epilepsy which grew increasingly worse until he was institutionalised for the final years of his life. He died in 1893. His father's alcoholism is reflected as a topic in his later fictional works.

Arthur Conan Doyle was educated both at home, and in a local Edinburgh school until the age of nine when he was sent to the Jesuit preparatory school of Hodder in Lancashire. Hodder was part of the Jesuit secondary school of Stonyhurst. Conan Doyle moved there two years later. He did well academically but did not find the strict and ascetic life of the Jesuit order very appealing; especially the corporal punishment meted out by the priests. The school offered him free education in exchange for a life of dedication to Jesuitism, but his mother turned down the offer. Instead, even though it was a major financial struggle, she paid his school expenses.

While studying in Stonyhurst, Sir Arthur examined all aspects of religion and their belief systems. He seemed firmly to reject Catholicism together with some disillusionment with Christianity as a whole. It may well have been the strict religious establishment that set him on the path to becoming an agnostic by the time he left school in 1875.

From Stonyhurst, Arthur travelled to Feldkirch in Austria, where he spent the year in a Jesuit school learning German. While staying there he found himself questioning so many aspects of the Catholic faith, and not receiving any conclusive answers, that it put him firmly on the path to agnosticism. Arthur left Austria and returned to Edinburgh in his beloved Scotland. With some good advice from his mother's lodger and lover, Dr Bryan Waller, Arthur decided to study medicine at the University of Edinburgh, which he attended from 1876 to 1881, and from where he achieved a medical degree. Here he met Professor William Rutherford, Professor of Physiology, and Dr Joseph Bell, Professor of Clinical Surgery, two of his greatest influences. Conan Doyle became a surgeon's assistant to Dr Bell in Edinburgh. These two men later became the inspiration for two of his most famous fictional characters. In ACD's novel *The Lost World*, one of the characters, Professor George Edward Challenger, was based on Professor Rutherford, while Dr Bell's incredible deductions and reasoning with regard to the history of his patients led to the idea for Detective Sherlock Holmes.

Doyle observed Dr Bell's methods to describe a patient's character with just a few glances in their direction. He cited a man that did not remove his hat must have been in the army, and was only recently demobilised, thus he was not used to the ways of civilian life. Bell could extrapolate far more information from his

47

observations than could be determined by Doyle's rapid questioning. The keen scrutiny he employed also enabled him to deduce from a working man's clothes the exact nature of his occupation which was often of an unusual kind that could not easily be calculated. This helped him build the Sherlock Holmes character and sharp deduction used with amazing affect when he wrote his stories.

In 1878, Doyle accepted some temporary medical assistantship positions with Dr Charles Sydney Richardson in Sheffield, and Dr Reginald Hoare in Birmingham. Dr Hoare treated Doyle like a son who in turn enjoyed his time with his mentor. It was at this time that he became interested in spiritualism and began intensively studying it.

In 1880, ACD enlisted as a surgeon on the whaler ship, *The S.S. Hope,* enjoying an adventurous life at sea. The voyage took him to the Arctic which "awakened the soul of a born wanderer" as he wrote many years later. This maritime adventure inspired his first story about the sea, the frightening tale, titled *Captain of the Pole Star*. It was evident that he enjoyed the life at sea; so much so that after he received his M.D. in Biology in 1881 he signed on as the ship's doctor on a West African steamer where he nearly died of a fever.

In 1882, Doyle, against his mother's wishes, established in Plymouth a medical practice with his Edinburgh medical schoolmate Dr George Budd. Unfortunately their professional relationship ended over concerns of Budd's ethical behaviour. Budd was an outrageous marketer of his medical services; his policy was to generate as much publicity as possible. He put out a rumour that he would see patients for free between midnight and 2am, and that bald men had to pay double!! He had to shoo away people from his door who turned up in the middle of the night. Budd generated his income from patients who came between 10am and 4pm which he would see for free, but made money from those who would pay half a guinea to jump the queue. He then sold all of them questionable medicinal remedies made up by his wife.

Doyle eventually had enough of his former friend when they fell out over Budd accusing Doyle that patients were being fobbed off by inferior advice from his junior partner. This from the man who was quoted to a patient 'Take your medicine, and if that does you no good swallow the cork. There is nothing better when you are sinking'. The accusation was too much for Arthur and he then moved to Southsea in Portsmouth where he set up his own practice. While there he married his first wife, Louise Hawkins, in August 1885 and they travelled to Ireland for their honeymoon. Doyle started writing his stories during the quiet periods in his practice where he successfully created Sherlock Holmes. The detective's first appearance in *A Study in Scarlet* was published in *Beeton's Christmas Annual* in 1887. Around this time he also started to attend psychic meetings in Southsea.

Success as a novelist came quickly with his first published historical novel, Micah *Clarke.* For Conan Doyle being taken seriously as a novel writer meant more than anything to him; certainly more than writing Sherlock Holmes stories which he found really tiresome. But in the end, Sherlock Holmes was his legacy and his bread winner. He felt that recognition finally came his way when he met Oscar Wilde at a dinner in the summer of 1889 and Wilde praised Doyle's latest novel, Wilde said he enjoyed it immensely. Subsequently the owner of Lippincott's monthly magazine commissioned Conan Doyle to write a short novel, and soon after he began the next instalment of Sherlock Holmes, *The Sign of the Four,* published the following year. In 1890, Doyle went to Berlin to write a review of Dr Robert Koch's cure for tuberculosis but found out that he was just a quack Doctor. He felt that he needed a change of career and under the influence of Malcolm Morris he suggested to study ophthalmology in Vienna which he found very lively, but the German instruction was difficult for him so he took further instruction in Paris.

In the early part of 1891, ACD left Southsea and moved to London where he opened an eye clinic at 2 Upper Wimpole Street. Unfortunately few clients turned up to his practice. In fact it was said in his autobiography that not one crossed his door. This failure left him with plenty of spare time to write stories about the famous Detective Sherlock Holmes. *The Strand Magazine* published the first six *Adventures of Sherlock Holmes,* which fortuitously for Doyle commenced its first publication that year. 1891 is a defining year for Conan Doyle where a bad bout of influenza nearly ended his life. He had an epiphany and realised that he couldn't combine his medical practice with a literary career thereby setting out to become a fulltime writer.

While writing the stories of Sherlock Holmes, ACD published another great novel that year titled, *The White Company.* His historical novels were more of a passion for Conan Doyle; in contrast, the Sherlock Holmes stories were aimed to provide him with fame and fortune. He confided in his mother that he wanted to eliminate Sherlock Holmes so he could concentrate on 'better' things; such as more literary novels. His mother advised him against this so he put it off for a few years. It was not until 1893 on a trip to the Richenbach Falls in Switzerland that Doyle became inspired by the location and came up with the idea of how to kill Holmes.

The story of Holmes' death is published as *The Final Problem* in *"The Strand"* magazine. Holmes dies in a struggle with Professor Moriarty, his arch nemesis, at the Richenbach Falls, leaving his many fans horrified. Many of his fans wore mourning bands and *The Strand* subsequently lost 20,000 subscriptions.

In 1893, Doyle's wife Louise was diagnosed with tuberculosis (TB), and the same year his father Charles died. He built a home at Undershaw in

Hindhead, Surrey, as the mountain air was supposed to be beneficial for his wife's health. Conan Doyle took up skiing at Davos in the Alps which he enjoyed immensely and also allowed his wife to benefit from the pure mountain air to help her illness.

In 1895 the Doyle's left for Cairo, Egypt, in the hope that the warm dry air might cure Louise's TB. While staying there in 1896 fighting broke out in the Sudan between the British and the Dervishes. Doyle sent a cablegram to *The Westminster Gazette* asking to be appointed their war honorary correspondent for the conflict. They duly agreed and he travelled up the Nile to the front line in Sudan to report first-hand on events. He learned a lot from the war which gave him the experience for war reporting on conflicts in later years.

ACD and Louise returned to England and settled in the house in Hindhead. With the outbreak of the South African war in 1899 Sir Arthur attempted to enlist in the Middlesex Yeomanry, but was rejected and put on a waiting list. He was disappointed, but not for long as his friend, John Langman, contacted him and told him that he was setting up a hospital at his own expense. He suggested that Doyle help supervise the operation in an unofficial capacity. Conan Doyle jumped at the chance to be involved in some way and set off for South Africa in February, 1900. He spent six months there and found the conditions in the hospital deplorable.

On his return from Africa the same year Doyle tried politics. He stood as a Liberal Unionist Parliamentary candidate for Edinburgh but lost by a narrow margin. He also wrote *The Great Boer War* that year. This was a five hundred-page report of the war and the organisational shortcomings of the British army at the time.

The war had led to an extraordinary outburst and denouncement of Britain's conduct in the war. Conan Doyle felt compelled to write a short pamphlet titled *The*

War in South Africa: Its Cause and Conduct which was translated worldwide. In 1902, Doyle's stance in defending Britain's role in the Boer War, in addition to his services to the crown during the war, earned him a Knighthood. It was rumoured that King Edward VII was a devoted fan of Sherlock Holmes and he added Conan Doyle's name to the honour's list to encourage new Sherlock Holmes' stories. Conan Doyle had seriously contemplated refusing the honour as he felt that he did not deserve it. Doyle thought he was just doing his duty in defending his country. His mother had her firm opinion and persuaded him to accept it for the 'good' of the family name.

Doyle set to work on a serialisation of *The Return of Sherlock Holmes* in *The Strand* magazine which was published in 1903. Three years later tragedy struck when his wife Louisa died. Sir Arthur went into a period of depression but managed to overcome it with his insatiable desire to fight injustice. This led him to undertake a new job and battle against the "Miscarriage of Justice", as he called it, which involved George Edalji who was convicted of savage attacks on cattle and horses in the district of Great Wyrley, near Birmingham.

Chapter Eight

Conan Doyle Becomes Sherlock Holmes

George Edalji, originating from an Asian Indian family, grew up in Great Wyrley. His family became the victims of racial intolerance and received disturbing anonymous letters. A disgruntled servant of the family later confessed to sending the letters. In 1892 more anonymous letters were sent to the family. The Chief Constable of Staffordshire who, according to rumours, had a grudge against young George implicated him by saying that he "knew" George was responsible for writing some anonymous letters, and that "he hoped to give the culprit a dose of penal servitude." As George was an excellent student and studied diligently to become a solicitor the accusations were preposterous.

In 1903 a series of animal mutilations occurred in Great Wyrley which involved slashing of cows, sheep, and horses. The animals had shallow cuts slashed underneath their stomachs and they bled to death. An anonymous letter implicated George as the culprit and he was arrested. He was found guilty on dubious evidence presented in court, and sentenced to seven years of hard labour. Not everyone was convinced that George Edalji was the perpetrator so the townspeople gathered a petition of 10,000 signatures demanding his release. This action pressured the system which led to George's acquittal in 1906, four years earlier than his total sentence, but he received no apology, compensation, or pardon.

Conan Doyle's articles helped review the case. Doyle reviewed the evidence methodically in the same the way Sherlock Holmes undertook his cases. He discovered that the bloody razor found in George's house which was presented in court as evidence used in the mutilations was just a rusty old razor blade. The handwriting expert who matched the writing on the anonymous taunting notes accusing George had made a serious mistake in an earlier case where a man was innocently jailed. The mud from George's boots used as evidence to prove he was in the field where the final mutilation took place turned out to be of a different soil type. Most importantly the mutilations and taunting letters continued to be sent after he was jailed.

Conan Doyle's absolute proof of George's innocence came when he arranged a meeting with him in a hotel. When Doyle arrived at the hotel he found George reading a newspaper very close to his face and a little to the side. As a trained optician, he knew immediately that this was a condition of myopia (near-sightedness) and astigmatism. This condition would have impeded George's vision to see clearly in the dark while trying to avoid farmers or police. He knew then, of course, that George was innocent. So he set about writing a series of articles outlining the case and the evidence, in *The Daily Telegraph*, which caught the public's attention.

As a result of the articles and as there were no procedures for retrials in those days; a private committee was established to review the evidence. The committee cleared George Edalji of the mutilations but found him guilty of writing the anonymous letters. Subsequently the law society readmitted him to the roll of attorney from which he had been barred. In addition, *The Daily Telegraph*, helped to raise the admission fee of £300.

Another important result of the whole process was that Sir Arthur's campaign showed the urgent need of an appeal process for convictions, and this led to the establishment in 1907 of a Court of Appeal. Sir Arthur paved the way to correct any miscarriages of justice in the future. In 1906 he attempted politics again when he ran as a Unionist candidate for Parliament in the Border Burghs. Unfortunately he was once again unsuccessful.

In 1907 Conan Doyle remarried, to a woman named Jean Leckie. George Edalji was one of his guests at the wedding reception and Doyle later said that "There was no guest he was prouder to see". Conan Doyle had known Jean since 1897 and it was love at first sight. They maintained a secret relationship for nearly ten years while his wife Louise was alive, but as Louise was ill he was very careful to make sure she never knew about the affair.

Following their marriage ACD and Jean moved to Crowborough, East Sussex where he built Windlesham Manor, a large house, in which he wrote more novels and spent the rest of his life. After his marriage he also tried playwriting, and wrote three plays that were unsuccessful. Undeterred he wrote a fourth play with Sherlock Holmes as the main character titled *The Stonor Case,* and later renamed *The Speckled Band.* It was a tremendous success and received rave reviews.

In 1909 Conan Doyle took up a campaign against Belgian oppression in the Congo by writing *The Crime of the Congo.* The birth of his son Denis that year prevented him from writing much fiction, and again in 1910 when Adrian was born.

However Sir Arthur couldn't keep quiet for long and he became involved in another high profile miscarriage of justice case. The suspect this time was Oscar Slater a man that Sir Arthur once described as "not a desirable member of society." Slater had a dubious background in illegal gambling and was well-known to the police.

The case concerned the murder of Miss Marion Gilchrist, a woman who lived in Glasgow. It started in 1908 when Miss Gilchrist was bludgeoned to death in her flat while her servant, Helen Lambie, went out on an errand. When Lambie returned she found her mistress lying on the floor covered in blood with her papers scattered. The servant also noticed a diamond brooch was missing. Oscar Slater was later identified as the man seen leaving the crime scene.

A massive public outcry over the murder pressured the police to bring a suspect to trial. Slater seemed to fit the profile of the murder, so the police announced that they were looking for Oscar Slater in connection with the case. Slater, in the meantime, had pawned a diamond brooch and fled to America under an assumed name. As far as the police were concerned it was an open and shut case. Slater, who heard about the warrant for his arrest, came back from America with the intention of proving his innocence. It was found that the pawned brooch was different to Miss Gilchrist's but the police stated they had found a small hammer in Slater's house and it was believed this was the murder weapon.

Slater went to court in 1909. He was found guilty and sentenced to death. After a plea for clemency from his lawyers the sentence was commuted to life imprisonment. Slater's lawyers contacted Sir Arthur to see if he could help Slater prove his innocence. Conan Doyle got to work on the facts of the case. Although he didn't approve of Slater's background or character he felt that he was innocent of the Gilchrist murder. He outlined the evidence point by point in the book, *The Case of Oscar Slater,* proving his innocence. The facts found by Conan Doyle were overwhelming. Slater used an assumed name to travel to America because he was hiding from his wife, not the police as was earlier assumed. The samples taken from the murder weapon on the supposed hammer found in Slater's possession, actually turned out to be negative. A medical examiner believed that a wooden chair leg covered in blood was the actual weapon utilised. Sir Arthur thereby concluded that Miss Gilchrist knew the murderer as she opened the door and allowed the killer inside. Although Slater and Gilchrist lived near one another they had never met.

Demand for a retrial faltered. The authorities said there was not enough evidence to reopen the case. It was not until 1914 that new evidence came to light when a witness could prove that Slater was not present at the crime scene. Although Gilchrist's servant, Helen Lambie, had identified Slater in the trial as the man seen in the hallway she had given the police another name which the police decided not to investigate. Officials refused to reopen the case. Sir Arthur was outraged and said "The whole case will, in my opinion, remain immortal in the classics of crime as the supreme example of official incompetence and obstinacy". The momentum for a retrial was lost for nearly a decade even though Sir Arthur had done his best. Nobody was willing to move ahead any further.

Slater contacted Doyle in 1925 and handed in a secret letter written on waterproof paper that had been smuggled out under the tongue by another convict. He pleaded to Sir Arthur not to forget him. Sir Arthur, always an honourable man, fired off some letters and lobbied any friends and MPs willing to listen. This may have resulted in the publication of the book, *The Truth about Oscar Slater,* in 1927 by a Glasgow journalist, William Park. He expounded Conan Doyle's theory that Miss Gilchrist knew her murderer. Park added that the killer was most likely her nephew but due to libel laws could not name him in the book. It generated many newspaper columns and there was uproar when police witnesses came forward to say that they were coaxed into identifying Slater as the man they saw at the building where the murder took place.

The pressure finally paid off, after 18 years and six months, when the Secretary of State for Scotland ordered the release of Slater in November 1927. Doyle set about trying to gain a pardon for Slater and a retrial was ordered. With the help of generous donations from Sir Arthur and his friends, Slater's legal costs were met. Slater was cleared of all charges and received £6,000 in compensation, a considerable sum in those days. Conan Doyle assumed that Slater would repay those who helped pay his costs, but Slater took a different view saying that he should not have to pay his court costs. Conan Doyle did not want, or need the money, but it was Slater's ingratitude to those who stood by him that really upset him. Conan Doyle later wrote to him saying "You seem to have taken leave of your senses. If you are indeed responsible for your actions then you are the most ungrateful as well as the most foolish person whom I have ever known." Although Slater maintained his attitude Sir Arthur always believed that what he did was for the right reason, and was at least satisfied that he had a victory with the pardon although Slater's attitude left a sour taste after all the effort he put in.

Chapter Nine

Conan Doyle Follows Natural Spirit Laws

Sir Arthur felt he did the right thing by taking on the Oscar Slater case. Slater was not an endearing character, as Conan Doyle later admitted himself. However Sir Arthur was a man of integrity and honesty who believed in helping others. He saw the Slater case as a miscarriage of justice; therefore he followed his natural spiritual instinct. These instincts can be defined as 'spiritual laws' which we follow through our life although we don't always know that they exist.

Humans have discovered, through science, the physical laws of Planet Earth, such as gravity, pressure, electricity, and thermodynamics. Unlike physical laws we do not really understand the universal spiritual laws which rule the universe and our lives. The so-called supernatural experiences we hear about are caused in part by the spiritual laws that guide those who live in the afterlife, also known as spirit world. These laws are also called the natural laws because when you follow them then a natural course of events will follow. They are guaranteed to be exact, perfect, ordered and harmonious. You cannot avoid them, but if you follow the laws described below then your life will be more spiritual and harmonious on earth, and in the next world. There are many Natural Laws but the following are three of the most important:

- The Law of Cause and Effect
- The Law of Understanding
- The Law of Attraction.

These laws are NOT religious laws but are natural laws related to the spirit body.

59

Unfortunately at the moment scientists have not discovered these laws and they will need to do so before our world changes from a materialist, mechanical world, where our God is really money, to a harmonious spiritual world based on Natural Laws. The Spiritual Laws that need to be applied to people's life are described below.

The Law of Cause and Effect – This is a fundamental law that applies to both the spirit world and our world here on earth. It is what is commonly known as 'what you sow, so shall you reap' or 'what goes around comes around'. If we would all apply this to our decisions in life it would make this world a fairer and less hostile place. This law means that you will get back exactly what you put out. If you think negatively then you will become a negative person, and those who think positively are generally positive people. Do we apply this principle to our thoughts every day? I suspect that we don't.

What about that familiar expression 'that's just my luck' when something bad happens to you. This so-called bad luck happens for a reason, and usually it's because there is something to learn from the experience. I am not talking about little things like dropping a plate on the floor, but important incidents like perhaps meeting somebody you did not want to see, or wanted to avoid because you owed them money. The simple reason this occurred is because you didn't apply the law of cause and effect in the first place. For example, if you owe somebody money they expect you to pay them back, but when you don't eventually the lender will start asking "Why hasn't that person paid me back?", "Why is that person avoiding me?" The law of cause and effect starts to operate when your thoughts of avoidance and the lender's thoughts of repayment of the debt start a chain of events to lead you to meet. The result may be embarrassing or cause friction in your relationship.

You cannot hide from your problems because spirit law demands situations are worked out and balanced. If there is imbalance between two individuals they both need to learn a lesson. In the above case the borrower's lesson is either not to borrow money, or to pay it back quickly. The lender's lesson is not to lend money or give money to people in future. If both the borrower and the lender would have known of Francis Bacon's maxim *"Neither a borrower nor a lender be...For loan often loses both itself and friend"* there would be no friction in the friendship or embarrassment when the meeting occurs. The loan of money has probably ended a good relationship as the trust has been lost from the lender, and subsequently one doesn't want to meet because of the debt. The law must balance itself. So while a debt may not be paid the result is that you have both paid a price and lost a friend. The cause is money and non-repayment; the effect is a loss of trust and friendship. We all borrow money but we must ensure we can pay it back. I know it's obvious, but this is how issues are resolved on earth with the Natural Law of Cause and Effect behind all actions. This law not only applies to our everyday lives it is also applied to the planet: environment, nature, the animal kingdom and our climate.

The 'El Nino Effect' in the Pacific Ocean, warm currents flowing around the west coast of South America, has a significant influence on the weather and climate in South America and the rest of the world. Other major currents are the *Gulf Stream*, which flows from the Gulf of Mexico to northern Europe, and the *Jet Stream* which flows above the British Isles. Any changes in the flow of these currents will have a disastrous effect on the climate of Europe. Recently these currents have been more intense which some scientists believe is due to deforestation of the rain forest in Brazil. The loss of these forests, which function like the lungs of the world, are causing imbalances in various places on the planet and creating hurricanes, typhoons, and tornadoes that seem to be more frequent and more intense. Every year the weather forecast establishes the hottest day or month,

61

coldest day or coldest month, breaking records from previous years.

We are experiencing more droughts and therefore seeing many more massive forest fires all over the world. Floods are also becoming increasingly common. Places that had not flooded before or for hundreds of years are now having problems caused by deforestation, global warming, and a reduction in the ozone layer. The Earth is one big ecosystem. Therefore an imbalance in one area causes reactions in other parts of the planet. The Law of Cause and Effect applies not only to Planet Earth but also to the planets in our solar system. All the planets interact with one another, and as you may already know, the gravity between the sun and planets also have harmony. Balance is needed everywhere, and by simply applying the Law of Cause and Effect it can change our whole attitude towards life thus resulting in a more spiritual and happier existence.

The Law of Understanding - There is logic to the natural spiritual laws. If I am nasty to someone I will get the same attitude in return. If you turn a relationship into a friendship when somebody is nasty to you then you are applying a spiritual law. To do this you must try to understand the person. Why are they being spiteful to me? Is it just me? Are others treated in the same way? When you look at the situation and try to understand the motive behind the meanness, rather than reacting to it, you may be surprised to find the answer. A good example might be at your place of work where a colleague is never satisfied with the work you do, no matter how hard you try. It's a very common scenario. How do you deal with this?

- First, since the aggressive person gets satisfaction from your discomfort do not react to their baiting. If you are calm and cool they won't understand why you are not reacting.

- Second, put yourself in their position. Watch them and figure out why they have this attitude. Perhaps they are being treated in the same way by their boss. A bully is usually insecure whether it's in the office or some other relationship. The result is that the bully takes out his or her frustrations on you because he/she feels you may be better than them. This may lead you to ask many questions, and importantly you must ask them questions and find ensuing answers. It is harder to do this while bearing someone's nastiness but this is how one spiritually grows. Look around: do you really know your friends? Do you know their likes and dislikes? What makes them tick? You can only get to know them by understanding them.

If you apply the same rule to situations in your life you'll achieve more insight and control over yourself. Reacting to situations is easy to do but by reacting in an explosive way you show that you lack control. It's much harder not to react. Once you learn to control your emotions you are starting to understand the situation. Why is this happening? How do I deal with this? Should I deal with this or walk away?

Sometimes one understands situations so well that it's just not worth staying to argue. You will recognise that some people just want to cause trouble and this is where you apply the law of disappearing; basically walking and not talking. We cannot progress as individuals if we don't understand ourselves or others; therefore understanding people is very important because it's a skill and a spiritual law. Do we understand ourselves? We know our likes and dislikes but do we really know whether or not we are insecure? If so why are we insecure? Are we secure with our own feelings and sexuality? We must ask questions about ourselves and hopefully we'll find the answers. If we don't like the answers we find, or we cannot deal with them we assume a negative, or even an aggressive attitude. In other words we take our frustrations out on someone else.

Some people hide their insecurities by speaking gibberish after a few drinks or sometimes even without drinks. One who acts as a know-it-all is most likely also hiding insecurities. So it's best to leave them when they start and find better company elsewhere. Drinking affects people differently; some become liars others become emotional the quiet ones become loud and aggressive and loud ones become quiet and sometimes intellectualise. This brings me to another spirit law: The Law of Attraction.

The Law of Attraction – The Law of attraction was talked about in a book called "The Secret" a few years ago. The book deals with how you can attract the things you want into your life by thinking about them, and this is absolutely true. However, there is always the caveat of "Beware of what you wish for!" Because what you think you want may not be really what you wished for in the first place when you get it. Our thoughts create our reality and our life plan. Our hopes and desires can come through but only if we initiate the actions with them. Dreamers never have their wishes come true because they never apply the actions to make their wishes come true. You have to take steps to make something happen. For example, it could be like having an idea for a business. You setup the company, develop a product, and sell it. If you don't do these things then a business will not grow. So, if we want our spiritual friends to help us, or angels, guides etc, then we must make the actions and thoughts so they can help guide us to what we need. But it's our decisions and actions that make something come true, or not as the case maybe.

There is another spiritual attraction. Like we can attract nice spirits to us, we can also attract some darker or astral spirits to us too which can result in a form of possession. Can you become possessed? Could this be true? Well, actually, yes you can. Possession can be temporary or semi-permanent. By this I mean that all possessions are governed by how you THINK. You can temporarily attract astral beings to your thoughts which in turn will influence you. If your thoughts convey negative feelings: anger, revenge, hate, and murder, you send out a wave of thoughts that allows similarly inclined beings to 'feed' off you. Astral beings become attracted to your way of thinking and feed from the energy that you emanate. When you have an astral being attached to you it's difficult for your spirit guides to come close to protect and influence you. It is as if you had a barrier surrounding you to bar any influence from them. The astral beings 'possess' by constantly manipulating you to think negative thoughts. It will keep occurring until you regain control over your thoughts. As an example, if you had forgotten about someone who hurt you earlier these beings will bring back those negative thoughts, but it will only work if you allow them to upset you.

The advantage the astral beings have over you is that they know that you are not aware of their presence; hence you think it's your own thoughts that are causing your distress. Of course their pleasure is derived from your pain, your anguish or any actions that they cause you to commit. Some people like to stress others on earth and the same also occurs on the spirit side! If these people have exactly the same feelings or thoughts on the earth plane once they cross over they don't become angels.

If you are shocked at the thought of somehow being possessed do not think of possession as something that takes control of you. The possession I am discussing is one of influence on your thoughts not control of your individuality.

How do you stop from being possessed? It's quite simple; guard and analyse your thoughts, control your emotions, try to be more understanding, and forgiving. It is only when you control your thoughts, or forgive yourself, or someone else that an influential possession ends. Sometimes it is not an astral being at all but your own mind that causes this to happen. You need to be aware that there are beings in the astral plane that enjoy upsetting people on earth. The likelihood of this occurring will reduce only when you have more control over yourself.

Research has been done on this subject by Dr Elizabeth Kubler-Ross, and Dr Carl Wickland, who actually spent thirty years of his career investigating and corroborating the phenomena. They were both absolutely convinced of the reality of this issue[1].

Keep in mind that what you think governs how spirit can influence you. If you have good thoughts then you attract guides of a similar nature, and if you do the opposite by having bad thoughts you will attract lower astral beings. There is an old saying "Like attracts like". This saying perfectly explains how one attracts good or bad karma to oneself. Positive things happen to positive people does it not? Thieves and criminals think and act alike. Peaceful minded people protest about similar issues. The reason we have communities of good, or bad, people is because their thoughts have attracted like-minded individuals together. We usually get what we deserve, in other words, the thoughts we put out create our future path or karma as stated in Indian philosophy. The Law of Attraction ties in with the Law of Cause and Effect as they are similar in many ways. However the attraction deals with those spirit guides who influence us from the astral plane, the people we mix with on earth, and more importantly, the next plane of existence we reach after we die.

(1) Dr Carl A. Wickland, *30 Years Among the Dead;1978; Spiritualist Press*

Chapter Ten

Life After Death

By choosing to read this book you may have some hope, or maybe a belief, that death is not the end of one's conscious life. If this is the case then I propose to you that it is possible to survive bodily death, and that we do continue living after our physical passing as spiritual beings. Once we die our spirit body, which is encased in a physical body on earth, is clothed in an astral body and it eventually sheds the astral body to be 'reborn' into an Etheric body, a lighter form, as we progress. It is a form of shedding skins. The astral body is heavier because it is closer to the earth in its material structure. We live in what the spirit world calls the 'earth' plane. When we die we move into the 'Astral dimension' Plane. If we have progressed as a spiritual being we can remove ourselves from the Astral Plane and move into the Etheric Plane a light and beautiful world.

As previously stated we eventually die and transform from our current existence into the Astral Plane. For example, if a friend or relative died and crossed over from the earth plane you would see this person exactly as he or she was on earth immediately after death. The main difference is that they would be whole and the body would be in perfect condition. There is one illness they could carry over and that is mental illness which can be treated through healing and resting on the other side. The person who passed will have exactly the same attitude, humour, character flaws, or loving ways they had on earth. If they were good then you see them as a good person, if they were nasty they are still nasty. In other words we do not become angels when we die - no chance! Our bodies have undergone a transformation but our spirit, or soul, is still the same. Why should we be any different after death?

No money or material items are needed after death. You don't feel hungry, but you may still feel the need to eat, drink, or smoke. These needs are psychological not physical. As we know nicotine and alcohol are drugs, but they are physical drugs therefore we wouldn't need them if we had a spirit body. So why would we still have these feelings? These feelings still persist in our minds after we die. There may still be a need to indulge in our vices like having sex. Our vices cause most of our pains and troubles on earth. This world would be a very different place if we didn't have drink, food, drugs, or sex. The spirit world that we live in when we die has no need for money as we don't need to buy material items. Spirit bodies do not decay like a physical body, nor do they have physical illnesses. Although we will go to a world described similar to this we still keep our vices until we 'feel' there is no need for them any longer.

If an Astral spirit, that is a spirit who lingers close to the earth, feels the need to drink he can still satisfy his vice from the Astral Plane. To do this, he or she, will normally go to a bar or pub and hang around for a victim. He will find many drinkers there of course happily indulging in alcohol to satisfy their earthly bodies' addiction. What our astral friends can do to have "their" drink is to partake in this feeling along with others around them. In order to do this the astral being attaches itself to the spinal cord of their selected earthly body thus merging their astral body with the victim's physical body. As the person drinks the astral spirit is able to taste the alcohol and feel the effects the victim is feeling; things like the gradual loss of consciousness, tiredness, and so forth. This is a form of possession, and it may be temporary since the astral spirit is simply fulfilling his need for alcohol just like he used to do before he died and went to spirit. I believe that some people are easier to possess than others. The possession depends on a few factors: the strength of the person's willpower and how intoxicated a person becomes which is usually down to ones tolerance to drink. The same cycle of possession applies to drugs, food, and sex. Astral spirits will normally try to possess people who are weak willed or have a lack of self-control.

How does this Law of Attraction apply? It is all related to how we think. As we think we will attract spirits who are like-minded. To some extent it could be described as a mental magnetism. Our thoughts have a force of attraction and repulsion which go out like magnetic waves and are picked up by astral spirits that surround this world. These spirits are attracted to the thoughts of a likeminded person thus forming a one-way relationship with them. This spirit attraction could be drawn to a person who is quite aggressive, or maybe a person who is very studious and likes books. It does not have to be a negative, there can be positive attractions. I said that it can be a one-way relationship because they are feeding off our thoughts; we are not gaining anything from them. Astral spirits can gain energy and power from our thoughts which have energy, creative, and destructive power. If we attract spirits they can start influencing us in many subtle ways.

Mental obsession is a good example of these influences. Where does it come from? An obsession is the domination of one's thoughts or feelings by a persistent idea and it can turn into a form of possession if taken to extreme. We have looked at alcohol already but there are many others that may not be as obvious. One example is fitness which keeps the body toned and healthy; it helps us relax and increases our metabolic rate so we digest better. But how much is enough? Some people are obsessed with their body spending strenuous hours on daily exercise. It's like a drug. As the adrenaline pumps the feeling they get from exercise is a form of high that astral spirits enjoy. They don't need to keep their body fit but they still want the feeling you get from physical exercise. Some people become obsessed about their body as a result of sexual inadequacy. They feel that they cannot attract another person unless they are physically fit. Everyone wants to look good but there has to be a limit an acknowledgement of what is sufficient and an awareness of when you are over-exerting. This acknowledgement is called 'control'. We gain control over ourselves through mastery of our five senses and our emotions.

The Laws of Attraction not only apply to the Astral/Spirit world, but they also have huge influences for our lives on the earth as well. As I said previously all our pain and pleasures are caused by the five senses and our emotions. Unfortunately we have more pain and torment than pleasure on earth. Can people distinguish between love and lust? How many relationships are based on lust? For example, when we have thoughts of lust these thoughts will go out to the ether and are picked up by people around us who are then attracted to lust. What is called 'love at first sight' is most likely 'lust at first sight'? We are receivers and transmitters of thoughts; sending them out like radio waves into the ether. This energy is used in many ways to build our future, in other words, we attract people that will help us create our future. People come to us from both the earth side and the spirit side.

Chapter Eleven

New Directions for Sir Arthur

In 1912 the year Conan Doyle's daughter, Jean, was born; and he created a character called Professor Challenger based on his novel *The Lost World*. This wonderful science fiction story was a roaring success and became a film in 1925. In the following years Doyle wrote four more adventures based on Professor Challenger.

Sir Arthur travelled to the United States and Canada in 1914 stopping first in New York. He seemed to enjoy Canada more than the US; however his mind was in England as he felt war in Europe was imminent. He didn't stay in North America long and returned after a month.

Doyle wrote a book in 1913 called *Great Britain and the Next War*. It was written as a reply to General Friedrich von Bernhardt's description of German policies. Conan Doyle warned the Navy of the need for a channel to Europe to safeguard supplies in the event of a submarine blockade. His warnings of a submarine threat that could lead to merchant vessels being wiped out, leading to a possible famine, were not taken at all seriously by the Navy. However, the German Naval Secretary later said of Sir Arthur that he was "the only prophet of the present form of economic warfare" when the Germans began to attack British merchant vessels.

Doyle had an inventive mind especially in relation to military topics. He was always coming up with new ideas to help the war effort. He strongly advocated body armour for the troops and was instrumental in helping to promote a 'tin hat' to protect the head from bullet wounds. Conan Doyle also suggested that the Navy use inflatable rubber collars that sailors could carry in their pockets, and inflatable life boats because most naval ships hardly used them due to weight and other considerations. His ideas were no doubt influenced by the experiences of the Titanic disaster several years earlier when it was discovered that there was an inadequate number of lifeboats on board.

Sir Arthur's knowledge of history inspired him with ideas for contemporary troops which he felt were inadequately protected against the range of firepower directed against them. In 1916 he wrote to David Lloyd George, UK Prime Minister, to discuss body armour. Lloyd George replied saying "I may tell you that we are giving very special attention to this question....but...our great difficulty is to get the soldiers at the front to take them into use".

Sir Arthur tried to enlist but at the age of fifty-five was considered too old. Instead he became a member of his local volunteer force, the Crowborough Company of the Sixth Royal Sussex Volunteer Regiment. He held the rank of Private with pride for four and a half years. (He had a rank because he was appointed Deputy-Lieutenant of Surrey.) He kept himself busy with writing eventually producing a six-volume historical compilation of the war titled, *The British Campaign in France and Flanders.*

By 1916 the war and its repercussions had caused millions of deaths on the battlefields of Europe. Whole villages and families were being wiped out and people were looking for answers to life after death. As a result there was a huge revival of spiritualism just as had occurred during the American Civil War, and again later in the Second World War.

Sir Arthur had been interested in spiritualism since the 1870s and was convinced of the survival of the soul or personality after death. He felt that now the time was right to declare his belief in life after death. He would need his faith in the afterlife two years later when his first son, Kingsley, died in 1918 and again when Sir

72

Arthur's brother Innes, a Brigadier General, died of pneumonia just after the end of the war. It was a huge blow to Doyle but evidently spurred him into action as he became a huge advocate of the spiritualist movement until his final days thus earning the title "the Saint Paul of Spiritualism." Doyle spent most of his fortune on promoting spiritualism, and it was said that he spent a million dollars promoting the Cottingley fairies' story, an incredible sum at any time.

Conan Doyle first started to speak openly about spiritualism in 1917 having held back due to his work for the war effort. After the death of his wife's brother Malcolm, a close friend, he went to a very gifted medium called Lily Lauder-Symonds. It was during a séance with Lily that he received convincing proof of the afterlife when she provided a message from Malcolm who told her about the story of the guinea coin he gave to Sir Arthur as a joke saying that "it was the first fee he would have as an army doctor." This story was of course unknown to any medium and even the close people around him so it was very convincing proof for him, and to make it even more fascinating Sir Arthur had actually kept the guinea given to him on his watch chain as a memento.

Sir Arthur announced his conversion to spiritualism in a 1916 article in *The Light* magazine, a publication dedicated to spiritualist philosophy. He received both plaudits and rebukes. The spiritualists applauded him while the sceptics and Orthodox Church disapproved of such a great writer being gullibly led by those 'mediums' that used trickery and fraud to prove life after death. At the time there was a lot of money to be made out of mediumship and many people were being regularly exposed of faking communication from the afterlife and giving evidential proof to those who were suffering the grief of losing their loved ones in the war. This obscured the genuine mediums that were actually giving excellent evidential proof. Doyle himself did his best to expose fake mediums as he knew how detrimental they were to his own cause. Although many bad ones were exposed the good ones never got reported in the press. Even after the initial publicity Sir Arthur was often ridiculed for his belief especially by his peers and the press in general. Many thought he was gullible and quite possibly mad.

However he was committed and determined to speak up for what he believed was the truth. Conan Doyle was passionate about his belief in the afterlife. He disregarded the critics, chastised those who committed fraud in the name of spiritualism, but mostly, never wavered once his secret was out. He truly believed in the afterlife and was not alone in his thinking. He had other great allies with great minds such as Sir Oliver Lodge (Inventor of Radio before Marconi took the credit), Sir William Crookes (Nobel Prize Winner), and John Logie Baird the inventor of television. They all believed the continuous existence of the personality, spirit, or soul, as most people call it. Once the spirit has no use for the physical body - the body is discarded. As Sir Oliver Lodge has often said "We are like caterpillars waiting to remove our outer skin and turn into beautiful butterflies."

Once the cat was out of the bag so to say Conan Doyle set off on a tour of the major cities in Britain promoting spiritualism to anyone who would listen, and at the time there were many. They may have come to see the man who created Sherlock Holmes, but many left with at least the knowledge that we live on after death. He travelled all over Europe, the USA, Africa, and Australia to spread the word of spirit spending one and a quarter million pounds on the cause during the 1920s.

The Cottingley fairies' case truly propelled him into the headlines. In a small village called Cottingley, in North Yorkshire, two young girls claimed that they had photographed fairies near to where they lived. The story was brought to Conan Doyle's attention by a letter from a spiritualist friend of his, Felicia Scatcherd. She told him that two young girls had photographs that would prove the existence of fairies. The girls, Elsie Wright, and her cousin, Frances Griffiths, claimed that they had seen many fairies around a beck, which is a small stream, near their village early in 1917. They first photographed two fairies with Elsie's father's camera. When he developed the photos he saw the two shapes and asked the girls what they were.

"Fairies, of course," they replied.

Next they managed to photograph a gnome standing next to Elsie. When the photo was developed the girls insisted that it was real. They were barred from using the camera again as Elsie's father didn't believe them.

Sir Arthur sent a close friend, Edward Gardner, to investigate the mystery. Gardner met the girls and obtained two photos of small transparent female figures. Out of embarrassment the matter had been dropped in Cottingley, but a seed was germinating in Gardner's mind as he believed the photos were real and the girls were telling the truth. With copies of the photos in hand he told Sir Arthur how he felt. Sir Arthur sought out other opinions. Sir Oliver Lodge felt they were fakes but others believed the girls were sincere.

When the newspapers picked up the story, Doyle was on a trip to Australia, so Gardner took the flak from journalists. In the 1920's the girls later took three more photos making the famous set of five that are now known as the Cottingley Fairy photographs. One looked like a fairy offering a flower to Elsie while another depicted a "fairy bower" described as an ectoplasm-like figure in a tree. The third fairy was captured leaping into the air. Sir Arthur asked Eastman Kodak laboratories for an opinion of the photographs. While waiting for the results to come back he published an article about the fairies in *The Strand* Christmas magazine of 1920 which was immediately deluged by numerous photographs of fairies. However none of them matched the 'purity' of the Cottingley photographs. Conan Doyle decided to write a book detailing the whole affair called, *The Coming of the Fairies*.

In the 1980s the two elderly women admitted that four of the photographs were faked. They didn't tell Sir Arthur at the time because they felt he was so nice they didn't want to upset him. The whole episode got out of hand and they were shocked at how quickly events unfolded out of their control. The girls faked the photos as a way of getting back at the people who didn't believe them and also teased them about the fairies. Between them they agreed that one day they would tell the truth, but not until all the main people involved had died.

Examining those pictures today one can see that they look like fakes. Sir Arthur and millions of others were totally taken in by the hoax. If Doyle had doubts about the validity of the photos later on he kept quiet about it. As he was such an honourable and spiritual person he would never have confronted the two girls about faking the photographs. He understood that there is much we don't know about which is as true today as it was at that time. I am sure he believed in the existence of fairies whether or not the photographs were real.

However there is a twist to this amazing story. The women admitted that most of the photos were fakes, but Frances always maintained even to her death there "were" fairies, and that the final picture titled "Fairies and their Sunbath" was genuine: 'I saw these fairies building up in the grasses and just aimed the camera and took a photograph.' Both of the girls always said that they had actually seen fairies playing in the woods near the beck. There was one independent witness, a writer called Geoffrey L. Hodson, who backed up the girls' claims. He later testified that he had seen the fairies himself, and confirmed the girls' observations in all details.

And In the 1980's a former wrestler (Ronnie Bennett), and then forester in Cottingley Woods admitted to having seen fairies in the woods. He claimed he saw the elf-like figures while working in the Cottingley Estate Woods. *"When they showed themselves about nine years ago there was a slight drizzle around. I saw three fairies in the woods and I have never seen them since. They were just about ten inches tall and just stared at me. There is no way the Cottingley Fairies is a hoax."* However, as with all paranormal events, it is capturing one of them in a photograph that is always the most difficult part.

Finally, in a TV programme called the "Antiques Roadshow" shown on BBC television on the 4th of January 2009, the daughter of Frances Griffiths appeared with one of the antique experts. She had brought copies of the original photos and the actual camera used by her mother to photograph the fairies. Her daughter told the presenter that her mother admitted the first four photos were faked, but she also said that there were fairies and her mother till her death said that the fifth one "Fairies and their Sunbath" was totally genuine and not faked. She saw a mist forming on the grass near the river grabbed the camera and instantly took a photo. The result was the fifth photo a real fairy picture.

(The fifth Cottingley picture "Fairies in the Sunbath")

Chapter Twelve

Mediums

It is my intention to share with the reader some of the secrets that Conan Doyle has passed on to me as well as the philosophy espoused by him.

Do you know the difference between a medium and a psychic? It is important to distinguish between the two. A person can be both, but most people are psychic and do not have mediumistic ability. So what is the difference?

A medium is a channel between the spirit world and this world. They allow spirits to inspire them with thoughts and relay proofs of survival after death through evidential messages, using techniques such as *clairvoyance* (seeing messages), *clairaudience* (hearing messages), *clairsentience* (knowing messages), and physical mediumship (projecting ectoplasm for spirits to use), which is very rare. Mediums have a conscious co-operation with spirit world entities or their own personal guides to channel messages from them.

A psychic, on the other hand, has the ability to read an aura and gain knowledge about the person's past or present experiences, and to a certain extent predict their near future. Telepathy is another example of psychic ability. For me psychics don't necessarily provide evidence of life after death, but they show me that we have latent supernatural abilities which are, in fact, very natural. A gifted fortune-teller utilises the psychic faculty within them.

A person can be a psychic and a medium at the same time. Mediumship is a higher form of communication, and I don't mean that in a condescending way. I mean only that you need to be more sensitive as a person to tune to the guides and spirits that surround us. It is one of the hardest and highest forms of mediumship, because it offers the highest form of proof of life after death, is physical mediumship which allows those who have passed over to use the medium's special physical energies to reappear in solid form.

A physical medium is a person who has developed the ability to produce large amounts of ectoplasm from their physical body and the material objects in their surroundings allowing a spirit person to re-form their physical body just as it was on earth, warts and all. Spirits appearing through physical mediumship can have any physical defects that they had on their body such as missing fingers or scars. These give an added proof to a loved one who knew the person as they were, and recognises them in their recreated form. Physical mediumship is normally done in dim light or darkness and sometimes with a low red or blue light. I can affirm one hundred per cent that it is real, and a wonderful, unique gift. I will talk more about this in a later chapter.

You may be wondering whether you could be a medium. The answer is yes of course! Every person on this planet is able to become a medium because everyone is a spirit form incarnated into a physical body. Perhaps one day there will be overwhelming scientific proof that we have a spirit body. I know that we all have a spirit body. The spirit body is a reality. I believe this without a shadow of doubt.

The spirits, guides, and helpers that a medium communicates with are always around ready to help us. Their world is of service to others. Their 'food', for want of a better word, is helping others in their world or people on Earth. By doing this the guides themselves grow in spirit through their service to others. So if you want to develop mediumship the spirit guides are waiting for you to ask for their assistance in developing it.

How do you start? First, you need to believe that you can do it. Second, you need to be patient as it can take years. Mediumship is earned by every individual not just given to them. Do not feel like it's not worth the time it takes because eventually your life will be more enriched. What will you gain?

• You will no longer feel like you are alone or on your own.

• Mediumship will help you face life's trials and tribulations.

• A new philosophy of life will help you understand more about this world and the next.

• Your emotions will be increased so that you have tremendous highs.

• When you connect with your guides you will feel a wonderful feeling of love and happiness in your stomach (this alone is fantastic).

• You will be able to help people around you as your guides will inspire you, if you ask them, to help friends or loved ones.

• Strange and wonderful things will happen to you whereby you know that your guides are looking out for your interests.

• You may start to see spirit lights and spirit forms during the day or night. It may shock and exhilarate you when this occurs but it will not frighten you.

You might say that this is all very well, but there must be a downside to mediumship. Of course there is. Everyone pays a price for being a medium. Some of the downsides of mediumship are:

• Your sensitivity will increase. You will find that your anger levels are greater in situations where you may not have got angry in the past. When reading books or watching films you will find yourself more emotionally touched, even crying at certain moments.

• Large crowds will drain your energy. You may find crowds unbearable and need to find peace and space or feel crushed.

• Hangovers are more acute and last longer.

• You will sometimes feel increased despair for the world at the senseless killing and unnecessary evil done by man.

• When giving readings you will have to be very careful about how you say things to people. One wrong sentence can offend or even cause heartache for somebody. After a reading you may worry about whether you have said the right thing or expressed yourself correctly.

• Sometimes you will have to miss out on events because your spirit guides need you to see someone who needs advice.

The benefits of mediumship outweigh the burdens. Life can be enhanced with a new sense of motivation and meaning. You really start to feel like you have a purpose in life and answers to all those questions about God start to make sense (Why are we here? Why are some people rich or poor? What's the point of good or evil?). There are lots of answers to these questions, and mediumship is a good way to get them.

In some ways the spirit world becomes a major part of the life you lead and might encroach on your own time. Would I give it up? Never! It's too important. The price is sometimes very high because it is a life of service, but it is the most rewarding thing you can do to give evidence that loved ones live on and want to communicate with us. Look at the comfort you can give to people especially when the spirit evidence becomes obvious. Seeing smiles on people's faces or tears of joy are irreplaceable.

All spiritual gifts have to be earned. Like everyone else mediums gain growth through life's experiences. There is no set path for each medium's development as they are guided by our spirit teachers beyond. They know what's best for us more than we know ourselves. One of the most important attributes for mediums is 'control'. "Control is everything" a guide named Tse Sing once said to me. A certain amount of control needs to be exercised with such a gift. The last thing a spirit guide wants is a medium that goes around upsetting people by giving them incorrect evidence. When all is said and done a person is a channel. You must put your ego aside and give what you get from your guides.

Remember that everything in life has a price - a cause and effect. Successful business people usually pay the price for success with long hours, sometimes up to seven days a week. Others may take risks with their money to invest in things they hope will pay off. Professionals go to university to gain a degree by studying for their exams and hopefully passing them. Tradesmen do an apprenticeship to learn their skills. This time of learning is well spent for most people. It is the same for mediumship.

Mediumship is a qualification you receive at the end of years of development. Indeed development should never really stop. With mediumship you should be able to bring proof of life beyond death to our loved ones on Earth. Mediums make a real difference to those who suffer what is usually the most profound event in one's life - the death of somebody close to you. Losing a child is probably one of the most harrowing things that could possibly happen in life. How can you express the feelings you have after a reading when you bring evidence to a mother who has gone through this especially when the child was young? To give somebody evidence from a lost child can only be described as miraculous. These moments are the rewards when you make a difference to someone's life.

As mentioned earlier mediumship is very different from having 'only' psychic ability. Psychic ability deals with supernatural abilities on the physical level or earthly existence. Mediumship connects with physical vibrations as well as the many different spirit levels. A medium should be communicating with spiritual beings in these higher levels giving evidence from those who have crossed over. Although a psychic can read somebody's aura providing them with 'evidence', it is not from those who have passed over.

When I communicate with the spirits, or my spirit guides, I can usually see them in a physical form with my mind's eye, also called *the third eye*. Because I see their spirit forms this ability is usually regarded as *clairvisual*. When I see my guides, for example, they impress thoughts into my mind. They can also show me images, whisper in my ear, or give me different feelings in my body, such as pains in my chest to indicate a chest or heart problem, pains in my legs to perhaps indicate arthritis, or shortness of breath to indicate lung or breathing difficulties. Those could be a condition that the receiver subsequently will die of, or possibly an earthly health condition the communicating spirit may have had while alive. The feelings usually come with a thought to make sure that the message is not confusing to the receiver or the medium.

Each of these forms of communication - clairaudience, clairvoyance, clairvisual, clairsentience - has what we call, 'vibrations' associated with them. Each of these abilities uses certain vibrations and the vibrations convey messages in different ways. As an example, *clairvoyance* is the most common form of mediumship but there are many ways to receive it. One vibration may show an image like a photograph of a blue car in a medium's mind. So you could say that "I am being given a blue car. Does that mean something to you?" And the receiver answers yes or no.

The second vibration may show a blue car moving like a video image and stopping by the side of the road. This could be interpreted by the medium who asks "Do you have a blue car that has broken down recently?" This message has more quality to it or a finer vibration.

A third vibration could be a blue car moving in a video image, pulling over to the side of the road with a thought or feeling that the car has broken down because it ran out of oil due to a leak although the medium did not see the leak. The question is put: "Do you have a blue car that has broken down by the side of the road because there was a leak in the oil tank?" If accepted this is very significant evidence and the vibration is deemed finer again. More evidence has been transmitted with these vibrations.

The fourth and final example is a vibration that I get sometimes. It feels as though someone has just spoken the words during a conversation and it is like a memory in your mind. This could come across as "I see you in a blue car that has broken down by the side of the road. There is a leak in the oil tank that causes the engine to overheat and the car needs a fuel injector replaced. I see a repair man pulling up to the car wearing a blue hat and he is talking to you about his wife's credit card bill." If this scenario is accepted by the recipient it is evidence of an even finer vibration received by the medium.

What I am showing here is that not all mediums can receive this kind of evidence because every medium is able to attune to different vibrations hence the evidence they give to receivers will be varied. All mediums pick up many different vibrations but much depends upon their sensitivity and the conditions surrounding them at the time. I can also say with confidence that the finer the evidence the more sensitive would be the medium.

Mediums are sometimes called *sensitives*; a term to describe people who are able to receive these fine vibrations from the spirit world. Unfortunately they are also very sensitive to conditions on Earth, and because of this sometimes find life a struggle. I am referring to the problems mediums have of picking up on people's thoughts, or feeling hate or anger coming from someone. They can sense trouble such as someone about to start a fight before it happens. Mediums like to avoid crowds because the noise or vibrations upset them and large crowds can also drain their energy (this is a frequent situation I find myself in when I go shopping in crowded areas. I need to take continuous breaks away from the crowds or my energy is drained). Vibrations and sensitivity are key attributes of all mediums. The difference between most mediums is the degree of sensitivity they have. The more sensitive a person is the finer the vibrations they receive, and thus the evidential messages they give to the receiver are enhanced.

Sensitivity is earned through service and sacrifice. You need to have humility to put ego aside and give service to your spirit guides as they are the ones who control the messages that come through you. As a medium you are always a servant of spirit. It is important to remember this or you will not progress properly as a medium. If you try and develop mediumship there is no doubt that your sensitivity will increase; usually with the help of your spirit guides who tune your aura to particular vibrations. While the qualities of humility, sensitivity, and service to others are the most important aspects of mediumship there are other factors involved, such as the interpretation of evidence, the expression of oneself, and the quality of the link between the medium and guide or guides. I really believe that mediums should be constantly developing themselves, or at least increasing their sensitivity through meditation or sitting in a psychic circle.

Age is no barrier. People can start developing in their teens, middle age, or senior years. Young people can be very sensitive so there is no barrier for them to become mediums, but some experience of the world can help especially when speaking to large gatherings. Quite a few mediums seem to develop their skills in their forties and fifties, or even later.

I love being a medium and I could never give it up or not use this gift to help others. With the knowledge I have gained about this world and the next I always feel privileged to have this gift that can be used by spirit. The spirit guides are the masters, and they will use mediums to help those needing to contact their late loved ones. There is no ultimate proof of life after death as yet but I am trying my best to kick the door open between this world and the next, and give people a glimpse of the truly wonderful existence beyond this sometimes hard, cruel, painful, and material world on Earth. It can be Heaven here sometimes, but at times, and for some people it can also be hell.

There are simply not enough mediums around and more mediums should be developing to make a bigger impact in today's society. Mediums are a small group of people who have developed their sensitivity nd allows them attunement to certain vibrations around us namely those with life force like people, nature, and animals.

The many distractions of the modern world such as TV, the Internet, hobbies, and sports, are preventing the number of mediums from growing. People do not want, or are not willing to take time to develop a connection with their guides by becoming sensitives. Mediumship is earned step by step, and our spirit friends are always ready to tune new mediums, but they will only do this when people are ready to develop.

If you want to develop mediumship I will explain some techniques to help you. However if you don't want to develop as a medium, that is also fine. What would be best for you then is to try seeking out the philosophy of the spirit world and apply it to your daily life. This philosophy is based on service to others, understanding, love, expression of one's artistic talents, and being a good person in your deeds and actions. It could mean just taking some time to help others where possible.

Experience has told me in my life that most people aim to be a good person. However many people who have knowledge about life after death do not apply it to their daily lives. I am not saying they have to be good all the time, but people can make decisions each day by applying their knowledge or philosophy of spirit to their activities. Whether or not you want to develop mediumship it is important that you try and live as harmonious a life as possible.

Chapter Thirteen

Evidential Proof

Arthur Conan Doyle was fortunate to have proof given to him at times but he had to wait until late in his life before seeing it. Everyone wants evidential proof of an afterlife which is very understandable in a world built on science and mathematical theories. Once Doyle had his evidence he believed from then on with absolute conviction that there was life after death. In the early 1920s he struck up a strange friendship with Harry Houdini undoubtedly one of the world's greatest magicians, and the most evangelical sceptic who made it his ambition to expose fraudulent mediums.

Doyle actually believed that Houdini also had psychic abilities which he wrote about in his book *The Edge of the Unknown*. Harry Houdini's attitude was completely opposite to Sir Arthur's in that he didn't believe in life after death and went out of his way to debunk it. Doyle and Houdini wrote to one another over many years each trying to persuade the other that their own position was erroneous. Neither man would budge on their opinion but they remained good friends, or were at least cordial because their relationship helped each other's public profile.

Together they actually exposed a lot of mediums who were faking their phenomena, but Houdini went further and actually damaged genuine mediums in the process of exposing fakery. The simple reason he did this was that Houdini thought every one of them was like him, a con artist or illusionist, with magic tricks at their disposal (a trick is really a con or an illusion). Houdini was brilliant at his art and believed that spiritualism was based along similar lines of illusion. Although he investigated hundreds of mediums, and had one of the largest psychic libraries at the time, he said he could not find one piece of evidential proof to support mediumship or the afterlife as being a reality, or so he said publicly. If he had seen the real thing he was loath to admit it. This negativity eventually caused a rift in the relationship between Conan Doyle and Houdini.

Houdini absolutely adored his mother and he was devastated when she died. After her death Conan's Doyle's wife Jean, gave Houdini some spirit messages from his mother through automatic writing, but he disregarded them and this was the start of a permanent rift with ACD. Houdini was totally sceptical and remained so until he died of peritonitis, due to a burst appendix which ironically occurred during a trick with a student in 1926. He asked the student to hit him as hard as he could in the stomach but the student surprised him and hit his stomach before he had time to tense his muscles, and he fell down injured. It proved to be a fatal blow.

The credibility of the afterlife and the paranormal has similar problems today just like in Houdini's day, in that no matter how many times a spirit is captured on film, there will always be people decrying its validity and asking for more proof. Undoubtedly there are some frauds and a lot of "evidence" is suspect, but the more we investigate and enquire the more questions are left unanswered. No matter what happens the message of spirit is still carried forward. Do fairies exist? Do nature spirits exist? I know they do as I have seen them with my own eyes. Both fairies and nature spirits are as real as anyone living in the physical world and they surround us everywhere. If you have the eyes to see them, the ability to open your mind and quicken your vibration you can see the trees, flowers, water, earth, and the air, all resonating in wonderful colours and sounds. Everything around us, even the smallest amoeba or the brightest flower, is filled with the infinite beauty and life force of spirit. We are surrounded with life that is beyond our normal frequency of sight and sound. With advances in science we may start to detect what mediums sense and it will be another provable fact. Hidden from us are dimensions of spirit beings who are trying to express themselves in this "sometimes" beautiful sphere we call earth.

Doyle travelled constantly during the 1920s. In 1922, while on a tour of the US, Sir Arthur reluctantly accepted an invitation by Harry Houdini to attend the Annual Meeting of the Society of American Magicians as an honoured guest. He was suspicious at first and fearful that he might be exposed to ridicule over his spiritualist beliefs. Houdini reassured him all would be fine and he accepted the invitation.

The gathering was held at the Hotel McAlpin and Conan Doyle had prepared in advance his own 'trick' which went down as an absolute storm. Prior to mounting the stage he had prepared a short film to show those attending that everything they knew about life was not actually what it seemed. Before the film was shown Sir Arthur told the audience that afterward he would answer no questions about the film. He said:

"These pictures are not occult but they are psychic because everything that emanates from the human spirit or human brain is psychic. It is not supernatural, nothing is. It is 'preternatural' in the sense that it is not known to our ordinary senses. It is the effect of the joining on the one hand of imagination, and on the other hand of some power of materialisation. The imagination, I may say, comes from me - the materializing power from elsewhere".

The film was played in front of an astonished audience including all the magicians present. On the screen the audience could see two dinosaurs battling against each other in a jungle. Nobody could believe what their eyes were seeing and they accepted it to be true. Following the presentation Sir Arthur said nothing. He stole the show, so much so that, *The New York Times*

90

ran a story about it the next day. The journalist who attended couldn't be sure whether it was real and Conan Doyle had used some sort of psychic projection from the past, or if he had simply been making fun of the occasion. The film looked so lifelike that all those present were naturally *convinced,* and afterward it was all they could talk about. *The New York Times* headline the next day was:

DINOSAURS CAVORT IN FILM FOR DOYLE
SPIRITIST MYSTIFIES WORLD-FAMED
MAGICIANS WITH PICTURES OF PREHISTORIC
BEASTS —KEEPS ORIGIN A SECRET —
MONSTERS OF OTHER AGES SHOWN, SOME
FIGHTING, SOME
AT PLAY, IN THEIR NATIVE JUNGLES

After the story appeared in the paper Conan Doyle explained that it was actually test footage from his upcoming film, *The Lost World,* and that Willis O'Brien had created the battling dinosaurs' sequence. O'Brien subsequently made the special effects for the film classic, *King Kong,* in 1933.

In 1925 Sir Arthur's book, *The Lost World,* starring his second most famous character, Professor Challenger, was made into a feature film and released. It was a great success, and Sir Arthur set about writing more novels with the character including *The Land of Mist, The Disintegration Machine,* and *When the World Screamed.* He needed an income to promote his spiritualism work so he carried on and compiled twelve stories about Sherlock Holmes in, *The Casebook of Sherlock Holmes,* in 1928.

His penultimate spiritualism tour occurred in 1928 when he went to South Africa for five months. In 1929 he set off on his final tour to the Nordic countries taking in Holland, Denmark, Norway, and Sweden. He was extremely ill and in such great pain that he had to be carried ashore when he returned.

Sir Arthur Conan Doyle suffered a heart attack at his home in the spring of 1930. He was found in his garden clutching his heart with one hand and holding a single white snowdrop in the other. He was such a romantic that he used to give his wife, Jean, a snowdrop every year on their anniversary, and even though he was very ill he went outside into the cold and picked one for her.

One of the last acts he did was to struggle to London to head a deputation to the Home Secretary to change the centuries-old law under which spiritualist mediums were prosecuted. He died on July 7 of that year in his Crowborough home. As he lay at home in bed with his family around him Sir Arthur whispered his final words into his wife Jean's ear "You are wonderful" then passed away.

ACD's funeral was more like a garden party with summer dresses and few people mourning. There were so many flowers sent that a special train was needed to bring them all, and they covered a whole field. His headstone inscription was brief. Written was his name, date of birth and four words: 'Steel true - blade straight'.

Arthur Conan Doyle was (and is still) an extraordinary man. Apart from his creation of Sherlock Holmes, which made him a very successful author with over sixty titles, he was an avid sportsman. He was a goalie and founding member of the Portsmouth football club, played cricket for the M.C.C, at the famous Lords Cricket Ground, and he also played rugby and golf. He was an expert at billiards, and a pioneer motorist driving his first car for the first time back to his house, a distance of over two hundred and seventy miles. Doyle excelled at boxing and introduced cross-country skiing to Switzerland. He never stopped writing; he wrote to the newspapers on all types of topics, and took a keen interest in photography which led him to write respected articles for *The British Journal of Photography*. He was always a strong campaigner for the underdog which helped release two innocent men from prison. ACD spent the last thirteen years of his life tirelessly promoting his spiritualist beliefs, traveling around the world giving lectures on this topic right up until his death at the age of seventy-one. He opened a bookshop in London and a museum, both subsidised by his income. He once famously said of that "I might play with a steam yacht or own race horses. I prefer to do this."

Sir Arthur had an extraordinary life and lived it to the full. He had many talents, as a doctor, writer, medical officer, war reporter, advocate for justice, unsuccessful candidate for parliament (twice), psychic investigator, and dedicated promoter of spiritualism and life after death. His missionary drive probably wore him out faster than if he had stayed at home as he was quite ill in the last few years, but against doctors' advice he continued with a punishing schedule right to the end.

It is my wish that in the afterlife I can accompany Sir Arthur to the many great libraries and halls of learning where the ideas and thoughts projected by him during his lifetime are still in existence. These ideas would be for example, plots, romances, and characters that he never used but perhaps had thought about. One could find out anything and everything to do with Sherlock Holmes and all the other books, like his historical novels, and *The Strand* magazine stories. Imagine the joy of seeing several hundred copies of your favourite story with these different characters, the twists in the stories, and the surprise endings Sir Arthur might not have used. The opportunities are endless!

Chapter Fourteen

What Happens When We Die?

What does really happen to us when the spirit body leaves this world? Generally before we die our spirit guides prepare for our death months or weeks in advance. The spirit guides will know ahead of time when a person is coming over to their side. As we are about to die our energy levels become lower and lower, and the spirit body starts to leave the physical body intermittently. This carries on until the silver cord snaps at the top of our crown. Somebody who has a clairvoyant ability may be able to see the spirit leaving the body, or at least the spirit essence or spirit light. The spirit usually leaves the body through the head area as the silver chord is near your crown on the top of your head. Never forget that the whole world is one big orderly spirit plan. If we take for example, people who are terminally ill lying on beds in a hospital spirit guides will be able to see how fragile their life cord is while still attached to their physical bodies. A person who is close to death tends to sleep a lot more. This helps the spirit guides prepare the dying person's spirit for the other side. On occasions there is a rush of energy into the spirit body two days before, sometimes the same day, the body dies. This force comes from the spirit world which helps detach the spirit body from the physical body. You could call it one 'final push'.

The person usually dies almost immediately after this experience. The silver cord snaps because it is so frayed that the person is basically dead. When I say 'dead' I mean that life has been removed from the physical body. When I say 'frayed' I mean that the silver cord has some fragments of life thread still attached to the physical body preventing the spirit body from being fully released. These threads usually wither away a few hours after the life force has left the body. However on some occasions when a person's time is not up, meaning he or she is not supposed to die but dies accidentally, it can take a few days for the silver cord to detach. This occurs because the cord was strong and the life force kept it intact. As the life force drains away from the body the cord begins to deteriorate. Subsequently with a little help from the spirit guides the silver cord is detached.

If a person's spirit is still attached to their body after death they can still move around and travel quite a distance. If a person is involved in an explosion or war-related death, where the body is disintegrated, the cord is snapped but the spirit body could be in a state of shock. In this case the spirit body is then moved to what is termed as 'the hall of rest'. This place is like a hospital where spirit bodies are treated with healing rays to help them adjust to their new world. Some spirits can stay there for the equivalent of a few days; others can be there for weeks, or months, or until they have fully recovered. Spirits that frequent these rest halls are those who have had such mental anguish on earth that it takes time to adjust and heal their spirit bodies.

Spirit bodies cannot be destroyed but they can be spiritually damaged and often need time to heal in spirit. Once a spirit has left their physical body it is normal to have family or friends waiting to greet them on the other side. Studies on pre-death experiences in many hospitals around the world irrespective of race, or practiced religion, found that people saw relatives or friends in the room before they died. A spirit guide communicated to me that ninety-five% of the spirits that cross over are greeted by somebody familiar as this helps them with the transition.

A sudden death provoked by violence can cause confusion to a spirit who dies in such a manner. War-related deaths can contribute to this confusion too. It is known that these wars and battles are still going on in the spirit's life even after these wars have finished on the earthly plane. This confusion is usually associated with an earthbound spirit or haunting. This incorporeal being does not realise that it is dead hence this spirit becomes confused.

The spirit of the deceased may see a crowd, possibly his or her relatives and friends, gathered around the corpse. The spirit if confused will normally try in vain to inform them that they are all right. However their loved ones cannot hear them. Moreover earthbound spirits are also those who are still attached to their families, businesses or other interests. They cannot 'let go' therefore they cannot move on. Eventually these earthbound spirits or hauntings perceive they are dead, and then a rescue guide may intervene and explain that what they are experiencing is, in fact, passing over from death. The guide may reach the spirit, but if he is not successful he will leave the earthbound spirit until he or she is ready to move on. It is not always necessary for the spirit to move anywhere. Spirits can stay anywhere as long as they like. There is infinite time to progress. As I said earlier time is measured very differently in the spirit world. What seems like days to a spirit can be the equivalent of months or years of our earth 'time'. Spirits can move backward and forward in time.

As we die in this mortal world we are born into the spirit world. When we die we have to go through a learning process like babies do on earth. It takes time for spirits to adjust to their new life as well. The spirit body is very subtle. How would people look once they die and cross to the afterlife? They would look exactly as they were before they died except they would have a smiling face filled with joy. There are exceptions of course, and I am referring to those who did not do well on Earth and left a trail of destruction behind them. Once you pass into the spirit world your body starts adjusting to the finer vibrations. These vibrations start to change your appearance. The wrinkles start to go, your skin is smooth, you get your hair back, and I am not talking only about men. The spirit body becomes younger and your appearance ends up looking like when you were in your prime years, anywhere between your twenties and forties. It depends on how you want to look. You definitely look youthful. If you died in childhood then you start to grow up to an age that suits you best. Some children like to stay the way they are for a while.

There are no rules, only natural laws, which means that you are bound by the limitations of the spirit world. However you can 'earn' the right to do as you please. When you earn this right you gain control over spirit 'matter'. So the natural law is not a rule, instead, it is a type of power earned by yourself as you take charge over your thoughts. Control is everything. For example, if you were a Dutch person who lived in the equivalent of Holland in the flat land of spirit world, and you wanted to build a castle on this land in spirit world then you have to earn the right to do it. This means you need to be able to control the forces of thought in order to construct a castle to your design.

Your thoughts create everything including any objects you would like to construct or have on spirit side. This means that you need to go through a kind of apprenticeship where you learn how to construct all the castle parts from thought. It is a step by step process just the way we do it here on earth: the foundations must be laid, then the walls, then the roof, the floors, the furnishings, and so forth. You need to be able to create the bricks, add the texture, the cement, keeping it straight hopefully, brick by brick added by your thoughts, the roof joists, and the stairs, etc. This is very much how things are constructed in spirit world. In the next world we create everything by thought. Everything is ordered. You earn the right to do things through service, that is, service to others. Service is the cornerstone of how things work in spirit world just as we need service on earth.

How does service work? You gain wisdom and love by servicing others. Love comes from the appreciation of the person you helped. If love is continually sent out to you because of your service then it will begin to surround you, and permeate your akashic record. Wisdom comes from helping a person through a difficulty. By doing so you gain the knowledge to deal with the situation at hand, and thus avoid a similar circumstance in the future. The thoughts of love are stored in your akashic record in the shape of dots made of light. This light makes you shine as an individual in the spirit world. On the other hand, if you have dark thoughts and people think negatively about you then you store dots of darkness in your akashic record. This means that your aura is dark and your spirit does not shine. When spirits come into your presence they instantly know everything about you as they read the akashic record that surrounds you. All the thoughts that you put out while on earth permeate the akashic field. For instance, if you saved a life or did charitable work your acts of kindness are there for everyone to see. Spirits can read each other's aura so there is nothing to hide. When you die you'll go to the vibrational level that you have earned; you will be surrounded by people of similar character and mind. This could be equated to your judgment day. In fact you'll judge yourself; all your acts of kindness or meanness will be exposed for everyone to see.

Based on this system you'll go to your own level of heaven or hell. This is done by natural law. In other words, you cannot ascend to the higher level you think you deserve because the spirit body with its akashic record cannot tolerate the vibrations of these levels. The thoughts you have on earth empower the vibration of your spirit body and tune it to the level it can tolerate. Spirits on higher levels can simply go down as they have earned the right, but the spirits on the lower levels cannot raise their vibration to go upwards.

There are many other factors and complexities involved which put your spirit in your 'vibration' of heaven or hell, or somewhere in between. Purgatory is for those spirits who have passed over but have not moved on to their vibrational level. These spirits have not accepted what 'they' judge to be their level. They refuse to go to the plane that has been earned by their actions, thoughts, and deeds. These spirits are resident ghosts who still haunt their previous dwellings. However not all ghosts are 'in purgatory'; some choose to stay there because they want to help others from their side, and still some others are not ready to move onwards, let alone upwards.

It is important for people to get away from the religious aspect of heaven, hell, and purgatory. It does not matter if you follow a religion or not. Is there a religion that holds all the answers? They all have some aspects of the truth, but all of them have been hijacked by man's interpretation which is mostly inaccurate and wrong. As you read this I will tell you not to take my word for what has been written here. Find out for yourself. Take what you can accept and leave behind that which does not make sense. The truth is to be found out if you look for it and it's there within oneself. I believe what I have written down is the truth. It comes from what I have read and from what ACD and other guides have told me.

If a spirit finds itself in a sort of purgatory, which is a sort of vibrational or dimensional level that they want to leave behind, then there is always a way to move out. Nobody is forgotten, and no one is left behind in the constant struggle to ascend to a higher spirit level.

All spirits have to earn the right to move to the next level. How is this done? The answer again is through service. We can move upwards to finer spirit levels of thought by providing service to others, and being able to control the extra senses that we earn. In the spirit world we all help each other out. We also help

99

those in the lower levels and on the earth plane through thoughts and guidance. As an example, when a spirit needs help designing a garden in the spirit dimension it would get help from spirits who design gardens with their thoughts. This includes everything from the soil, flowers, shrubs, trees, to the green house, which has to be built from scratch. These spirit gardeners give service to others and in turn they grow as a result of it. They could teach you to do it too. Everything is possible because you don't need to earn a living. Life here is simple and rewarding. If you don't feel like moving on or progressing then you don't have to. You are your own master.

It is often said in the spirit world that we are the dead people and they are the living. Our world is the dream world, and the spirit world is the real one. As I said before we come from spirit and go back to spirit. The earth is a learning ground, another school of life, but it is a growth of a spiritual life through the trials and tribulations that we encounter. Those in spirit don't need to sleep, eat, earn money, or have material objects. Money is the root of all evil. It's not hard to see why. Most crimes are related to money. Many of our pains and pleasures are caused by money. If the need for money is removed think how different this world would be. This world is about learning lessons, striving to survive, and developing our character. The needs of the spirits are immensely different to the needs of our physical bodies. Their energy is derived from their surroundings. The spirit body does not decay; it only becomes more refined as each individual grows as a spiritual being by servicing others. Service is the key element that makes the spirit world work. Everyone works for one another; souls lift each other up the ladder. It is a utopian world. The spirit world has order, purpose, and infinite time.

We seem always to need time on the earth plane. We always need to be somewhere. Unfortunately we

100

cannot travel instantaneously to our destination the way spirit beings do through the use of spirit locomotion. When a spirit goes to another dimension or another part of the spirit world to meet somebody, for example, they just think about moving there and they arrive in an instant. This is spirit- locomotion. The spirits shrink or contract as they travel, and expand once they reach the other side. Spirits travel much faster than the speed of light. In fact spirit beings don't have to travel as they can project their mind and tune in to their destination. It is another form of telepathy, but more sophisticated as they can see, hear, and feel at the same time as their thoughts are processed. If a meeting is needed in the spirit world then all those who are involved just tune in to each other's thoughts. They don't need to move, but they can travel to meet each other if they wish to do so.

Spirit beings dwell in their own dimensions, their own heaven or hell. Those who inhabit what is supposed to be hell cannot move up to the higher levels on their own. The vibration from the higher level is unbearable for their bodies. To enable them to do this they need a spirit from that level to take them there. Before going there they'll need 'a cloak of protection' placed around them to shield their bodies from the intense vibrations that they are not yet attuned to. These vibrations become more refined and rarefied as a spirit travels into the higher planes.

As previously explained, there is order in the spirit world and each spirit belongs to a class structure. This is not based on material possessions, society, status or intelligence. Intellect is treasured on earth; wisdom and spirituality, however, are the equivalent treasures in spirit world. The spiritual dimension you achieve is based on all your deeds on earth. We attract those of a similar vibration. The vibration of spiritual growth that we have achieved attracts us to the dimension of thought in which we are 'comfortable'. We encounter a beautiful world that is bright and colourful, filled with mountains, rivers, valleys and incredible buildings created by thought. We can also find halls of learning: art, music, literature and much more.

However this is only one side. What about those people who have not been so spiritual? What have they created for themselves? I will give you an example of a spirit who spent all his time making money on earth. It concerns an actual conversation from a spirit in the afterlife with a friend of his on earth. These psychic circles are direct voice communication. The voice speaks out of mid-air in the original voice and accent they had on earth. It takes a special medium to provide this sort of mediumship. The spirit came through speaking as a confused individual. His first words were *"It is cold and dark."* These were the actual physical conditions where he was 'living'. He continued to say: *"There is around and about me a wall of money nothing but money; it shuts out the light. It is so dark, and wherever I go I cannot get away from it, around it or over it."* A man in the psychic circle recognised the voice which belonged to a gentleman he knew who had died five years previously. The deceased man had been a very successful person on earth. A spirit guide then took over the conversation and explained that the man in question had spent all his life accumulating money so much that he created piles of money in the afterlife as well.

Unfortunately he did not develop his spirit while on the earth plane which meant the conditions he created in the spirit world reflected his spiritual growth: cold and dark. He told the psychic circle that he was surrounded by vast sums of money, and as a result he could not climb over it or go around it. A spirit guide helped the confused soul out of his own 'hell' by asking the people in this circle to send him positive thoughts. When they projected light to the spirit he found a pathway was created for him. Thus you can see how thoughts can help all those who have passed over to the spirit world. Don't forget their world is a world of thought; ours is a material and physical one. This spirit had to earn a new spiritual life by rendering service to others. He was now beginning his spiritual journey the one he had neglected to do on earth.

Bear in mind that guides and spirit helpers are always ready to assist us. Spirit guides or guardian angels, if you prefer, are usually around you most of your life, if not all of your life. Sometimes you will have one permanent guardian angel that is with you from birth to death while other guides, called spirit helpers, come and go. Spirit helpers come for brief periods only and they help you through a certain experience. For instance, in childbirth a particular spirit helper can influence your thoughts when necessary and move on once your child has been delivered. So spirit guides grow while we grow, by helping us they help themselves. When things go right for you, or when you are saved from a difficult situation don't forget to thank them just in case you meet them on the other side! They will always be there for you no matter how sad or alone you might feel one day.

When you die none of these guardian angels judge you for your 'sins'. They want you to progress therefore; they will be there for you. What you do in life is up to you; your spirit guides will influence your thoughts if you ask them as long as they are positive thoughts. Guardian angels will not help you with vengeful or harmful thoughts as it is not spiritual or good for your growth. The natural laws of spirit such as 'The Law of Cause and Effect' will take care of people who harm you. It may not happen immediately, it may take years, but it will balance itself. Finally remember that you are responsible for ALL your thoughts and deeds. Every action has a reaction, cause and effect, what goes around comes around.

Chapter Fifteen

Thoughts

When writing about his most famous character, Sherlock Holmes, Sir Arthur Conan Doyle was inspired by and based the character on one of his professors in medical school, Dr Joseph Bell. But as he wrote the wonderful stories were all of the Holmes' creation coming from the mind of Conan Doyle? Did Doyle have help in creating the detective's complex personality with his sharp deduction skills and fine logic combined with personal character flaws? Yes he did actually have help.

Our thoughts are sometimes inspired from beyond this world, and we may be a conduit for other inspired individuals who help great writers like Conan Doyle and J.R.R. Tolkien. The latter's books, *The Hobbit* and *The Lord of the Rings,* with their Upper, Middle, and Lower Earths sound like dimensions of another world that exists in a spiritual domain. In fact they are based on dimensions of spirit in the afterlife, and the thoughts about these worlds, with the characters that inhabit them, would have been imparted to Tolkien by spirits who had been to these dimensions and had seen the characters such as the 'Grey Elves' and 'Orcs' from Middle Earth. We all similarly attract spirit beings who impart thoughtful influences in all parts of our life. Some are to do with work or home life, others are good with relationships, and of course some are helping us express our artistic talents just like Doyle and Tolkien. There are naturally many other kinds of helpful spirits as well.

As we go through life and mature we eventually (hopefully) start to gain control over our thoughts and feelings. Then the natural law of attraction will bring helpful spirit guides to us. It is not that we don't have good guides with us at the moment, we have, but as we try to become more and more spiritual we sometimes need new guides with a greater spiritual understanding who can then influence us as we spiritually mature through our thoughts. Just as in school our teachers changed as we progressed it is the same in spirit. These spirit guides become attracted to our progress.

We can attract nasty spirits as well. Our thoughts have a magnetic attraction on the spirit side. We send out waves of thoughts just like radio transmitters, and the receivers are those spirits of a like mind. Those who are attracted to our thinking may well have been in our positions before so they can readily understand and influence us going forward.

This is why control of your thoughts, especially if you are a medium, is very important. If I am giving a spirit message to someone I want to be able to have the best communication with my guide, or the guides around me. To do this I say a prayer of protection which develops a link between them and me. In our world it could be interpreted as a secure or encrypted channel. I need it to be safe and stable since the information coming from my guides needs to be accurate so I can prove that somebody's loved one is indeed here communicating with me. My guide acts as a relay from those who have passed on since the spirits who have crossed over recently have to learn how to develop these new skills to interact with mediums. The prayer of protection acts like a force field and blocks any external thoughts from reaching me. Thoughts can come from the people on Earth as well as the spirit side so I need to be sure that what I am receiving is accurate, and true.

If you are inclined to think in a negative way be it with emotions of hate, revenge, jealousy, or greed then you will start to attract what are called *lower astrals* to you. These are spirits that live in the dimension called the *astral plane of existence*, or normally called the *astral plane*. Of course you don't want to bring lower astrals to you so you should always try to veer away from any of the feelings that would attract them. I know it's very difficult on Earth sometimes not to have these feelings, but you just have to keep trying. For example, I think some of the thoughts that I would have the least problems with are thoughts of jealousy and greed as I am not really a person who thinks them. Accumulating money and being jealous of other people does not come into my way of thinking so I already feel that I am mastering some of my emotions.

One thing that I would ask you to remember above all is that when sending out positive or negative thoughts be sure they are creative. Thoughts really do create things for us if they are positive, or destroy things if negative. I have been told this by a particular guide named Sandy, and other guides have confirmed that all thoughts travel out to those we think about. If they are not 'accepted' by the individual, either through insensitivity or ignorance, they will travel back to the transmitter (that's you) in this case. What I believe is meant by 'accepted' is that the person who has wronged does not feel guilty or remorseful either through ignorance or innocence. If the person believes that they were right to teach you a lesson this could also cause them to not accept your thoughts of revenge or hate. These will circle around the individual and eventually come back and cause illness in your body or mind. They also stay in your akashic record so be careful with your thoughts to others. It's not easy to hold your tongue sometimes, but it is even more difficult to hold a thought if someone has really upset you.

Due to my sensitivity it is difficult to be in unpleasant situations where there might be unsavoury individuals. I tend to pick up and sometimes see these horrible spirits hanging around nasty people. These astrals usually know what a medium does, and for them it's like a picnic so they try to torment me. When they come near me I start to feel my vibration speeding up; I become dizzy, sick to the stomach, become very hot or cold, and as I pass individual people with these lower astrals around them I literally get terrible feelings from them such as anxiety, nausea and depression.

It is possible to look at unpleasant individuals and see their faces changing to expose the inner self. Beauty is only skin deep and the soul or spirit is much more subtle. Think about this: if most of the people you know are good people and they die and pass over to spirit they go to people of a like mind (good, thoughtful, loving, generous people, for example). What happens to those who die and whose every thought was nastiness, greed, spite, revenge, and jealousy?

For all of us, it is really down to an individual's character that will determine the dimension of thought they go to on the spirit side. The place that you earn in spirit depends on many factors such as how you lived, whether you grew as a spirit, if you helped people along the way, how you will be missed, whether you loved and were loved in return, whether you had control over your emotions, and so on. Our thoughts specify our spirit world and shape our destiny on Earth. They have power and creative forces. Our thoughts shape everything that happens to us because the thoughts are our decisions which guide us on our path.

One of the reasons why prayer or positive thinking is so important is because we think so shall it become. 'Beware of what you wish for; you may get it' - this is such a true statement because sometimes we wish for something and end up being sorry. You can of course be absolutely delighted when something positive happens like passing exams or graduating from school or from university, but how many times have we thought about something that we would love to have and eventually ended up being disappointed?

Having a positive mental attitude is a very special gift. It is important to think positively not only for yourself, but also for others around you. Selfless

107

thoughts are the best kind you can have such as those that a mother would have for her family always putting their needs first. How much do mothers sacrifice for their children? Always looking after them, washing, cleaning, cooking, and homework - sorry Dad! Their thoughts usually become ours as mums have a huge influence on how we develop as characters, don't they? But sometimes their thoughts have a negative effect. Their fears or protectiveness, for example, can also be transmitted to us and cause insecurities.

My mother was overprotective and had quite a few anxieties. Over the years I came to understand this, and re-evaluated my thought processes to think more positively. Her insecurities came from her father's death (he died when she was only ten-years-old). She also had an obsession with clocks and we must have had over a hundred of them around the house. My father was certainly kept busy winding them up!

It was only in my mother's later years that I understood the significance of the clocks. The love of clocks related to the time that my mother saw her father lying in a coffin in the living room. She was very young and this had a profound effect on her. As she looked into the room there was silence with the exception of a ticking clock in the corner so the ticking clocks reminded her of her father and the sense of loss. I never realised this until I was talking to her one day and she told me the story about her frequent visits to the coffin laid out in the front room. Because of her loss in early childhood she became overprotective of us. I brushed off most of her fears as I grew up, but I picked up her anxiety and impatience and they are still with me today.

It would be great if we could see our thoughts in action but it is only later when we see the results of our thinking. If we could actually see our thoughts going out into the ether we would have such a different world here on Earth. Our guides and spirit friends can see these thoughts. They can use them to help us, or help others if that is what we wish. I don't know how, but it works.

The thoughts we put out are a material substance that can be manipulated in spirit. Part of it is left behind in our akashic aura when we think. I know that some experimentation with healing thoughts during the 1960s showed that they do exist. Dr Bernard Grad of McGill University in Montreal[2] proved that if a psychic healer held water in a sealed flask, and when this water was later poured on barley seeds, the plants would significantly outgrow the untreated seeds that had normal water from a container. The intriguing part was that if depressed psychiatric patients held the flasks of water the growth of the seeds was retarded.

In Belgium the government became interested in a healer when they heard that by holding his hands over a piece of fresh meat the 'healing treatment' thoughts he put out seemed to preserve the meat. It did not decay or deteriorate for a month and was not refrigerated. The Soviets, in the latter half of the twentieth century, did experiments with two Georgian healers from Tiblisi, and found that while healing was successful in many areas such as ailments, infections and illnesses of the central nervous system, results were not instantaneous, but took about a month's worth of treatments. [2]

Even now, as I write, there are spiritual healers being employed by the National Health Service. Healing thoughts work, but we need more experiments and investigation into it by the scientific community. It's been shown in traumatic operations like heart and other major organs that if classical music is played during the operation the patient recovers three times more quickly than a patient who is operated on without the music being played. Some hospitals are now introducing this in their surgery theatres. It's the musical waves or vibrations that helps the healing process.

Prayer is a form of positive thought projection. Why is it that most people pray only when bad thing happens to us? Why don't we pray when things are going well? Our prayers should be structured and not just said. One needs to construct elements of what is desired and build the thoughts by using mental visualisations. If you wish to be successful in a career you need to imagine yourself in that role confidently overcoming any challenges that might arise. See yourself as confident and in control and then put more feeling and emotion into your prayers. Visualise good things that are happening to you, and feel happy with that thought perhaps by envisioning your face with a smile, or if you are praying for them seeing the same on another person. Use imagery with feeling to make these prayers (thoughts) stronger. Do not pray in a mechanical way for example, reciting lines from a prayer book, because this is fruitless. Use your own words projected with mental imagery. Go into a chapel or church, synagogue, temple or mosque, because these houses of worship have concentrated prayer energy. Remember it is not important where you pray you can do just as well in a nice comfortable environment in your own home. Successful sportsmen and women use visualisation imagery before their events and literally dream their way to winning.

We are what we think, and what we think we become. Most people who reach the top of life's ladders be it in sport, music, the arts, entertainment, or other, would be strong thinkers who are passionate about what they do. Their 'thoughts' will be constantly focused on what they want to achieve. They set their goals early in life and worked through a plan to achieve them. I know this is obvious to most people, but it really is our thoughts that create luck or help us to overcome obstacles placed in our way, and which bring us to our ultimate goal.

Thoughts imparted from spirits can be good and bad. Is it possible to come under mental attack from these thoughts getting subsequent physical feelings such as being unable to relax or clear your mind? I am not talking about once or twice a day, but twenty-four seven. I get this myself on occasions from lower astrals or 'the dark side' as I call them. Sometimes they may start speaking in your ear after you wake up, or when you are about to go to sleep telling you that you have cancer or heart problems exploiting anything that you may be worried or anxious about. They blow in your ear sometimes poke you or grab your foot. Because I am a physical medium dark astrals can sometimes gain my energy and use it against me. I have a lot of protection from my guides on the spirit side, but the dark astrals are always looking for weaknesses in my defence. It is a constant battle. It is important to be aware that sometimes, if you allow them, dark forces can influence your thoughts (The Law of Attraction). If you are thinking positively, with thoughts of goodness, they cannot harm you. Always ask for protection from your guides if you are afraid or are in a difficult situation. They will put a barrier around your aura to protect you.

We do not realise it, but we can shield ourselves from nasty thoughts. Prayer is a little like a magic spell, and because spells are projections of thoughts, good or bad depending upon the person, these thoughts protect us from other negative ones. So when we pray we put out this (spell) energy around us that we, of course, cannot see, but it is definitely seen on the spirit side since that is a world of thought energy. The thoughts of positive prayer help us as individuals. Negative prayer also exists, but since it has its own energy it can cause problems for people. If we put out negative thoughts it can create trouble for individuals and eventually will make us ill (The Law of Cause and Effect).

We are responsible for all our thoughts. This is why we should not send out negative ones for they will be stored in our akashic record, and given the cause for the same thought to come back to us later in life, or even sooner. Don't think badly of people even though it's difficult when they have wronged you. It is better to ask the Great Spirit, or God, with a prayer to teach them a lesson so they do not do the same harm to somebody else.

As previously discussed all our thoughts are stored in our akashic record that surrounds us. Thoughts can actually make our physical appearance change. If we think positively, and are basically happy you can see this just by looking at our faces or features. Sensitive's like myself have extra gifts or abilities that allow us to read a person's aura. I can tell whether they are ill and where in their body the illness is located. This can be helpful to know when giving a message, but it is not proof of life after death. Reading a person's aura is a psychic ability. You can pick up on their health, their personality, or whether they are anxious, high-strung, wise, peaceful, depressive, nasty, and all the emotions and characteristics of people. When people are in a bad mood it's like they have a dark cloud around them and you can pick up on it.

It is better not to judge people because they may have some of these characteristics as "you can never know a person's situation until you have walked a mile in their moccasins" to quote a famous Native American expression.

We all have to learn lessons as no one is perfect. If we think pleasantly of others and ourselves we will have a light aura that surrounds us. If we harbour dark thoughts and think negatively our aura will be dark and heavy. Once again, however, remember that it is important to guard our thoughts.

Positive thinking is also prayer, but unfortunately people don't pray because of the religious connotation. People these days believe less in religion because they are distracted by everything around them. Young people feel they lack something in their lives but cannot describe it. They have more disposable income to buy more material objects like TVs, DVDs, MP3 players, or to use the Internet. But they don't want or feel that they need organised religion but they feel a spiritual pull thus they focus this energy on things like environmental action, anti-globalisation, and animal welfare.

Everyone wants to believe that a God exists but not everyone is willing to believe the current religious interpretations. Often the current view is seen as outdated and narrow-minded and one cannot take the literal interpretation of the Bible anymore because it is full of contradictions and is quite bigoted and narrow minded.

We have increased our knowledge of the world and can see how it works beyond the subatomic level. Our space probes are reaching to the furthest points in the galaxies that surround us, but still we lack something to link all this wonder with our daily lives - spirituality. The essence of our being, the spirit that drives our physical bodies, gives us all our joys and pains, and yet we have no clue that it even exists. This spiritual essence is as real as the physical body, but how many know it is within all of us? Every living creature has a spirit body, animals, plants, trees and even rocks. We have knowledge, science, technology, entertainment, and many wonders but we are missing spiritual growth, the nourishment that our spirit body needs. Our needs for the physical body, like food, clothing, and exercise are well known. *What does the spirit body need?*

[2]*Psychic Discoveries Behind the Iron Curtain*, Sheila Ostrander & Lynn Schroeder, Bantam Books, U.S.A., p. 224; also read chapter on 'Healing with Thought', p. 293.

Chapter Sixteen

The Spirit Body Within

If Sir Arthur Conan Doyle is living on the other side how does he survive without a body? When we die or pass over to the afterlife we take the form of a spirit body. We have all heard the number of expressions about the word 'spirit'. Here are some examples. What about the *'spirit of man'*, *'the spirit of a nation'*, and the *'Holy Spirit'*. The spirit that *'drives us forward'* or is *'his spirit crushed under the pressure'*, *'his spirit has been broken'*, or *'the spirit is released'*. These are familiar expressions, but we don't know the real meaning. I think most people believe that the spirit is something tangible. I believe, in fact I *know,* it is real. I have seen a person's spirit in front of me after they had died. To me it is a real body just like the physical body. Just because most people cannot see spirit it doesn't mean the spirit is not there. It means that the spirit body exists beyond the visible spectrum of the physical eye. The spirit body can be seen by the 'Third Eye' or spiritual eye, but this needs to be opened first.

Why can I see spirits but you cannot? Am I mad? Am I seeing hallucinations? I am not mad and I am certainly not seeing hallucinations. I have communicated with spiritual entities who have told me about their lives, or more importantly given me evidential proof to their loved ones who are left behind. Because it happens so often or is repeatable then it must be true. The whole of scientific progression is based on repeatable experiments. All the readings I do are repeatable and very specific. And the evidential proof from these encounters is backed up as well. For when I tell people who are strangers that I have never met before evidence that is personal, and sometimes incredibly profound with information that could have

114

happened as a child and forgotten about, or even happened an hour ago, this shows that there is an intelligence behind the reality of an afterlife. The problem with proof and evidence from spirit is that it needs to be personal before you can believe it, and sometimes it is very personal. When a spirit communicates with evidence it's sometimes the little things that usually give the best proof.

So why do some mediums see these spirits while most people cannot? It's because they have opened themselves up to spirit and they can communicate through certain parts of the brain sometimes called the mystical 'third eye' located in the centre of the forehead. It is considered a spiritual eye as opposed to a physical one. The brain is an interface to the mind and the mind is the area where all our thoughts and experiences are stored. The mind is outside the physical body.

To start the process of opening up to spirit you really need to consciously make an effort. You can start to open these centres up through meditation or by just believing that it is there. Once it starts to open you begin to see two worlds: our physical world and the spirit world. How much you see depends upon how much you develop, and as you develop your sensitivity will increase. If you open up your third eye you are starting a new path in life because you will begin to become a sensitive. The third eye is not just about seeing spirits it also receives thoughts from spirits, and thoughts and emotions from others around you on earth. You will start to pick up on other people's feelings, their emotions, even their illnesses. The eye does not distinguish whether what you are receiving is good or bad just like your physical eye allows good images and bad images to enter your brain. We can close our eyelids to stop us seeing things that upset us, but it is more difficult to do this with the third eye.

It is not uncommon for mediums to receive negative thoughts from time to time and there is a need to be able to defend oneself. These negative thoughts are never acted on, of course, but mediums need to be aware that they are like radio receivers that pick up lots of thoughts from other people and external astral spirits who are not very nice. The mediums mind need to distinguish exactly where these thoughts come from, and although they know they would not act on these negative thoughts the more sensitive the medium is the stronger they feel these thoughts. This is one of the prices paid for developing mediumship which means you will need to have a strong will so as not to succumb to these thoughts.

The spirit body is an exact replica of the physical body. If you died and left your earthly body anyone who saw you one minute afterwards would see an exact copy of your physical body, clothes and all, but without any physical defects. On passing over cancer disappears, arthritis is gone, Alzheimer's disease is removed, and people can see clearly. Those unfortunate to have lost limbs, for example, would actually regain them the moment they crossed over to the other side. Many elderly friends of mine who found it difficult to walk in their last years would come back and skip around in front of me, and I have often seen people who had canes or crutches throw them away as they appeared in front of me.

Although there are no physical illnesses in the spirit world there can be a residue of mental confusion left over from a persons earthly life which gradually disappears with time and the help of other spirits. This could be a person's reluctance to believe that they have actually died. There are communities of spirits who still go to a place of worship and follow the rituals they did while alive. My spirit guides have often told me that eventually the confusion is lifted from these people, and they start to look for other things to do. This is when rescue spirits pick up on their thoughts and show these spirits all the wonderful things to do on the other side.

The spirit body is attached to the physical body with what could be described as a silver cord which is very flexible and can be stretched for hundreds of miles or more. As long as the silver cord is intact and attached to the physical body we will live on the earth. Once the silver cord snaps, our time is up, our spirit body is disconnected from our physical body, and we then pass from this world into the next. There is a quote in the Bible which tells of the silver cord "...*before the silver cord of life snaps and the golden bowl is broken*" (Ecclesiastes 12:6-7). When you leave your physical body during the sleep state, just like when you are dreaming, the cord keeps us connected to our physical body. Have you experienced the effect of your spirit body being quickly pulled back into your physical body making you jump? This is usually caused by the spirit body having to return unexpectedly from the astral plane before it was ready. Generally the spirit body comes back very smoothly so you do not normally have this shock during the return.

Our dream world is located on a level of the *astral plane* closest to our Earth. It is a place where our dream thoughts can actually create a reality that seems as real as our world and usually bring to 'life' an obscure representation of incidents that are worrying us at the time. The dream-state usually puts a story together that can help us understand the reasons for our problems. If you can remember your dreams they can be analysed with some logic, and a good dream interpreter can help you work out the dreams meaning. For example, many people have dreamed that they have actually lost some of their teeth. It is a common and very distressing dream that normally indicates anxiety, insecurity, and a lack of confidence, and because you are on the astral plane your worries create the images of teeth falling out. It can seem very real while you're dreaming, and it can be a real experience, but it's a spiritual experience rather than physical.

117

Dream interpretation is a science unto itself. It was a very highly regarded gift in Greek and Roman times. Unfortunately a lot of my dreams can be a little like nightmares. Because I am so open to the astral plane I get good and bad spirits in equal measure. The good ones are great, bring in wonderful feelings, and surround me in a golden light, but the bad ones attack me, sometimes physically, while I am entering or leaving my physical body. Apart from the physical attacks, which sometimes leave me with bruises or scratches on my body, they also attack me mentally by using any of my insecurities against me. For example, if I was worried about a pain in my chest they would torment me by putting thoughts of death in my mind or whispering in my ear that I have a heart problem and am going to have a heart attack. Mediums have to be very aware of the darker side and how it operates. Above all they need a very strong will to counteract these opposing forces otherwise they could end up in a lunatic asylum. This is a reality for some psychic mediums that could not control the forces.

Our thoughts cause our actions, what we think is usually what we do, so it is vital that we think positively. Remember our thoughts have power and have energy. We can create our future which can be good or bad depending on our attitudes towards it. Send positive thoughts out for yourselves and your loved ones. Send healing thoughts to those who may need it even something as small as saying, 'God' or 'Great Spirit', 'please send healing to my friend'. Our spirit guides can use these thoughts to help that person. Can you imagine what could happen if thousands or hundreds of thousands of people sent out these healing thoughts? Maybe miracles could happen. It's not just an idea!

Chapter Seventeen

Developing Mediumship

Would you like to be a medium? It's hard work to develop and become a medium. In many ways your life will not be your own and you will have to make sacrifices. Your sensitivity will make living on this planet more uncomfortable. You will try to seek peace and avoid arguments but your health may suffer in some way because of the increased sensitivity. You will need to think more about what you are going to say and be in control of your emotions, but the rewards are priceless. To be able to bring communication from a loved one, such as a child, back to their mother is a wonderful thing to achieve. In fact bringing back any loved one is a miracle because it is very difficult to do.

Wouldn't it be wonderful if you could actually communicate with your spirit guide (or guardian angel if you prefer)? Developing mediumship is open to everyone. There are only a few requirements:

1. You need a peaceful room or somewhere quiet, even the toilet if it's free! I would suggest sitting in a comfortable chair for about twenty-five minutes a day or every second day if that is not possible. This is your time so use it wisely. You need to be free of distractions as much as you can. Playing music is also a good idea though if you want to have silence that is also all right. Personally I prefer classical music — choral music or Gregorian chants are the best for me because of their resonance, but if you prefer something else that's fine. Play it at a low level like background music.

2. Try to clear your mind. Don't think about work, family or anything else. This allows our

119

spirit friends to work on your spirit body starting to 'tune' your aura to their level by adding vibrations to your spirit body. This can take a while and there are no quick fixes as everyone is 'tuned' at the level they can accept. The vibrations will cause your sensitivity to increase, and you may find emotional changes in yourself later on such as being quicker to temper, avoiding noisy environments, even crying at some sad moments in films or TV shows.

3. After a while start to ask questions and see what kind of answers come back. You may be surprised at the results. Ask a question that you don't know the answer to perhaps something about a brother, sister or friend, such as what colour car they will buy, or how many people they work with in the office, and ask their names assuming you don't already know. The questions are up to you but I think you can work them out. Be creative the harder the better. When you receive thoughts you will almost certainly doubt whether they came from your mind or elsewhere. This is natural but if you ask questions remember them or write them down. If the answers turn out to be exactly what you thought maybe it's not your mind after all! Keep practicing. The spirit guides are *always* ready to help you. Even if you don't want to be a clairvoyant it is a great way to relax, get some healing, and if you link with your guides you might experience a wonderful high like you have never before experienced. This is really worth the effort. As long as "you" ask the guides, they will help you to heal your body. Always ask them for help if you are having trouble.

Think about how nice it would be to have a friend always looking out for you. Healing, inspiring, sending love to you, and never judging. All our guides are here in service, which basically means they are here to help ease our burdens. But remember, they are not servants – they are special friends. We must learn our own lessons in life go through life's experiences and gain wisdom while increasing our knowledge. If you look at the progression of your life it starts at birth; you start growing, learn to walk, talk, gain new experiences every day and understand more about the world around you. You go to school and perhaps to a university. It's a non-stop learning experience, or at least it should be. There are so many mysteries to life, space, and the universe that sometimes it's overwhelming.

Most people believe in a god of some description a creator who links everything together in some way. As a child, I remember having an image of somebody or some being looking down on us the way the movies portrayed the Greek gods peering into the pools of water to see visions of life below. This might have been a Hollywood interpretation but I went along with it for a while when I was younger. Another idea I had was that our solar system was possibly like a grain of sand on a beach in another world larger than ours. This is actually quite close to how our world could be described from the spirit side. One very wise guide, called Tse Sing, said to me once that "you think that your world is so sophisticated and clever, so advanced with its technology, a shining beacon in the solar system, but the Earth from our side looks very insignificant indeed. Compared to our world of wonders, infinite realities, and glorious colours which are indescribable your Earth is like a piece of dirt in the corner of a dirty, neglected, dusty room in darkness."

It may humble a few of us to think that the earth is not the centre of the universe. The Earth is really not a very nice place. Half the world is starving when they go

121

to bed and another quarter lives in poverty. By virtue of reading this book you have advanced to the quarter on this planet that are educated and well fed. You are probably able to earn a decent living. Are we really sophisticated? No. We are not actually that clever. We are allowing forests to be cut down, oceans to be fished out of existence, and hundreds of species of plants and animals to become extinct every year. The Earth is polluted from the ground to the sky, and the most beautiful natural regions of the world are being turned into tourist resorts.

What causes this to happen: money, greed, recklessness, indifference? No it's thought! Yes, *thought*. Everything comes from us thinking about it whether it's constructive or destructive. We think therefore we create. We want to have children - a thought. We want to change our jobs - a thought. We want to help somebody - a thought. All of our imagination, the arts, architecture, and wonderful gardens, absolutely everything – comes from our thoughts. Unfortunately we can't actually see our thoughts, but we definitely see the results.

Thinking is a complicated business. It has pretty much been proven that telepathy exists so we know that thoughts can travel from one person to another. You may have heard about this odd stuff around us called 'ether' through which radio and television waves travel. The spirit world exists in a world of ether and other dimensions of finer particles. Spirit beings live there because that is where we end up after we die. Their world is a world of thought ours is a physical world of matter.

If thoughts can travel between us and if the spirit world exists (it does) why can't thoughts come from their world to us? In fact thoughts come to us all the time from both good and bad spirits. Good and evil exist on the spirit side so we can be influenced from either direction. We draw in those spirits of a like mind, but the type of spirit we actually attract always depends upon our thinking.

Let's assume that we all want good spirits to help us, but they can only do that if we think in the right way. Our thoughts are like building blocks. They are put together and things are constructed from them, but they can destroy as well. Everything is balanced; black and white, good and evil, hot and cold. By thinking in the correct way, that is, in a positive way we can cause energy to build up so that good things start to happen. Think of it as a chain of events that combine culminating in reaching our goals. It could be compared to studying for a degree. You think about which degree you want to achieve, that's the target, and all the thoughts from your decision to your graduation are the building blocks; the studying, partying (let's be honest!), cramming sessions, missing the odd class. All these thoughts put together in the right way, constructively, will help you achieve the degree. I am not saying it's easy - effort is required. The more you think positively about a goal the more chance you have of obtaining it because our thoughts start the chain of events. We also need physical effort because we live in a physical world. It's not brain surgery, but you need to understand that the things that happen to us start on the spirit side in the ether. Understanding and accepting the simple rules to live a good life, as revealed by Sir Arthur Conan Doyle, will really help you achieve good things in your life.

Chapter Eighteen

Differences between Ghosts and Spirit Guides

Ghosts are Earth-bound spirits who have died and are still hanging around for their own reasons. Sometimes they don't even realise they are dead; they are confused because things in their world look very real to them and they see a carbon copy of life on Earth. Everything on Earth, and everything that ever existed on Earth, has an etheric double or duplicate copy on the spirit side. So when you die just like the scene depicted in the film *Ghost* where Patrick Swayze (who died) can see exactly what is going on around him but cannot communicate with his wife. As a spirit you feel alive you *are* alive, but nobody can hear you. When you pass over to the next dimension, or spirit world, you live in a world of thought. While we communicate on Earth through physical means like speaking, and through visual images, the spiritual dimensions communicate through thought. There is no language barrier as there is no language. Thoughts do not have a language. There are some mediums that pick up thoughts of spirits who have passed over, and there are those who are described as *sensitives*, those with the ability to pick up feelings, thoughts, smells and much more, but even with these abilities they cannot necessarily see spirits. Personally I have seen many ghosts in my lifetime. Ghosts are those spirits that are living so close to the earth that they sometimes appear in our dimension when the conditions are right.

A medium or psychic can be more sensitive to the 'ghostly' or astral dimensions and a medium or sensitive can see ghosts more than others. Sometimes ghosts are seen by people without any mediumistic or psychic ability because a tear between their dimensional world and ours briefly occurs. Some ghosts are described as a 'visitation', and are seen in places where they once lived. They will come from a higher or different dimension of spirit to their old homes where they can relive or experience periods of their lives like if they want to remember memories and experiences of what happened at a particular time. The visiting spirit can link with vibrations within the house and absorb all the moments, feelings, thoughts, and more, from any particular period in their life. This review is used by these spirits to go over lessons learned, or perhaps not learned, while they were on the earth. The spirit can experience the thoughts and feelings of those concerned at the time. A spirit could visit their home simply to remember happy times and experience those periods that made life worth living. These spirits in visitation are sometimes heard and seen by people presently living in the premises, and therefore experience a 'haunting'.

Spirits can also be resident within a home and 'haunt' the house or location. When they passed over they were in no hurry to move on to their next destination, and decided that they liked living within their old premises which is usually an exact replica of the home they lived in on earth.

There are also ghosts seen that are not actually ghosts, but powerful emotions or memories of an event in time and these are called 'looping ghost' events. There is no interaction between a looping ghost and a medium and it is considered to be like a video recording of an event.

What are spirit guides? Spirit guides are spirits or spiritual beings who have previously lived a life on earth before passing over. They come to help us through our current life from birth until death. They can be considered our true friends as, no matter what we do, they will always stay with us. The guides will begin their 'mission' after a period of learning in spirit on how to communicate with people in a physical body. Once their training has finished they will agree to help a person who is going to be incarnated into a physical body to progress on a spiritual path. When you are born you will have a spirit guide already appointed as a guardian, or guide (it is generally agreed between yourselves before you are born that you will know your guide before birth), and they will stay with you for most, if not all, of your life on earth. They will guide and guard you through your ups and downs always keeping you on a particular spiritual pathway or destiny. The spiritual pathway or destiny would have been agreed by yourself before you were incarnated as a baby and born into your earthly family.

Throughout your life you will have other guides called 'spirit helpers'. They come into a particular part of your life where you need certain experiences that they can provide and influence you through your 'thoughts'. For example, as they have been through this already, and know exactly how to guide you through it, a spirit helper could give you guidance through a particular relationship which might be a challenging experience. They know exactly how you feel as they have that experience, and thus can provide the necessary advice to help you make your decisions.

As an example, if you started a new business and had no experience of running one before you could have a 'helper' from spirit who has been through this experience and they can impart their business knowledge to you. Once you have gained the necessary knowledge they will leave and help another individual. Spirit helpers come and go throughout your life. If you don't learn a particular lesson a helper might come back again until the lesson is finally learned. Sometimes we never learn a particular lesson in this life and may have to come back again. This would be through reincarnation which we will discuss in a later section.

Time doesn't exist in the afterlife the same way it does on Earth. What may seem like a day in the spirit world can be a hundred years or more for us. Time is an Earth invention. We measure everything against time. With time everything decays, our food, our bodies and our buildings. Some ghosts who have been dead for hundreds of years think they have been dead only hours. They don't need to eat or drink, go to the toilet or sleep, and there is no night and day, so there isn't a way for them to measure time. It's hard for us to understand this as time is a basic measurement every second of each day on Earth.

You might well ask "Why can't a spirit guide tell them they are dead?" There are a few problems with this. A spirit guide may be able to contact a ghost by moving into their reality or vibration, and the spirit guide may tell the ghost they are dead, but the guide's advice will not always be believed. For an example, imagine you were a materialistic person (someone who only believes in things you could touch) who always believed that when you are dead there is only blackness, nothingness; how would you feel if someone came along and tried to convince you that there is life after death after all? In answer you may think that you're on drugs or it is all a dream, and tell the spirit to go away and stop bothering you. When that situation occurs, the guide or guides will leave the ghost be until it realises it may be dead and starts to think that they need to get out of wherever they are.

Other ghosts think so strongly they put up a barrier or a 'force field' around themselves. It is so solid that it makes contact almost impossible with the spirit guides who are trying to get through to the Earth-bound ghost. The barrier or 'force field' comes down when the ghost starts to question his surroundings or is looking for answers. Spirit guides also use mediums on earth that are closer to their vibration to help release them from this barrier they create. If the lost spirit changes their mind then the guides who may have tried to help them the first time 'feel' the call, or are attracted to the thoughts of the ghost, and come back to help it into the lighter levels or a level suitable for their vibration.

Vibrational levels are the infinite realities or dimensions of spirit that surround us right now. Think of radio stations transmitting a signal they all surround us right now, but we can't hear them unless we tune into them. And we have different levels of quality like LW/AM/FM. All these frequencies are existing together in our space, but all are separate, and all are unique. We go to the level or dimension that we have achieved or earned, but the spirit level that we earn is also the one that is most comfortable for us. This is a natural law as we cannot go to a level we have not earned the reason being that we could not live or exist comfortably there. A simple analogy would be a group of athletes who love to run and exercise. All they talk about is exercise routines, types of vitamins and diet. I am sure they would not be comfortable with a group of academics who love to sit around discussing Einstein's theories and quantum mechanics.

We have levels of reality here on Earth just as they have them on the spirit side. The reality of the farmer in the countryside, close to nature, is very different from that of a man living in a 10-storey building in an inner city. A person living in a tribal village in central Africa has a different reality than a Hollywood movie star, or those living in the Caribbean live very differently from those in Alaska.

These levels are what are meant by one's heaven or hell. As we move through our existence on Earth we build up a sort of record around us often called the *akashic record*. This tells a spirit guide everything there is to know about us as individuals. It holds all our thoughts, good and bad, our experiences of pain and joy, so that if one spirit comes into contact with another they instantly know everything about each other.

Although everything on Earth looks solid it is made up of fine subatomic particles which some scientists are now calling 'strings' because that is what they look like at the smallest quantum level. The strings in this universe vibrate at many different frequencies depending upon what they make up, and those in the spirit world also vibrate on infinite levels. The spirit world can be solid, like it is on Earth, or made up of energy which is manipulated by the thoughts of the spirit beings. The etheric world they live in is made up of finer subatomic particles than we have yet to discover. I am sure we will discover more answers about how these vibrations 'work' in the future.

Because the next world is a world of thought and not of matter our thoughts are treasured and valuable. Our thoughts create everything once we die. They shape appearance and mould the reality we live in, and attract friends that surround us (like attracts like). When you think about friends or family on the spirit side these people will hear or pick up on your thoughts or feelings and make contact with you. Spirits don't have to physically appear although if they choose to they can. Sometimes they simply tune into thoughts and speak through telepathy.

One could write whole books about the spirit world, but one thing that I have always been told to remember: *this world is the dream and the spirit world is the reality*. Remember this! We come from there, are born into this world, and go back there once our lives are finished.

Chapter Nineteen

How Do We Begin Our Spiritual Growth?

When you die your vibrational level changes depending on what you did in your life, your kindness to others, the love you gave and received, help you provided to people, the expansion of your mind, control of your emotions and physical senses, and overcoming your fears. To be truly considered as being on a spiritual path these are some of the lessons on which we need to work.

Tse Sing the spirit guide told me "Control is everything." To be in control of one's life is very desirable, but to achieve this we need to plan things, take responsibility for our actions, and have control over our emotions, desires and feelings. To truly grow in the spirit world you need to have mastered the basic five senses on Earth: sight, sound, hearing, touch, and taste. You also need to free yourself of obsessions, jealousies, envy, greed, perversions, hate, revenge, and sloth. These characteristics are not desirable on Earth and are far from spiritual. If you have any of these feelings and regularly express them in your emotions you are not on a spiritual path. To get on to a spiritual path you need to try to attain mastery over desires and feelings that are negative and regressive for us on Earth, let alone a spiritual being.

Everyone has had some of these characteristics, and that's one of the reasons why we are here. We need to learn how to control and remove these negative feelings from our lives. In the spirit world we learn how to develop more spiritually. On Earth we learn a degree of control through opposition and hardship. Once we have mastered this to a certain level we move forward into the spirit world taking what we have learned and earned to further our growth and development.

Before we come from the spirit world we map out what we want to do in life including the family we will live with (yes you choose your family), the sexuality we will have, the race into which we will be born, whether we will be rich or poor, the relationships we will encounter along the way, whether we will have fame and fortune, whatever we need to grow as a person, what skills and abilities we want to learn or develop, and even whether we will win the lottery. This becomes what we call our 'destiny'; we are all destined in some way. We cannot all be famous or rich, but we can all be loved. If we have only one life to develop how fair is it for the baby starving in Africa, while a child is born into a wealthy family with all of its advantages? This would not be fair, of course, if we only had one life, but the fact is we have many lives each different from the other. We learn different things and develop our character through each lifetime.

As an example, we can look at Mozart. How could a boy of four have been able to write a symphony without any tutelage and experience? Perhaps there are two parts to this answer. The first is that he was a musician in a previous spiritual incarnation where he gained the experience of the instruments and musical scores which enabled him to write. Second he used this experience to channel his wonderful music from the spirit world. He was a medium. It doesn't otherwise make sense. Mozart's genius was inspired by the spirit world, but his experience from a previous life helped him understand what he was writing. Also he was placed in the best conditions for him to grow as a musician. His father had a musical ability and Austria had a climate of classical music creativity which allowed his skills to flourish.

We have experiences or talents (natural abilities) locked away in what we call our subconscious or

131

unconscious. The subconscious holds many things that we do not seem to obviously know. It holds the basis of the character we are today. As we grow up some of us seem to have a natural gift for things. We may have an aptitude for languages, or sports, mathematics, music, or history. This is because we have previously learned or experienced them. Through the growth years of childhood we start to be aware of information leaking through our subconscious into our conscious. We start to develop a certain character or individuality as we begin our teenage years, growing until maturity, whereby we hopefully begin to understand more about ourselves.

While piritual growth is very important, we cannot learn all of our spiritual lessons while living on Earth. There are too many distractions around us to grow spiritually especially in this high tech age. It is a much more self-centred world. We think less of those around us. Many times it comes down to "What's in it for me?", or "I am too busy to help you; I have my own life you know!"

Material items are fantastic. I love the world of computers but I'm currently seeing that it makes young people too reliant on possessions such as high tech phones or television. Two of the best things in life that many have lost are innocence and self-discipline. We grow up too quickly now and know far too much too early, about sex and the world. Because big businesses are targeting youth with fashion, cell phones, semi-alcoholic drinks and more, peer pressure leaves them feeling insecure if they are not familiar with the latest fad. There is huge pressure on teenagers now and it is all material. There is no room for spiritual expression. I very recently read about a 14-year-old girl who committed suicide because she heard a rumour that her boyfriend was going to dump her. It was only a rumour and there was no truth in it. I can only imagine that at her age she felt ashamed about not being able to hold on to a boyfriend!

The imbalance is immense between the material and spiritual aspects of life. The material world carries much more weight these days. There is too much peer pressure and loss of innocence; young people are growing up far too fast, leaving a vacuum of respect and self-discipline, and spiritual connections. It is not just the young who are missing spiritual balance in their life. Those in their late teens, twenties, and thirties are also searching for something. They don't realise that what they are missing is a lack of spiritual growth.

How does a person begin spiritual growth?

Responsibility - Spiritual growth begins with a change of thinking. If you believe that there is life after death, and that the reality here on Earth determines your reality in the next world, it will have a profound effect on your life. Knowing that there is another reality after death should make one think more about future thoughts and actions. When you realise that you are responsible for *all* your thoughts and actions it should make you change your opinion of your role in the world around you. By thinking about each thought or action, good and bad, you will find that you will start to become more cautious about how you think and what you do. This awareness also makes you think about the thoughts that you send out making your aura shine if good, or become dark and dull if bad. You will realise that you want only thoughts of good deeds. The thoughts of people who think well of you because you are loved, or for whom you have done a good deed empower the spiritual fields that surround your body, your aura and akashic record.

However the reverse also applies for those who wish you harm whose thoughts can affect you if the harm was intentional. Innocence or rejection of any harm causes these thoughts to rebound back to the sender. Likewise if you do the same these negative thoughts come back to you. This is why you should always be

133

careful of having negative thoughts and actions. By just acting on this lesson it will have a profound effect on your life and spiritual growth.

Experience - We have incarnated our spirit into a physical body. We are here to gain experience in all of the things life in this world has to offer. The experiences we go through are usually determined beforehand; our destiny will map out what paths we are going to take in life. There is never a definite path for us, but some paths are more certain than others. We have free will which allows us to change our path to a different one at any moment, but even that is restricted to certain paths.

We go through the experiences of falling in love, overcoming pain, facing insecurities, pushing away embarrassments, passing exams, and so on. Every experience should teach us knowledge and wisdom. One problem we will find is that if we do not learn our lessons they come back to us later. You cannot hide from the lessons that need to be learned. If you avoid dealing with a problem it will return to you sooner or later. How many times has this happened before? We cannot cheat our destiny. There are karma guides who help construct our pathways in life, and cause any of these problems to reappear just when we thought we had finally got rid of them. The karma guides, or the Lords of Karma, as I have heard them called, are not concerned with any individual spirit's circumstances, but will apply the law that is right for the spirit on its path at that particular time.

We all try to avoid problems; it has happened to me many times even though I understand how the law works. This is the Law of Cause and Effect. You cannot cheat yourself. By not dealing with it you will find it grows and grows and you will begin to get depressed about it. Is this not true? Therefore I have learned that if you have an issue the best thing to do is just stop, clear your mind, and say "OK I'm going to sort this out". Once the momentum builds up to solve the problem it becomes so much easier and you feel a great sense of achievement once you've overcome it.

It is very common for us to hide from our problems, but they are really there to help us grow spiritually. By solving our problems we gain energy and vitality, and with determination we gain 'will power' which is a real substance and very much a power within an individual. We would do well to develop this but it takes faith in oneself. You will develop this only by preparing to take the steps that determine that no matter what happens, you will pursue it to the end. By overcoming adversity we can add to this power within our spirit which is also supplemented by every little achievement made. If we do not have strong will in the first place its power is strengthened by the guides around us. If it is in our destiny to increase our will power we will have adversity put in front of us. At times it may seem quite unfair and unjust, but the problems are there because we need to strengthen our will and learn from them.

Wisdom and Understanding - One of the most important spiritual growth techniques is the use of the Law of Understanding. As you go through life you meet a lot of people who upset you. It can make life very frustrating and tough sometimes when people do you harm, physically, verbally, or unjustly, and you can sometimes end up feeling bitter towards a person or situation. Once this kind of experience happens to you how do you deal with it? Take for example, a person who is arrogant and full of himself, who professes opinions about everything, which are invariably wrong and usually not even their own. They may try to outwit you, verbally abuse you, and continually put people down with what they believe are superior abilities.

Why are they doing this? What makes them tick? If you start to ask these questions instead of lashing out you are learning a spiritual lesson. We must try to look at the reason for this individual's insecurity. It is a typical case of a person who is very insecure about himself. He feels inadequate and lacks confidence. Most people carry personal insecurity of some kind but do they realise this themselves? Would you recognise these characteristics or similar traits within yourself?

Our insecurities usually develop from childhood, and unfortunately we pick up many of them from our parents. They can often stem from subtle words that were said to us at an early age in negative situations such as our parents berating us for not achieving good grades in school or not being good enough in sports. This can cause a lack of self-confidence as years pass by. As can comparisons to others with comments like, "If you were to work as hard as little Jimmy you would get better results". Words can cut our confidence like a knife through butter so we begin to develop a sense of failure combined with negative thinking. We start to measure ourselves against the achievements of people like 'little Jimmy'. As we move through life we meet similar characters and try to prove ourselves to them. Sometimes it is not even obvious that we are doing it and we only learn about it when someone else tells us.

Did our parents ask themselves why we were getting poor grades? Could it have been because we were not academically inclined, but preferred creative, artistic subjects? We cannot all do well with academic subjects and many take on other professions. It is unfortunate that peer pressure is so strong these days that we feel we must all go to college and get high grades. The simple answer is that we can't all do this. If our parents had understood us better they could have tried to learn why we were not performing well in school. Understanding works both ways. We must understand ourselves as well as others around us. By trying to understand we gain wisdom which helps us avoid pitfalls and overcome problems. We can learn a lot from other people's problems without going through them ourselves.

Wisdom is learning from our experiences. It is a spiritual characteristic because it helps us avoid trouble, deal with people and their problems, feel confident about ourselves and our abilities, and expand our knowledge of the world. If you know how to deal with people you can relate to anyone in the world. We are all learning the same lessons but in different cultures. Wisdom is above language and far more treasured than intellect. I have found that intellect does not have emotions, whereas wisdom does, which is why you should try to understand people.

The Law of Understanding not only applies to yourself and people around you, but also should be applied to problems that you encounter. It may not be anyone's fault that you find yourself in a difficult situation. If you try to *understand* why you might have gone through a rough patch and look for the lessons that you need to learn then spiritual growth is occurring. It is no good blaming everyone for the situation or looking to blame somebody. Try to see what lessons need to be applied to a problem. Say to yourself "Okay this is a bit messy but I will try to figure out what I need to learn as I don't want to repeat this lesson again later on".

When we look at a typical loving relationship that breaks down there is usually blame on one or both sides. Do we understand why it broke down? Was there real love or was it lust? Relationships should grow with acts of selflessness on both sides where you do something for the other person without any reward and it is simply for their love. If one person is making an effort to grow and expand their relationship but the other half does not change there will obviously be conflict. Only when people start to really think about, or 'understand' the other person do we start to foster a loving relationship that will have loving and spiritual growth. If you cannot become true friends it is unlikely that you will be in a great loving relationship. Understanding, selflessness, love - you need these three spiritual qualities to make a relationship work.

It is not surprising that so many relationships break down these days. We all want our partner to be the smartest, most caring, trusting, handsome or beautiful, honest, generous person around, but do we aspire to have the same characteristics? With so much information available to us from TV, the Internet and magazines, we are distracted by the relative ease of how we can change relationships. A few decades ago people made the effort to stay in relationships. If things got difficult people would work harder to stay in the relationship although they sometimes stayed together because of peer pressure. These days it's so much easier to break up and there is less of a stigma attached to it. It is possible that in this new, liberated age, we are more emotionally insecure. Many women are now financially secure enough to choose men without having to worry about their financial future. In some ways men now feel less secure themselves and more emotionally vulnerable. There is a greater balance of the sexes today which is good for everyone and we are more honest about our feelings and aspirations.

Where does this attitude come from? Well it is actually spirit-inspired. Most of our influences come from the spirit world. There is a higher plan involved but knowing what it is really is unimportant. The most important thing is what we want to do during our lives. If we begin to really believe there is no end that we don't die we survive in another dimensional reality, and what we do here governs how we will progress on the 'other side'. We should be thinking about the spirit world and the far reaching influences of our thoughts. This philosophy for life affects, or should affect, everything we do. There is no creed, no dogma or 10 Commandments, no rules to be followed. We all know what is right and wrong and how to be good people. This is the best way to live your life.

If you look at most lives on this planet since half the world is starving at any one time the great majority have bad lives. People in Africa and Asia have very hard lives and encounter many difficult experiences that make them despair; they might look at the lives of others and wonder why they could not have an easier path. We choose our destiny and path in life although for some people life does seem very unfair and full of injustice. For others life is wonderful and full of luxuries, good schools, decent jobs and good family lives. Why do some people have luck and get the best start in life, while another is a poor, abused orphan that turns to crime? If the orphan swapped life half way through with a rich child would their life lead to the same results? Does a good start in life result in a good person, or does a rich person have the money to pay a good accountant or lawyer to hide their misdemeanours? Every now and then situations cause us to fall by the wayside. We try to be good but life throws us a curve. Why is it so unfair that some people are born rich while others are born poor? As mentioned earlier we choose our spiritual path or destiny, and the experiences we go through, good or bad, in order to grow in this lifetime.

Is the spirit world just? Yes there is justice, but not if you believe that you have only one life. How can everyone learn everything in one lifetime? The simple answer is we cannot. It only makes sense if we have 'many lives' which brings me to the next topic of reincarnation.

Chapter Twenty

Reincarnation

Reincarnation is a wide topic and frankly I don't know everything about it. However I will explain what ACD and my spirit guides have told me.

The first point is that we are spirits incarnated into a physical body. As previously stated we come from the spirit world and we go back to the spirit world. The spirit world is the reality; our world is considered by spirits to be the dream. If we complete the circle once why can't we do it multiple times? Well we *can* do this. We can even incarnate into other dimensions. Earth is not the most significant dimension.

What is a spirit? For me a spirit life is a part of the god, and the essence of life in development. It never stops growing or expanding, taking on new knowledge, and living in many dimensions. The spirit cannot die or be destroyed, and even the most evil spirit will eventually turn toward the path of light. A spirit expresses itself through the soul which is the manifestation of mental and emotional bodies.

So why do we incarnate into a physical body and why are we here? There are three basic explanations:

- To gain experience from all that life on Earth has to offer. This includes eating, drinking, walking, driving, sports, falling in (and out of) love, friendships, family life, procreation, learning, and much more. From this we may begin to see how large the universe is and start to ask questions.

- To master our senses. We need to be able to control our senses with self-discipline and not eat or drink excessively. We need to master our emotions, control our anger, express love,

140

and overcome loss or negativity. As we gain mastery over our senses our consciousness develops further due to a greater awareness of the things that affect us.

- To express our creative abilities. All artistic feelings should be developed and expressed. If we do this we are using the god power of creation where our thoughts and actions transmute into wonderful achievements. This could be done through practicing sports, painting, writing, developing computer games, or anything else that is an expression of creativity. We should add part of our spirit to this world, but how we do it is up to us.

If we are in the spirit world we might decide, for example, to incarnate into a physical body to learn new lessons and have new experiences, or if we are an advanced spirit we may want to help others to progress by incarnating as a family member, or possibly a teacher, a writer, or a scientist. Many incarnating spirits choose to have influence over other earthly spirits.

Incarnations are planned because there is a perfect order in the spirit world and nothing happens by chance. We are guided by higher spirits who are guided by even higher spirits. There are 'Lords of Karma', very high spirits, who work out karmic pathways without any bias to the incarnated person as they know what burden each person can carry, and the experiences, good and bad, that must be fulfilled if they are to achieve their desired destiny.

The word 'karma' simply represents the law of cause and effect, or 'sowing and reaping'. A spirit's earthly pathway involves experiences of good karma and bad karma which balance the energies of the individual spirit. When I say 'energies', you could think of the karma energy being held in the akashic record that surrounds your spirit body. I will use an analogy to explain the akashic record.

Akashic record - Imagine that your akashic record is made up of dark and light spots. Positive thought energy looks like white spots which have impregnated all the good thoughts sent out from your mind. The opposite of this is negative thoughts which are heavy and have dark energy that results in black spots on our akashic field. What a progressive spirit should desire is to turn the black ones white and increase the amount of white ones. The more light or white spots that you have the brighter your aura or spirit shines, while dark ones make you heavy and unspiritual. If you think dark thoughts you will surround yourself with a dark aura.

These dark spots need to be removed. To achieve this, you need to go through spiritual experiences and learn from them, and help others without receiving anything in return. Thoughts of selflessness should be your aim. Some of the spiritual virtues we should be trying to reach are: doing service to others, lifting people up, being kind, not simply with money, but by spending a few minutes of your time to help a friend when it may be difficult and you are tired or busy.

Karmic incidents don't have to be doom and gloom; they can be very subtle. Good karma is rewarded just like bad karma must be excised. For example, if you stole from somebody you would lose the equivalent material possession through the destruction of something you treasure, or its theft from you in the future. Good karma can be gained if you helped a friend paint his house for no money, and that help will be reciprocated by an equivalent deed later in life. Karma, good and bad, can come quickly or take many lifetimes, but those negative spots will eventually need to be removed. Sometimes when a bad incident happens it is for good reasons although at the time it does not seem that way. Karma is like a material that is created and destroyed. It is similar to a material that attaches to your spirit body under the laws of cause and effect. Karma is created when you need to learn lessons, and destroyed when you have learned them. In a way it has more to do with balancing spiritual energy than to do with good and evil.

Why do we incarnate? Maybe we could learn everything in spirit world?

Incarnating on Earth means that you are here to accomplish certain tasks before you leave for the spirit world once again. The incarnation of a new spirit begins about three to four months after conception when the chosen spirit starts to merge with the aura of the expectant mother. It is often said that a mother looks radiant; this is because people who are sensitive pick up the spirit child in her aura. The baby spirit begins a new conscious period of its spirit life, and will 'forget' its previous existence so that it will have a fresh start. From birth the baby will 'grow' a new consciousness which will contain all the experiences and thoughts created by the incarnated spirit, but will also have a certain amount of past life experiences that become apparent as time goes on. These come from the subconscious, or unconscious, where all of the spirit's previous lives are kept.

All of our experiences make up part of our character. As mentioned earlier an aptitude or natural ability for languages or sports, for example, comes from having learned these skills in a previous incarnation. Our previous hopes and fears may also start to appear stemming from things that we may not have achieved or mastered in another incarnation. A lot of likes and dislikes come from our subconscious memories, from our previous experiences with fashion, writing, history, hobbies, and so on, as do our attractions to certain things. Many people feel very comfortable in other countries to which they have travelled even feeling a strong affinity to a particular country although they have not previously been there. Some people have an easier time than others when learning a language. Is it because some languages are easier, or because those people spoke them in a past incarnation?

It is true that many hopes and fears are sometimes transferred to you from your parents, and academic achievements run in academic families which may have nothing to do with reincarnation. Or does it? Some people do reincarnate with like-minded people. Remember like attracts like.

So why don't we know about our previous lives then?

The simple reason is that we are not supposed to know. We are here to learn new lessons and master old ones that we have not previously learned. There should be no distractions from past lives. Imagine how you would act if you knew you were a particularly wicked person or a very famous person. You would try to discover everything about yourself and this would naturally have a major influence on your current life even perhaps in a disastrous way. You could become arrogant or depressed over past incidents causing yourself to lose track of your goals for this incarnation. I am sure people would look differently at you if they knew you were Adolph Hitler or Abraham Lincoln. In fact Abraham Lincoln was a big believer in the afterlife and attended séances with mediums. Therefore we must start each new incarnation with a clean slate so to speak. I like to think of our incarnations as an onion; each of the layers represent our lives lived already each separate in their own way when peeled away, but put together the layers make up the whole of the onion. We are currently on the outside layer with the brown skin representing our physical body. When we die the brown skin is peeled away and we are left with a lovely onion!

If we have incarnated so many times when do we stop reincarnating?

It is up to the individual to decide whether it needs to incarnate or to stop reincarnating. Incarnations on Earth can be compared to the many years of education from primary school up to university. One can spend many years learning at different levels of education and passing exams to prepare for living in the world after secondary school. The spirit world could be described as having infinite levels of learning. Earth is just a small part of it. We continually incarnate learning our lessons by returning to the Earth until we do not need to come here anymore. It's just like a school.

Based on my understanding from Arthur Conan Doyle most incarnations are evaluated and agreed upon beforehand. Which kinds of lessons will we need to learn or what lessons we should teach to others? Will we be rich or poor, male or female, or even transgendered? Which race and nation will we be born into and in which religion? Every aspect, to the tiniest detail, is planned. One thing you must remember is that we have free will to choose even though we have a plan or destiny that is laid out before us. Most of the time, 90% or more, things are certain to happen. However we have free will to make changes. The question is where does free will start and where does it end? We are also guided by our guardian angels or spirit guides who keep us on our chosen path with their thoughts and influence.

When we have a reading with a psychic or medium they will pick up details of the current pathway laid out before us. As I said there is a 90% certainty that the pathway before us will occur. Sometimes a psychic may appear to interpret wrongly the events before us; although a psychic can misinterpret something it can also be put down to a change of direction by our free will.

What are group souls?

Group souls are many soul-spirits who gather together for a collective of experiences whereby some incarnate into a physical body, while the other parts of the group help and encourage from the spirit world. For

145

example, the incarnated spirits may be of different genders, races, or professions and may have different or even similar experiences to reach a certain level of spirituality. Some souls may meet and form a soul mate relationship.

Group souls follow a plan agreed among themselves. The souls in a group can number from two or three to a dozen, twenty or hundreds, and even thousands. The group soul is like a diamond with each facet representing an individual spirit which is either an incarnation on Earth or living in spirit world. Each facet part makes up the diamond or soul, but each has its own individuality. Group soul theory is quite complex and my explanation is as I understand it from my guides.

What about religion?

There is no religion in the spirit world. We are judged on our spiritual growth not on our religious persuasion. How does religion fit into our destiny? Religion is man-made and it has a purpose. If you look closely at the messages from all major religious writings you will see that there is an element of truth in all religions which over time has been distorted, lost, or changed. However religious writings are often made of opinions that are often wrong and unspiritual.

You can learn many lessons from religion. It has a force for good but it is used by people who want power and interpret the writings for their own motives. Take the simple case of a man born on a desert island he will never see the rest of the world, or come across any religion. Will he enter heaven without following a religion? It is often said in Christianity that you cannot enter the Kingdom of Heaven without knowing the Lord's words. What happens to the man who does not know any of this? His spiritual growth is the important thing — how he lived his life, what his thoughts were, and the actions that resulted. Nothing else really matters.

We need a framework on which to live our lives and the natural spirit laws are there to provide it. It is always said by nearly all spirits guides *"Take what you can understand discard what does not make sense, and search for the truth"*. I have had so much proof of a life beyond this world that to me it is as natural as eating, but I don't take what I know for granted. I try to live it every hour of every day. Sometimes I fall by the wayside, but with the reality of the next world staring me in the face, quite literally every hour of every day, I quickly get back on track. I am not perfect, no one is perfect, and that is why we are all here.

Chapter Twenty One

Physical Mediumship

Mediums receive evidential proof of life after death from our loved ones who have passed on to another dimension of existence which I call 'spirit world'. Physical mediums are mediums that create the conditions for people from the spirit world to materialise corporeally for a brief period of time thereby enabling physical contact and communication. Materialisations can also be through voice communications from mid-air (called *direct voice*), and other forms such as apports, psychic smells, and raps on tables which include table tipping.

Physical mediumship really took off in the mid-Victorian period around the 1850s, and continued up to the 1950s, but has become less popular and well-known due to the many distractions of our modern world. This makes the sacrifice not as rewarding. Although it is still practiced today it has become almost hidden like an underground movement. I am trying to help revive it but it takes years to develop. For me physical mediumship is the highest form of mediumship one can attain because the results can be truly spectacular, even magical. But it is the most difficult to 'earn' by which I mean that all forms of mediumship are merited by each individual.

Physical mediumship is very unique in that the medium needs to have certain 'vibrations' and an abundance of a particular substance called *ectoplasm* which is drawn from the body and mixed with chemicals from the spirit side. Once the spirit guides have mixed the ectoplasm into a workable form spirit entities start to cloak their bodies with the ectoplasm thus allowing themselves to materialise as a full body (rarely), or more often bodily parts like a hand or a face that people can see or touch. The spirit guides also use ectoplasm to create what the spirit world call *ectoplasmic rods*. With the help of spirit chemists the rods are made into a solid substance used in physical circles to move objects and distribute energy among the participants.

Spirit helpers sometimes construct, again from ectoplasm, spiritual devices on their side such as a direct voice box. These are used to talk directly to circle members as they enable spirits to talk out of mid-air in their original accents, and with their same unique and characteristic way of talking. It is so real that you would not believe it was anyone but that person. The voice box allows a spirit to project their thoughts into the device which then vibrates the air in our atmosphere causing a voice to be heard. It has been said that spirit entities have to remember how they used to speak before attempting this (there is no language in the spirit world only thought). Direct voice will come through in any language of course as long as we can understand it on our side.

It is my opinion that a direct voice circle is second only to a full physical apparition of a spirit entity. Direct voice and physical mediumship are usually found together but this is not always the case. Some mediums, like the great direct voice medium Leslie Flint; he could not take the stresses and strains of physical mediumship so he concentrated only on direct voice. Other physical mediums focus on physical apparitions only while others do both, like Alex Harris. [3]

Physical mediums are very rare, indeed, due to their bodies having an excess of the ectoplasm used in materialisations. Most people have this substance but only in very small quantities. It could be that as few as one in half a million people have enough of this energy to become physical mediums.

What is it like in a physical circle? One could compare it to the séances of the Victorian and Edwardian periods but modern circles are more sophisticated. The

149

term *séance* conjures up images of horror movies and Ouija boards. Most people now call them *physical circles* or *psychic circles*. We are not communicating with the dead because nobody on either side is dead. We cannot die, we don't die, and we only change our bodily form from physical to spirit.

Psychic circles are a scientific experiment and I try to make them light and entertaining with humour and fun as the main elements. The participants and I sit in a circle with our fingers or feet touching. A circle of energy needs to be created so if the members maintain contact energy can flow around them. Usually the medium feels whether the circle flow is broken by somebody removing their hand, and if they need to break contact for a moment it is advised that people make another connection with the person next to them. Holding hands for up to an hour or two is very difficult because hands can cramp and become sweaty if it's hot so I prefer people to touch fingers.

When materialisations and direct voice occur mediums need this physical connection to allow energy to flow and create the phenomena. Over time the energy will start to wane. This is especially true with direct voice where the speaker's voice becomes low and distant as the energy diminishes. A good way to replenish the energy is for everyone to sing for a little while, preferably with some music, as this will give the spirit guides the necessary energy to continue the psychic circle. Connecting with each other even with fingertips, and creating energy are vital to making a physical circle work properly.

The conditions to create physical mediumship have to be perfect; the vibrations of the medium and sitters must be in harmony. If a person in the circle is ill this can have a severe draining effect on the energy produced. Negativity, frustration, impatience, and fear can all have a bad impact on the circle's energy. In certain cases the materialised forms will not materialise fully with some spirits appearing as a decapitated form, or with a half-sized head and shoulders, or with a three-quarter length body which in itself is quite spectacular to see. I have heard a quote from a spirit guide saying that it can take the equivalent energy of a hundred nuclear bombs to create materialisations.

Remember that ectoplasm comes from the medium. It is a large part of his or her bodily substance, and the manifesting spirit clothes itself in it. Any shocks or light flashes can destroy the ectoplasmic energy causing pain or illness to the physical medium. Everyone including myself would like to see spirits appear in daylight as solid as you and I. However materialisations are done in darkness, unfortunately for everyone, because of the sensitivity of the ectoplasm to white light which destroys its structure. This irony means that most psychic circles are held in darkness with a red light which allows people to see the materialised forms appearing. Red light and blue, as well, will not destroy ectoplasm like white light. Undertaking a physical circle in these lighting conditions can leave it open to allegations of trickery and fraud from sceptics and magicians. No matter what a medium does there will always be those who want to disbelieve or prove fraudulence. I suspect it will always be so. But when you have seen it with your own eyes there is nothing that could be more wonderful than bringing people back to be reunited with their loved ones if only for a few minutes. I want to help take the fear of death away from all people. This is what my mediumship is all about.

Physical mediumship has many side effects: the drain on energy, illness, mental fatigue, mental attacks, and even early death due to the stresses and strains of materialisations literally wear out the physical body. Not many people can spend years developing their physical mediumship abilities due to these stressors.

There are many facets to physical mediumship. These are direct voice, materialisations, apports, transfiguration, psychic smells, raps, people being touched, and levitation of the table and other objects. The medium usually goes into a trance to bring these about but this is not always the case. A brief explanation of each follows:

Transfiguration - With transfiguration the face of a spirit person can be seen forming over the faces of the medium or other sitters. It is best to do this type of mediumship in a red light so the ectoplasm can form over the faces without being destroyed. The spirits' faces can be very clear at times with the medium's face completely disappearing. On other occasions many faces can appear over a medium's face quite rapidly but each one is distinct from each other. Features like beards and moustaches can be clearly seen, as can objects like glasses or earrings, a smoker's pipe or hats. Hair can change shape and size, as can body shape, which can appear large or small. It is not an optical illusion, as people in my circles can see the ectoplasm forming on the faces opposite or their own hands. Fingers can extend or diminish in front of everyone's eyes. It is truly fascinating to watch and you need to see it to believe it.

Direct Voice - Direct voice is another very interesting part of physical mediumship where the voice of a spirit speaks to sitters out of mid-air. Most mediums have a speaking trumpet sitting on the floor of a circle or table if one is required. These are conical-shaped objects with holes at both ends, and are placed in the centre of the circle of people present. When the atmosphere is right for the spirit they will sometimes make the trumpet float in the air and fly around the room stopping at a person they may want to address. More often the trumpet is not really used for communication or amplification, but it makes the psychic phenomena very interesting and helps concentrate the mind.

Direct voice and independent voice are basically the same, but some people have different ideas about how these work. The voices are created from an artificial voice box formed from ectoplasm again taken from the physical medium. Psychic power needs to be generated from the sitters to help form ectoplasm for the communication so music is played and a singsong helps bring the energy up. Once the power is sufficient it can take a few minutes for a spirit to master the voice box, but when the voices come through it's as clear and powerful as anyone talking in the room. Men, women, and children of all ages can speak in many languages and accents. Direct voice mediumship, unfortunately, requires complete darkness to function but again it offers direct proof of life after death as questions and answers can be made to the spirit individuals.

Apports - Apports are physical objects materialised by spirit guides for the group of people sitting in a psychic circle. Usually this involves a physical object that has been dematerialised in one location, transported to another, and re-materialised. It has been known for objects to appear to individuals who are not in a circle, have nothing to do with mediumship, or have no contact with psychics. The objects can be almost anything from flowers and books to jewellery, and even money, usually coins in small denominations. Remember financial wealth is not important to spirits. I have even heard the story of an umbrella, which had been left outside of the room, being dropped onto its owner's lap. Apports occur for particular reasons and psychic circle sitters do not usually sit for the purpose of bringing through apports. They just happen during a psychic circle if the spirit has the energy or a particular reason to do so. One strange peculiarity of apports is that they have an extended life if the object was once living; there are reports where flowers have lasted for months or up to a year in some cases. Apports are great fun and it can make you wonder whether the 'transporters' from *Star Trek* will be a reality one day!

Levitation of Objects - Levitation is the movement of objects without normal means of support. This can be done by either psychokinetic energy (*telekinesis*) or through the use of ectoplasm. One of the most amazing examples of levitation was through the mediumship of D.D. Hume. On more than one hundred occasions from the 1860s to the late 1870s he was levitated up to the ceiling and often around the room above the heads of the sitters. On one occasion he was moved out a third storey window and in through the window of an adjacent room.[4]

In a psychic circle ectoplasmic rods are created and are used to move objects, such as tables. I have seen tables move in many different ways with people lightly touching them so lightly that you can see fingertips gently touching the surface. The rods sometimes form out of the solar plexus and stomach area of my body as the medium is the significant source of ectoplasm. But the rods can also be connected to the other sitters if there's a need for extra energy resources. Sometimes sitters feel a sharp pain in some areas of the body, normally the legs or arms, when these rods are inserted.

Raps or Knocks - A very common phenomenon is table raps or knocks. These sounds range from soft finger-like taps to large knocks, like knuckles banging on a table. Quite often you may also hear a sound like wood splintering or cracking. On other occasions ectoplasmic rods can cause raps to occur. With all of these raps or knocks you can establish a code for yes or no answers. I use one rap for "yes" and two for "no". It is quite an effective form of communication and if you ask the right question it can also be very informative. I have even had prophetic questions answered whereby the answer was verified weeks or months later.

Spirit Lights - If the people in a circle are very harmonious it can create conditions for some wonderful phenomena. One of these is the appearance of spirit lights. Spirit lights come in all intensities and colours,

154

commonly blue, white and red. The colours can be spotted as bright spots from time to time, however, on rare occasions; they can have incredibly intense brightness. The lights are considered to be a representation of a spirit's presence and their vibration. The brightness of the spirit light usually indicates higher levels of spirit development.

Ectoplasm - When spirit operators withdraw the etheric energy-matter from a medium's body this is known as ectoplasm through the use and manipulation by which the physical phenomena occurs. Ectoplasm can be created in many different forms, visible and invisible, white and coloured. The form chosen depends upon what the spirit guides wish to do with this incredible substance. Once created, the ectoplasm generally emerges from the medium through some bodily orifice (nose or mouth), or through a psychic centre located near the navel known as the *solar plexus*.

Ectoplasm can be used to move objects. During a demonstration, such as those I've just described, the spirit operator might mould the ectoplasm into hardened rods. The ectoplasm is 'collected' by spirit helpers and mixed with chemicals on their side to create a refined ectoplasm which the spirits then use in physical phenomena such as materialisations, or table raps and movements.

Materialisation - For materialisations spirit guides collect ectoplasm from inanimate (furniture, materials in the room) and animate objects (the medium and circle sitters), and mix it with etheric chemicals on their side to form a stable moulding substance that spirits can use to create an exact physical replica of how they looked on Earth or how they now appear in spirit. The degree and strength of the materialised form varies. A fully materialised form, or head-to-toe materialisation of a spirit, when seen live it is perhaps the most amazing phenomenon witnessed in mediumship. There are countless recorded cases where spirits have materialised fully [5], with full dress, facial features, and any distinguishing marks they previously had on their body. They can look as solid as our earthly body. On some occasions materialised spirits have gone to the extent of creating fingerprints of their materialised hands, moving heavy objects, or dancing with sitters. Materialised spirits can walk among the sitters, talk to them via direct voice, touch, hug, and kiss them, allow people to touch them, pass through walls, and dematerialise.

During the manifestations physical mediums usually sit within an enclosed area called a 'cabinet'. This is basically any area that allows a physical medium to sit away from the sitters. It also helps focus the energies and creates a type of battery from which the phenomena can be formed and energised. In front of the cabinet there is usually a curtain which can be spread to enable people to see what is going on inside. When materialisation is about to occur the curtains are closed for two reasons: first, as the spirits are using part of his bodily energies to mould the ectoplasm into a form it protects the medium; and second, the curtains obscure the build-up of the materialised form which can be quite disturbing to see. As soon as the materialised spirit form is ready it will step out of the cabinet into full view.

At the start of materialisation the lighting in the room is usually very dimmed or completely extinguished - a low or bright red light normally provides the only light source. I sometimes use a blue and red light. My spirit guides have told me that white light tends to inhibit the phenomena, while dim red light energises it and will often tell me how much light I can have as they will know the strength of the ectoplasmic energy that has been collected. The conditions around us always determine how good a sitting will be.

One of the most interesting phenomena seen during materialisation is the physical link between the materialised form and the medium. After a spirit materialises and walks away from the medium, a cord of ectoplasm linking the spirit with the physical medium can often be seen. This ectoplasmic cord can be likened to the umbilical cord of a foetus. Through it the spirit operator receives a supply of etheric energy-matter from the medium. The spirit may dematerialise by withdrawing the ectoplasm back into the medium's body via this cord. There seems to be no limits to what a spirit can do through physical mediumship provided proper conditions prevail.

Why is Physical Mediumship so rare?

Physical mediumship was common during the last century until around the 1930s but it declined rapidly in the 1950s. In the early half of the twentieth century the power and range of seen phenomena was amazing. Unfortunately these days it is quite rare to see the same levels of phenomena. It seems that people are just not dedicated enough to sacrifice their time and effort to develop physical mediumship because it really does take total selfless devotion.

In the early years of the twentieth century a psychic circle was a social event. Most of the great pioneer mediums began by sitting in a home circle. Since the start of the twenty-first century it seems as if there is an increase in development circles but not necessarily physical mediumship circles. In fact we may be on the verge of a new growth in the former, and hopefully some of these may turn into the latter. During the end of the 1990s there seemed to be a resurgence of interest in physical mediumship but it still tends to be like an underground movement with closed circles, and mediums who will sit for years to get the phenomena and do not wish to have any publicity. I can understand this as I have run a few physical mediumship circles for many years, and although they were not closed as such not all members were willing to continue year after year.

Why has physical mediumship not continued from the early part of the twentieth century?

The first reason for this is that when spirit phenomena started appearing in the Victorian and Edwardian periods it was relatively new and people naturally wanted to see it live. They needed objective evidence of the spirit's presence, and of course spirit guides were quite willing to provide evidence of physical manifestations. When people began to accept the reality of life after death, and mediums' evidence, they yearned for more spiritual teaching and philosophy. This gradually reduced the occurrence of physical mediumship. As a counterbalance to physical mediumship, mental mediumship began to predominate. In other words the needs of humanity dictated through their thoughts how spirits responded to those needs and created the conditions we see today. It is always the case with spirit that if enough people think of these things then thoughts start to create new realities. Perhaps new promotion of ideas could help the cause of physical phenomena to grow again.

The second reason for the decline of physical mediumship is the fact that its development can be a lengthy, sometimes tedious, process with no materialisations occurring in the circle for years. It requires great commitment on everyone's part and generally revolves around the development of one or two people in the circle with others sitting to help them in their development. Some very interesting things usually occur even if they may not be materialisations. There will certainly be raps, table movement, psychic smells, spirit lights, transfiguration, and other noteworthy physical phenomena.

In the physical circles that I have led some very unusual things have happened, such as strange sounds, clinking of a knight's armour after he was seen clairvoyantly, shuffling of a Victorian woman's pannier dress across the floor, birds flapping their wings, footsteps walking around the wooden floor of a circle, and voices from mid-air. I have seen tables moving of their own accord and lights turning themselves up and down or off. I have also witnessed psychic smells that fill the whole room. One of the most amazing phenomena was the blue lightning figures which were seen by at least a dozen people under a red light. These were two or three rod-like lights about fifteen inches long which looked wavy, and for at least a few minutes appeared set against an empty fireplace.

Every night is different, but for a physical medium it is extremely draining both physically and mentally. The next day can feel like a hangover for me as I am extremely sensitive to crowds, noise, and light, and only start recovering in the evening. In the nicest possible way my energy is used and abused by the spirit guides. The medium requires a lot of tenacity to cope with the physical energies and rise above the harshness of the world. On the plus side the experiences last a lifetime –actually, an eternity, because we never die.

What makes a physical medium?

Mediumship itself is not exclusive to just a few people because it is a very natural aspect of the spirit body. To a large extent anyone can develop mediumistic ability to link with their spirit guides thus becoming receptive to the influences coming from those in spirit. But not everyone can become a physical medium. That requires certain elements to be present within the physical organism of the medium namely the elements to create ectoplasm. Either you do or don't have them. You also need an abundance of patience. Additionally it will help immensely if you have a strong will to cope with life as a physical medium usually has increased sensitivity.

In my experience as a physical medium I have often found that illness and physical exhaustion tend to weaken the energies necessary to produce the physical phenomena as do long periods of cloudy weather. On the other hand good health, sunny days and vigorous circle members help the mediumship to appear more dazzling and energised. Other mediums that I have met also noticed these conditions to be true in their experience.

[3] *They Walked Among Us* by Louie Harris 1980 – Psychic Press
[4] *Experiences in Spiritualism with D. D. Home, by Lord Adare Private print 1869, 2nd print by the SPR 1925*
[5] They Walked Among Us: by Louie Harris 1980 – Psychic Press

Chapter Twenty Two

Photoplasm

For nearly a decade or more I have in conjunction with my spirit guides been developing a new form of physical energy for materialisation in light. This new substance is not like the 'old' ectoplasm which I would describe as a very crude form of material used by mediums in the early twentieth century. Spirit chemists have been working on their side to develop new substances that are not so sensitive to light. Both worlds progress together so spirit guides do not always have the answers to every question, but they are obviously infinitely more advanced. It is we who are falling behind always trying to catch up.

When photoplasm starts to generate around me it's a process which I call 'the quickening'. I call it the quickening because its vibration is faster than that of the heavier older ectoplasm. The difference between these two energies means that, given the right conditions, this photoplasmic energy can be produced from both the medium and the sitters. The real bonus is that the formation of the spirit can be achieved without the medium going into a trance, and without the aid of a cabinet or the room being in complete darkness. This new ectoplasm is structured in such a way that it cannot be grabbed or manhandled, but will dissolve or disappear on contact with anyone other than the medium or anyone else who is producing it. Indeed should the spirit wish to touch somebody it will form into a solid structure just like any physical body. This new physical and spiritual substance can be seen as clouds of energy with faces in them, or even a structured net-like substance similar to fine lace with cross-connecting strands.

My experiments have found that the more harmonious the circle the more powerful and tactile the energy. I call this substance '**Photoplasm**' because it has more properties of a holographic light that can turn into a solid form. This is not to say that it cannot also be transparent like a hologram. It comes out like a mist that condenses from the body, turns into a pliable energy form, and can be light or solid. This is why it has two forms and is more flexible. This energy can be felt around individuals as a tingling electrical charge. At times it can be seen as a light blue colour with little sparkling lights within it. Photoplasm with spirits help can move objects like flowers in people's hands. I have captured this phenomenon on film and there are clips on the internet. Photoplasm also distorts physical bodies and causes strange affects like hands shrinking or expanding, and even x-ray like affects whereby people can see objects through their own hands. Before something can move *the etheric or spirit body must move first then the physical moves.*

Under low-wattage red and blue lights in the presence of more than twenty-five people I have produced several spirits that are seen at the same time. The light is strong enough so that you can see a large black letter A on a white piece of paper. Photoplasm has been used to lift a very heavy table while I was walking around the outside of the physical circle, which is very unusual, as most physical mediums are literally tied to their chair (to prevent trickery) or in a trance. Independent witnesses who have viewed this photoplasm have described it as literally clinging to me like a cloud on my back pulsating backward and forward as I moved around the circle. This quickening photoplasm can be seen in a strong red or blue light and very rarely in white light or even sunlight. It is still being developed and refined by spirit chemists.

There are other mediums that currently have this ability, but have not yet realised what they have. They are manifesting this photoplasm in private. Because of these complex energies and trying to work with this

162

difficult phenomenon most mediums tend to have a very close group of sympathetic people who have a similar aim of proving the existence of life after death. However large sitting groups are not a problem for me and I have had hundreds of people attend my circles witnessing what I have described above.

This photoplasm energy will, in the future, be developed in the aura of a medium which will allow it to be manipulated in a much safer environment compared to how it was developed in the past. It will remove the frequent problem of exposure to white light which causes the ectoplasm to become unstable and rush back into the medium's body thus causing potential physical injury, and even death in some cases. The photoplasm will hopefully reduce injury to the medium as it will simply dissolve without causing any distress. I have been informed that in the near future the photoplasm will be drawn out of the aura and manipulated to allow a spirit to appear in a holographic projection form that can change density as described above. What we would expect to see is a spirit forming from what would look like an electrical field of energy and light. The field will also have sound frequencies and light combined with the ectoplasm. A holographic projection machine will be invented to allow this to occur and there will be a combined effort from both worlds to make it happen. It sounds very exciting and I am sure the results will be spectacular. Arthur Conan Doyle told me this will be coming in the near future.

The Photoplasm energy has allowed me to provide some amazing physical phenomena in my circles which includes; the moving of flowers in peoples hands. This can be seen on my website www.ghostcircle.com. People have been able to feel a spirit presence by actually feeling the characteristics of a human body with heat and shape which they follow around with their own hands. Strange phenomena has resulted in hands shrinking or growing and people have seen right through their hands like an x-ray of the bones in their fingers, or no hand there at all, it has completely disappeared. There are lost more different phenomena that has been captured on film and saved for people to see now and for future generations to view.

People don't always appreciate how much effort goes into creating this phenomenon on our side and the spirit side. Every occasion is a new challenge fraught with constant difficulties because of the barrier between the worlds. If it was easy you would have heard about it much sooner. I have, on perhaps hundreds of occasions, seen thousands of people on the spirit side watching all the events connected with our '**Ghostcircle**' psychic circle. Even though a room may be physically small on our side there is no space limitation on the spirit side.

Why would there be so many spirits looking on? Well, if you suddenly died tomorrow you might not believe that you are dead, but if you did actually believe wouldn't it be very interesting to see some spirit communication in action with people on Earth? How would you prove to a spirit that he or she was dead? What better way to prove your death than to see this communication within a psychic circle? When you die you do not change as a 'person' in any way with the exception of the shedding of your physical body. You are exactly the same person one minute after you pass over. One of the first things you would do after realising that you had died is try and communicate with your loved ones and friends to let them know you are alive and tell them what it is like in the afterlife.

Unfortunately this will be a frustrating experience as most people on Earth will undoubtedly not be able to hear you. Also the afterlife is so real that you initially will not believe you are dead. Spirit guides will try to convince you, but you may not accept what they say. Going to a psychic circle will help to remove this illusion and frustration as it will make you realise that you have passed over. With hundreds of thousands of people dying each week I am sure a large proportion of those who have passed on would like to see this - I would love to see it myself. Of course it is probably a 'good night's entertainment on the spirit side for those who wish to see it. I can't wait to see this myself one day, but not just yet!

When I hold a psychic circle it is primarily composed of three parts. First, I ask everyone to send out some healing thoughts to their loved ones and friends. Second, I will try to give clairvoyance and last, we do physical mediumship. All parts are necessary. As an example, doing the healing first allows everyone to relax their mind and forget any problems they may have had during the day. Once the healing is complete I will give some clairvoyance and ask if anyone else has some to give. Finally, I switch on the red or blue lights under direction of my spirit guides and allow the physical phenomena to occur.

There is one thing that is common through every circle I have ever done: *no circle is ever alike.* Anyone who has sat in my circle will agree. Because no circle is ever the same it proves again how difficult it is for our spirit guides to predict what will occur. I love doing them as they are always fun, and I try not to be too serious which helps everyone relax. You should treat a circle like an evening with friends who are communicating with more friends. There is nothing scary or spooky about it.

Chapter Twenty Three

The Dark Regions

As previously discussed, in spiritual growth you earn everything through your deeds and your spiritual growth is assessed by all the good and bad that you do in your life. To physically do a good or bad deed you first have to think about it. Your body reacts directly to your thoughts which are stored in your *akashic record*, the "mind field", which surrounds your body and is like a computer memory that cannot be wiped and has infinite capacity.

Proper thinking helps you to live a good life here and earn a good life in the spirit world as well. It has been said that to enter the Kingdom of Heaven you must be, or think like a child. A child has pure thoughts of innocence, uncorrupted by the evil of the world, at least in their early years. We need to find that childish wonder, that thirst for knowledge.

There are many regions or dimensions of light and darkness. We pass over into these when we have taken our final breath and hope to end up somewhere beautiful with all our loved ones. Unfortunately this is not always going to be the case because you could agree that everyone on Earth is not necessarily good. We are not all going to the 'Kingdom of Heaven.' There is as much evil as good in this world although most strive for the latter. Leaders who have dark thoughts and cause harm and upset to their followers have a surprise coming. These people might think that death is the end and they have no qualms about destroying everything that gets in their way. Those who are taking no responsibility for their actions like the dictators of this world; they are in for a big surprise.

Evil for me is like spiritual regression, or spiritual backwardness. There are many fundamentalist movements like the Islamists, Orthodox Jews, Scientologists and Christian fundamentalists to name some common ones; they all basically want to control and repress people through religion and their dogma. Many cults or religions are evil in that they suppress ones spirituality. I am also not singling out religion - some governments are just as guilty. If a society is not free the spirit is normally repressed and those in power want to control the people's lives. I personally class this type of regime as evil.

We should always be moving forward as a society, fighting for freedom, and helping our fellow man. For those who want to turn the clock back on humanity there is no light for them. For when they die, a dark region awaits those whose thoughts and actions are evil. Their black thoughts have earned their own dimension of darkness. The natural law of cause and effect is their judge and jury. I must emphasise that this is *not religious preaching* but a natural spirit law; it is the science yet to be discovered and will be through a greater understanding of the subatomic world. This new world which is based beyond the subatomic particles that we currently know of is located in finer particles or vibrations within the ether. Once we start seeing this ether and these vibrations it will be based on a new understanding of our world and the spirit that interacts with us. It will be a "new science" of the ether or **Etheric Science** as I call it.

Perhaps you can see here that there is a natural order and selection when we die based entirely upon the life we lead as a person and the thoughts we have had are stored in our akashic record. If you are a good person why would you want to be around nasty, evil people when you pass over? The natural laws prevent this from occurring because we earn the dimension of our own creation. Good people are surrounded by light, happy conditions of extraordinary beauty. If you are evil a dark region awaits. It seems logical and natural to be with people of a like mind like dictators with dictators?

What are dark regions like? Sir Arthur has informed or inspired thoughts to me about these dark regions located in the lower astral levels. Once a spirit has achieved a position of spirituality where he has earned a beautiful dimension of thought he can travel around dimensions or go down to the lower regions and help those who are in a less fortunate spiritual position. The lower regions become darker as you travel downward and are quite often colourless. The astral regions closest to the Earth begin to look like a light grey fog. The higher spiritual dimensions are lighter and as you gradually move to the lower ones they begin to become a darker grey, and eventually black. The buildings look like a war zone. Any landscape to be seen is devoid of nature which could easily be described as a barren desert with no sunlight. You start to feel colder as you move deeper into these dark regions just as the opposite in the lighter regions where you feel warmth. And in these darker regions the spirit bodies become distorted and hideous. People or spirits in these lower astral dimensions are dressed in ragged clothes and hang around in groups. They cannot hide their feelings. You feel their hate, spite, feelings of revenge, and any kind of dark thoughts emanating from them. These thought pictures that Conan Doyle communicated into my mind are of dishevelled people cowering in hovels and caves, carved out of what looks like black coal. The rivers that flow are full of dark sludge.

Fear and oppression rule the lower astral regions. There are many warlords of evil who have their own gangs. Their members cower under the influence of these leaders. They cannot escape from the gangs because being on their own leaves them open to attack from their own or other gangs. These gangs attack or find their victims and torture them. In the astral planes you cannot be killed of course although you do have a

168

body. Instead you can be tortured and beaten until you fall unconscious. When you awaken, this can continue again and again until these evil astrals have had enough of torturing you. Does this not happen on Earth? Of course it does. Why would it not happen after death? For people who have tortured and killed poor souls on this earth those victims will be waiting for revenge on their torturers unless they have progressed spiritually so that revenge is not part of their base instinct. I am talking about those of like minds, spirits who kill, inflict pain, or torture for pleasure. Only spirits of the most evil nature would be in these lowest regions, some of the darkest you will find. It is certainly not for those who have killed due to circumstances such as war or in their own defence. A good person who has killed for whatever reason is still a good person. But being a good person they will most likely have a conscience and will suffer the mental consequences of their actions until they accept an outcome that they can live with.

My guides have told me that there is no Devil or Satan, but I know there are many evil souls that could be considered as evil as the Devil. They rule regions of the lower levels and look as grotesque as one could imagine the image of a devil. Dark spirits do exist but they will only be attracted to people of a like mind. There is no reason to be scared of these dark regions because if you are reading this book it is very unlikely you will end up anywhere in them. It is the people who scoff at the message spirit puts forward who are the most in need of help. As my guides have told me before a person can grow spiritually the ground must be prepared before the seed can be planted. One of the many ways that spirits prepares the ground is through love for a companion. All the feelings generated by a loving relationship produce a strong base for spiritual growth through which we all advance at different levels and at different times.

Since there are infinite levels of spiritual dimensions spirits are graded to their own dimensions by the natural laws. Some people graduate to the misty grey regions with spirits who congregate with similar unspiritual souls as opposed to the pure evil spirits in the lower regions. Again the level to which you graduate comes down to how much spiritual growth you have achieved in your life. You judge your own actions. You can only live in the level you have earned, but spiritual progress upwards is always open to every spirit no matter what they have done. Even if you are evil you can progress out of these regions. Once you start to hunger for change this light is picked up by what are called rescue spirits who travel to the dark regions to help those out of the dark regions.

Good spirits or 'rescue spirits' travel to the astral and lower regions on rescue missions. They look for people beginning to feel the need for a change who have a spark of spiritual growth emanating from their aura. A spirit rescuer will help guide these unfortunates into a better dimension where they can start to grow or develop their spirituality. This shows that nobody is forgotten and everyone is open to progress no matter what they have done. But remember this is very important; you have to *earn* your progressions through your spiritual growth.

The conditions around you become lighter as you progress from one dimension to the next higher level. As I have explained above there is a sort of heaven and hell, or I should say, many heavens and many hells. These are of your own creation. You are the judge and jury. You graduate to the level you have earned. You cannot go to the higher regions until you are ready as the conditions will make your spirit body uncomfortable. Imagine it like standing in front of an intense fire with no protection for your body. You do not want to experience these kinds of conditions. Lesser developed spirits will need to go back to a dimension in which they feel comfortable. Just as on Earth you feel comfortable with like-minded friends or those of a similar position in society.

On Earth we tend to have a mix of spiritually developed friends. Some are wise, some foolish. Some are in control of their lives, while others are like rudderless boats in choppy seas. The lucky ones find love but their friends are always looking for it. All situations, good and bad, are lessons for us. Unfortunately most people only learn from bad experiences.

Some people are afraid to fall in love and I quote Alfred Lord Tennyson's poem *In Memoriam*, "it is better to have loved and lost than to never have loved at all". Love is the greatest emotion it is a positive emotion. It makes people do and feel things like no other feeling. We talk about it so much but do we really understand it? Love is exactly what we need to grow as spirits because your spirit expands when you give or receive love. When a loved one leaves earthly life and passes into spirit they are always remembered. A person who gives their time and energy is always a loving person because they want and need no reward. They have attained a level of spirituality where they want to help lift those around them. When you start to think like this you are on the right path.

Earth could easily be described as a very dark region by many, let's face it, half the world is either starving or living on the breadline with little or no hope for a bright future, so it would be correct to say this. Earth can be heaven when things are going well but for some it's a hellish place to live. Sometimes it can be hard to imagine that there are infinite dimensions beyond this one. Everything looks solid, but it's not. The world seems to have a lot of love but it is sometimes brief and fleeting. Peace is not very common either. There are wars going on every day in many parts of the world. Unfortunately for some money and power is the God of Earth. Perhaps we can begin to change this so that living

171

a good life and welcoming the afterlife becomes our goal.

Chapter Twenty Four

The Electronic Medium

The Internet has been around for nearly a decade. It has brought much to the world, making it a smaller place and enhancing communications. The Internet has its problems of course, but it is a force for good. My webpage for example, has enabled me to help many people who have made contact by searching for specific information. People have sent emails to me and my subsequent replies have had a great impact on many lives because my spirit guides have helped me to give so much hope to those who have lost loved ones.

The most amazing result of the Internet, for me personally, has been the development of two new forms of mediumship. These are what I call, 'electronic clairvoyance' and 'electronic healing'.

Electronic Clairvoyance- I established my Ghostcircle website with some of the ghost pictures, photos of orbs, and videos of spirit lights that I have collected over time. After a while, people started to contact me about photos with spirit orbs taken with their own camera. Looking at them I started to pick up information. It was not simply about the orb in the picture, sometimes it was detailed information about the person who sent it, including their family and environment. I had no idea from where this knowledge was coming. One particular person who contacted me was a man who was a father, named David H. Months earlier he had lost his son Josh, to suicide. David had been taking photos of his family at home and captured some orbs in several of the photos. I had no other details apart from the name of the county in England where David was from, and that his son had committed suicide. I looked at his photos and started to pick up information. This is what I wrote to David:

I see what looks like a...fuel gauge of a car, problem with a set of keys, the letter M, a pair of boxing gloves on some hands, which are then removed, there was a smell of paint with him, and lastly a pawnbroker's symbol indicating a debt owed.

Dave wrote back and said he was astounded. He could not relate to some of the points I made but he responded with the following:

Hi Patrick,

Well, you have astounded me. Josh was always short of petrol (EMPTY FUEL GAUGE), and that night, he was supposed to have taken some from his girlfriend's house and used that to kill himself. He had a lot of money problems...had a problem with his CAR KEYS after he died as there were 3 keys to his car but only 2 keys were on the key ring when he was found....Also, about the boxing gloves, Josh was getting into fights up the town 2 weeks before he died, but his brother is buying a gold BOXING GLOVE from a local PAWNSHOP/jewellers. The SMELL OF PAINT... He was always spraying his car or parts for his car and he even used to spray bits in the house…..

Yours,

Dave

Dave was eager to get more information so he took additional photos and I gave him another reading from the orbs in the new photos:

Hi Dave,

I see a torn t-Shirt. For some reason Josh is saying that he has been to America, don't know if he was planning to or wanted to go, but he has gone there since(in spirit). He is also indicating something is wrong with somebody's teeth. Two air tickets are being shown, and a wrist watch. He is also talking about giving away his jeans to somebody. I am being shown

174

some books with writing sketches. I don't know why, but I have just seen a glider plane.

I received a very good response from Dave:

Dear Patrick,

Well, once again you have astounded us.

...I wear quite a few torn t-shirts and Josh had a few too. He had wanted to go to America to see his aunty Lisa who has been working out there for a long while now, his brother has had problems with his teeth and has a dental appointment next month but he has been in a lot of pain. I had been wearing Josh's wristwatch until last week. I did give some of Josh's jeans away to one of his friends.

Josh was always the one for leaving notes and keeping a diary of everything he had done and all the times that he saw his girlfriend, his brother is also one that keeps books and writes and draws in them. As for the glider, I have been thinking about taking up hang-gliding or micro lighting and have been looking on Ebay over the last 2 weeks to see what is for sale.

I was very pleased with the response and my spirit guide's help, of course, and Dave wrote a follow up e-mail thanking me for my help:

Hi Patrick,

Well, all I can say is that the whole family are amazed, as we have been charged a fortune and told nothing that related to Josh, and then out of the blue I speak to you and everything that you have said is FACT and has happened to Josh or some member of our family in the past. It makes us very reassured that there are people like you in the world. I hope the other pics arrived ok.

All the best from us all here and Josh

Dave

I have had many correspondences with Dave and his family since but one e-mail stood out:

Dear Dave,

I am getting a pair of headphones from Josh, and suede shoes. (They are not blue :-)) I see a set of car keys for a change of car. One of the children has a problem with their chest and is getting healing for his side. I see a roll of blue carpet and Josh tells me somebody is laying a carpet or taking it up. Somebody is dyeing or highlighting their hair blonde. He is talking about Aaron's weight.

Regards,

Patrick

I was again very pleased with his reply as it hit home so accurately:

Hello ....

Well, this time you have sent us both cold, Josh's headphones are in the back bedroom and our youngest, Rhiannon age 3, keeps playing with them. The shoes, we buried Josh in BROWN SUEDE SHOES. As for the new car Josh was supposed to be getting a new car the day that he died. As for the child with the chest problem, Josh's cousin has got cancer in the chest and she is very young. The roll of carpet (BLUE) from Josh's room is in the garage and we are going to lay it in the back room. This afternoon, about 4 o'clock, Debbs started to give Kristy blonde highlights and the light on top of the computer was flickering all the time, and we jokingly said "there's Josh", Aaron came over a couple of nights ago and was complaining about his weight.

You have just excelled yourself and put Derek (Derek Acorah) to shame.

For God's sake take care of yourself, as we can't do without you.

Lots of love

Dave and Debbs

176

So, what I have found is that spirit communication does not necessarily need a physical contact, although it works best with one. The really astounding thing is that the electronic communication on the Internet carries people's vibrations which allow spirit guides to connect to a medium and provide evidence. I spoke to one of my guides and he said, *"The key to an email, for example, is that it is like a prayer because people are putting thoughts and emotions into it as they write. It can be compared to a paper letter as well, because mediums can get a vibration and reading for people from just holding a letter."* The orbs that were sent to me in photos allowed me to expand the connection and create a very good evidential link. I also noticed another phenomenon when I was writing the emails.

Electronic Healing- As I sat writing I found that I was getting extremely hot and tired, although I felt perfectly normal before I opened the email. There was a definite drain on my energy while reading and replying. I can only compare it to the feelings I get when I am giving healing to people. I always found that my replies seemed to uplift people in strange ways. It was not that the evidence put a smile on people's faces, because the evidence obviously encourages them, but they always felt 'energised' in a way that is indescribable. I know how giving clairvoyance can be draining, leaving one mentally and physically exhausted after some long sessions. This drain was definitely a healing drain.

It seems that the Internet has expanded the capability of spirit communicators and mediums to reach more people in a way not available in any previous century. Distance provides no barrier or limit for mediums to give evidential proof. The world is now certainly a smaller place because of the Internet. The electronic world will bring even more opportunities for our spirit friends to communicate with us. Even as I write this I am being told that new technologies are waiting to be inspired in the mind of scientists who are willing to experiment in new forms of communication. My spirit guides say to me:

"Embrace those souls who have passed over before you, who now know the reality of the worlds beyond yours. We are always ready to help those who are willing to listen. We live in a world finer than the subatomic particles that you have found. The secrets to this world will be given in good time, but man must change his attitude first. If mankind can spend billions discovering the world of outer space, then can he not find some millions to discover the world of the inner space, the finer, subatomic world?"

Chapter Twenty Five

Finding the Wallet

On July 7th 1930, Sir Arthur Conan Doyle suffered a heart attack and died. He finished one very successful journey only to begin another one communicating to others from the beyond, the spirit world. A few days later he returned. On July 13th of the same year, there was a large gathering of 10,000 people to honour Sir Arthur at the Royal Albert Hall in London. A chair was left empty on the stage, and one of England's finest and most respected mediums, Estelle Roberts, said that she was communicating clairvoyantly with Conan Doyle, who was sitting in the chair. She gave a personal message from the great writer to his family, who accepted the message as evidential proof.

Conan Doyle has come through many mediums since that time and is still very active promoting his views on the afterlife. One day I asked him about all the money he spent promoting spiritualism, as most of his fortune went to that purpose. He replied "I don't regret one single penny spent on it, as it brought so much hope to those who had loved ones in spirit." I couldn't agree more. I have spent a lot of my life and money doing the same. I want people to believe that we do not die. I don't expect people to believe everything I say but I wish that everyone would keep an open mind. If your mind is open, I hope that for those who read this book, one day something inexplicable will happen that can only leave you with the answer that it was not caused by forces of this world, but by the next, to which we are all going. This leads me to the reason for writing this book.

During the summer of 2004, I read in the newspapers that a 'lost' archive of Sir Arthur Conan Doyle's papers and some personal effects were being auctioned by the famous Christie's auction house. Each

179

week for two months before the sale date of May 19th, I seemed to read and hear about this event. It was on TV, in the newspapers, magazines, and on the Internet. It was so well publicised that I knew it was going to be a very successful and expensive sale, with items going mainly to Sherlock Holmes' collectors and museums.

I kept an eye on it, but had no idea I would be there. My friend Karl is also an avid Conan Doyle fan and he decided he wanted to go to the viewing. It was a once in a lifetime event as there was much material on spiritualism and mediumship, and it was a good opportunity to view these items before they went into a collection. On Sunday, before the Wednesday sale, Karl and I went to Christie's to view the sale lots. It was very busy for a Sunday.

On entering the room I could hear a loud booming voice in a Scottish accent coming from behind a large black curtain. I quickly peeked behind the curtain, and set up like a mini cinema with seat laid out I saw a black and white documentary film of the life of Sir Arthur Conan Doyle. I watched the reel as it described ACD's trip to New York in the 1920s with the liner pulling out on its way to New York from a port that looked like Southampton in England.

I can recall that the next frame in the film was Conan Doyle arriving at a banquet in his honour for the magic circle. I saw him being greeted by the great Harry Houdini and his magician friends before Sir Arthur sat down at the banqueting table. While he had the camera focused on him a few magicians walked up to ACD and performed card tricks, and disappearing object tricks. One magician had some paper or white sheets of cloth which vanished and then reappeared out of his mouth.

In retrospect, I now realise that the magicians were mocking this great man by pretending that physical mediumship was fraudulent, full of trickery and that ectoplasm in a psychic circle was faked by using sophisticated, or, as it seemed in their opinion, not very sophisticated magical tricks. These were the tricks that had supposedly fooled Sir Arthur and the others who believed in physical mediumship, or life after death. There was a great deal of fraud in those days because there was money to be made from mediumship. Sir Arthur Conan Doyle knew this and was happy to travel to different séances with Houdini to help expose these people, as they were no good to anyone, especially those like himself who were trying to promote life after death. Houdini, while being an arch-sceptic, actually raised a lot of publicity to attract attention to what Conan Doyle was doing, so in a way, he was also a good promoter of life after death.

In the film, it appeared from Sir Arthur's face that he was very uncomfortable but he knew what was going on and accepted it. Moving away from the film toward the sale lots I noticed that some people were pouring over letters and manuscripts on the seats and tables that were laid out for viewers. This was probably the only time they would ever be able to see these manuscripts. Several Japanese women were feverishly writing down the details; I expected that there would be Japanese people attending as Doyle has had a huge following in Japan. There were also some Americans around as he has always been very popular in the US.

It was strange to see all these people, myself included, looking over the last, large, unknown collection of ACD's works. They had been stored in a lawyer's safe for decades due to a family dispute over how to sell the collection. Conan Doyle sold his own manuscripts before he died as he knew the value of his work, and even then people wanted to collect his writings. After he died Sir Arthur's son sold more of the remaining manuscripts from time to time to various collectors. Now, with this sale, the lots were to be the last remaining items of Sir Arthur Conan Doyle's life. It had taken nearly seventy-four years for the collection to come to this sale.

As I perused the manuscripts one interesting item caught my eye. It was the wallet Sir Author had used up until his death. I found it fascinating to be holding the wallet that Sir Arthur Conan Doyle last held. I believe it was in his briefcase, which was on his desk before he died. The contents in the wallet were left exactly as when he last used it. His wife Jean, had written on a brown envelope, which was still with the wallet, "My beloved's pocket book – left as found in his attaché case".

It stated in the catalogue that several months after ACD's death, Jean had placed all his papers in a box. The wallet, therefore, had also been stored by family members for almost seventy-four years. Another interesting item that caught my eye was Conan Doyle's passport, which contained travel stamps of the countries he had visited. Both his name and Jean's were on it.

As I looked around, I felt there was very little chance of being able to buy anything in the sale. There was so much interest that with nearly 140 lots, museums, collectors, and people with very deep pockets would probably be the only ones to have the opportunity to purchase the items. There was huge interest in the sale and there were TV cameras lined up at the back wall. Although the estimate of the wallet was £3,000 to £5,000, I felt that its eventual price would move well beyond. To me the wallet was special, and therefore I thought that many others would feel the same and bid for it.

I spent about an hour at Christies but left feeling a little disappointed because it seemed that I would have very little chance of being able to purchase any of the items. I truly felt that it might be a waste of time going to bid, only to be disappointed. In the end though, auction day turned out to be a triumph!

Chapter Twenty Six

The Sale

The Sir Arthur Conan Doyle sale was hyped up by the media. There was a real international flavour to the people interested in Conan Doyle's sale items, which in some cases were unpublished. The lots for sale really summed up his life from the very start, with a picture of him and a manuscript of his first story, the beginning of his writing period after he left the medical profession, and on to his maturity, where he investigated mediumship while promoting it worldwide. There were ACD's diaries, passport, driving license, and ideas for inventions including a fascination with the channel tunnel to France. There were family letters, letters to and from friends, like Rudyard Kipling, Jerome K. Jerome, Winston Churchill, Theodore Roosevelt, George Bernard Shaw, H. G. Wells, J. M. Barrie, Oscar Wilde, P. G. Woodhouse, and many more. ACD unsuccessfully ran for Parliament on a number of occasions. There were details from his correspondence as a war reporter and a diary of his life as a surgeon on a whaling ship. In effect there was something of interest to everyone.

Karl and I were particularly interested in four lots, including a letter for Karl's brother, Gary, Gary wanted a personal letter written by ACD to James Ryan, Sir Arthur's best friend, in which he discussed several theories that Charles Darwin had put forward. Karl and I had a limited budget, so we agreed that out of the four lots we wanted, the wallet was the one we most desired. Therefore, if we could pick up a 'bargain', we would bid for it. The auctioneer rose to the podium and briefly welcomed everyone, checking with telephone bidders that they were ready, and then began with lot number one, a pencil drawing of Arthur Conan Doyle, aged five. The drawing was sold for close to its highest estimate.

The first item of interest to me was a silver trowel, presented to Sir Arthur *"as a memento of the laying of the stone of dedication in the spiritual church, Brisbane, Australia - Dated 11th January 1921."* It was placed together with a lovely certificate from the church of New South Wales. I don't know what it was about this item, but I really wanted to bid for it. Unfortunately, it went way over the estimated budget that we had allocated, so I had to let it go. ACD's passport came up quickly, but it also went well over its estimate of £1,200, ending at nearly £4,200. It would have been great to buy this, but it also would have meant spending most of our budget on one item.

The next lot we were looking at was a letter from Conan Doyle to the Irish writer, Bram Stoker, author of *Dracula*. Karl was most interested in this because of his Irish connection but he let it go, as he didn't think it was worth the price reached.

We were now on lot 127, Sir Arthur Conan Doyle's wallet. The reserve price was £3,000. The opening bid was around £1,000. Bidding went up in monetary increments of £100. I could see that it was a three-way bid between us and two other people in the room. Fortunately, there were no telephone bidders. "This is good" I said to myself my heart racing. The bids went over £2,000 and one of the bidders dropped out. £2,200 with us then £2,400 against us. I bid £2,600, the bidding increased to £2,700 against me, and then I bid £2,800. I put my head down, waiting for the next bid. It never came. I looked up, expecting somebody to put his or her card up. The auctioneer was panning left and right. "Are there any more bids? Selling for £2,800." No takers. I felt he was a bit desperate and holding back on selling this lot for £2,800. For what felt like two minutes, but was actually 20 seconds, he repeated that he was selling the item at £2,800. I watched in slow motion as the gavel in the auctioneer's arm hit the table as he yelled, "Sold!" *Were there other forces controlling the sale?*

Karl and I headed to the collection area downstairs. I couldn't wait to get my hands on the wallet. There were a couple of people in the line ahead of me. I spoke to a woman behind us who, as it turned out, had bought the passport that Sir Arthur had used when traveling. After paying I laid the wallet out in front of us. To me it was like a huge diamond jewel, glistening like sunshine reflecting on water. I didn't open it, as I wanted to immediately take it out of the premises. Karl placed the wallet in a backpack, zipped it up safely, and we headed out to celebrate. Leaving Christie's was the best feeling in the world. One might say that it is only a wallet, but I felt I had a piece of history. I had bought a time capsule of history but also, with my sensitivity and psychometric ability, I could touch the past by just holding an object (Psychometry allows you to sometimes see what those in the past saw, along with their emotions and thoughts). The wallet was like a time capsule; Sir Arthur Conan Doyle's thoughts would be impregnated on its surface, stemming from all the times he carried it and held it in his hands. So it seemed that somebody upstairs was looking out for us. I believed that the wallet was destined for us, but I had no idea why until later that month.

Chapter Twenty Seven

The Contents of The Wallet

After the auction we went to a pub and ordered a drink, while looking briefly at the wallet in a clear plastic folder provided by Christie's. The barmaid saw the Christie's bag and asked if I had bought anything nice. I replied that I had bought the wallet belonging to Sir Arthur Conan Doyle, "You know the writer of the famous detective Sherlock Holmes?"

"Oh, that's interesting," she said and added, "you know that he wasn't a real person?"

"Oh yes I know that," I said with a puzzled smile. Of course, I knew he wasn't real. But I suppose that some people do believe that Sherlock Holmes was a real person. I have heard stories of tourists looking for his address at 221B Baker Street in London, an address that never existed but is there now as a tourist attraction. Everyone knows who Sherlock Holmes is, or at least they know that he was a great detective. The problem is that one hears about him so much that he really does take on an aura of reality. Conan Doyle put so much thought into the character traits of Holmes that the detective could have been a real person. When you count all of the movies, dramas and plays made about Holmes, he has become a part of many lives, even if they haven't read Sir Arthur Conan Doyle's books.

Later I pulled out the wallet from the protective folder and laid it on the table in the pub. There was a brown envelope inside it, quite worn and ripped at one end.

Written on the envelope was an annotation by Lady (Jean) Conan Doyle. In black pen it reads, *"My Beloved's pocket book as left by him in his attaché case."*

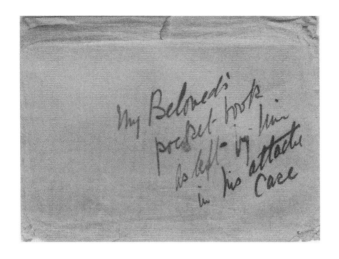

(The Envelope which contained the Wallet)

His wife Jean had placed the envelope in the wallet after his death and the contents were exactly as he left them before he died.

ACD's wallet is 6 ½ inches long by 4 ½ inches wide, or 16 cm by 11 ½ cm. and is made of lizard skin with silver corners protecting the edges. The silver hallmarks contain a small "i" with a London lion and leopard head, which dates it between 1904-1905, and the silver maker's mark is PB & Co. The wallet has a lovely smooth touch to the skin.

What I really love about the wallet is how close I can get to this man from the contents he left behind. When the wallet is opened the first thing one sees is several items neatly stored in the pockets. A rather pleasant, smoky, leather smell wafts up. There is a smudge of ink in the top corner presumably from a leaky pen. As the wallet folds out you can see two large pockets on each side with papers and photos folded neatly into them. One side has a leather pouch that folds over and is secured with a small leather strap. On opening the strap I found three 5 franc notes, but noticed that there were no English pounds - they must have been

187

spirited away by Lady Conan Doyle, if there were any at all. I replaced the francs and closed the pouch with the strap. On the right there was a one and a half pence stamp with a pocket specially made for it. Looking closely at the picture of the stamp I could see a profile of who I believe could be King George V. All around his head is writing, which states, "Postal Union Congress London 1929." Next to the stamp pocket is another one specially designed for calling cards (we now call them business cards). The card inside has written "*Sir Arthur Conan D*oyle" in italic script. Below to the left is his address, *Bignell Wood, Minstead, Lyndhurst*. To the right it is written, '*The Athenaeum Club*', a gentleman's club in London. In ACD's days a person would sometimes leave his calling card with the butler, maid or wife to say that he had visited or to make an introduction. It was very formal but it was a much more polite society in his time. However it was not necessarily a better world for most people unless one had a lot of money.

From the first pocket below the calling card I removed three photographs. They were all family photos, the largest of which is of Lady Jean and her two sons. On the back it reads "*This my beloved often carried in his pocket-book*." Next, there was a picture of Kingsley, the son who died at the end of the First World War. On the back of this photo was written, "*I (Kingsley) and D McMurray Dickson - Jan 16, 1915*."

(Kingsley Doyle and D McMurray Dickson)

The third photo shows Arthur Conan Doyle in a garden, sitting on a wooden bench next to his two remaining sons, Adrian and Denis.

(Arthur with sons, Adrian and Denis.)

189

As one can tell through the photographs he kept Sir Arthur thought greatly of his family. Indeed the remaining contents of the wallet show his love for them, as I will explain further.

The second pocket, below the photographs, contained two letters. The first was from his daughter, Jean (also called 'Billy'), for his birthday, and the other was from his son, Denis, who wrote about life at school. His daughter Jean's letter is so touching that it is obvious why he always kept it with him. The letter reads:

Windlesham,

Crowborough,

Sussex.

To my own darling daddy, wishing him many happy returns of the day.

Treasure one- I simply <u>Love</u> you, but I love You so much, it's impossible to express in words.

<u>*Billy*</u> *xxx*

It is a beautiful letter and it really moved me the first time I read it; I could feel the love coming from the words in the letter. I believe that Jean was in her early teens at the time she wrote this note. There is such a lovely simplicity about the words which expresses her absolute love for Sir Arthur. Even as I write this I am stirred once again to read it. Sir Arthur carried this letter everywhere to remind him of his daughter and perhaps when things got him down or when he was missing his family on his many trips abroad he took it out and read it. On Jean's death Sir Arthur's papers that were entrusted to her went to the British Library.

(Arthur Conan Doyles Wallet.)

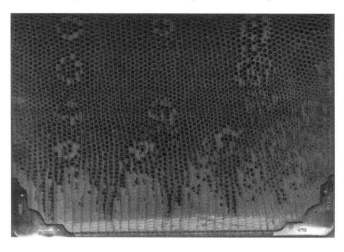

The second letter was sent to ACD by Denis who was boarding at a school in Eastbourne and wished him many happy returns for his birthday on May 22nd. It is a three-page letter with Denis' personal monogram of "*D*" written in gold script with the background of an emerald green oval. In the letter he discusses swimming practice and improvements in his cricketing. The letter provides a really good idea of family life around Conan Doyle, which one can see meant everything to him, as he kept so many mementoes in his wallet. This is what the letter said:

I

Thursday May 21st 1925   *"Berrow"*
                                            Carew Road
                                            Eastbourne

My Darling Daddy,
Very many happy returns of the day!!! And all the best in the coming year!
You won't have many more birthdays in this world, nor will any of us.
I am so looking forward to Saturday, when I will see you, Darling.
It was so nice to hear your dear voice over the phone on Sunday,
and sweet Mumty's. [Mummy]
I heard from Olive the other day; she is coming back to England
in early July.
Malcolm and I are getting on fine with our swimming. The other day
we had a race with Diplock's son, who is a very good swimmer –
we each did 1 length, and

II

he did 2 lengths. We had both been in some time and were fairly tired,
but he had not been in at all, and was quite fresh. Well, in the first
length (38 yds) he beat me by about 10 feet, so that when Malcolm started,
he was 10ft behind, and he only lost about that much
in his length. Yesterday Granville House was swimming there, and
we saw several girls we knew.
I am getting on with my batting better now, and last time the pro.
[Professor?]
said that I got on very well. My bowling, too, is improving,
I think. Some of the men at the club were very nice about it,
and said that I would make a good bowler. Someone told me
that my best ball was on the leg stump, which swung at the last moment.
They also said that I..

III

would take a lot of wickets with it, but I doubt it, very much.
Malcolm is getting on splendidly with his batting and fielding.
Well, I'm afraid I've no more news, Darling; please give my
love and kisses to Sweet Mummy, with ever so much of both
to your dear self,

Your ever-loving son,
                                            Denis.
                                            XXX

P.S I am getting on well with my work – In Latin I have just been
doing some Tacitus, who is supposed to be about the most
difficult authors.

(Letter from Denis.)

192

You can see the letter is written by a private schoolboy and is of its time. His use of language, his class, and breeding are very apparent. Having been born in 1909 Denis would have been around fifteen or sixteen-years-old in 1925. It is very well written with no misspelled words!

From just one part of Sir Arthur's wallet you can literally see that his family was central to his life. If you look at the first pocket on the other side of his wallet you will see the other love of his life: spiritualism or the proof of life after death.

(Jean Doyle with Children Adrian and Denis Doyle)

I opened the first leather pocket and found a collection of folded documents wrapped together with two folded postcards, the first of which showed the Carlton Hotel in Johannesburg, South Africa. Written in pen on the back of both postcards is what I can discern as descriptions of the spirit world or the afterlife that Conan Doyle had described. On the first card the description reads as follows:

193

> *I was glad to find animals and trees there. That was better than harps and clouds. I had feared it might be weird.*
>
> *When I found it here it was 1000 times more beautiful than the earth, tho' in some ways like it, I knew I could be happy.*
>
> —
>
> *Much is eliminated by our likes. For instance, with us there are no congested areas, no slums, no public houses, prisons, workhouses or asylums.*

On the back of the second card the text is written in the same handwriting. At the top left hand corner is the word '*Lower*'. From reading the content, it is clear to me that the second postcard describes what conditions are like in the lower astral worlds, the ones that are created by those who lack spiritual growth. You have lightness and darkness in this world so it is the same once you die. If you live a life of light you will go to a light world, so to speak, and those with a dark path gravitate to the darker regions. It is a natural law.

Below is the text written on the second postcard:

Lower

But on the lower spheres, there are more correspondences with your towns. Here one finds undesirable features, and these will persist while their counterparts remain on earth. So long as people live and think in undesirable ways, there must inevitably remain those undesirable places, to which they gravitate on coming here. When your earth has risen mentally and spiritually above such habits of life, the corresponding places on the lower spheres will disappear.

By using the word 'correspondences' Sir Arthur meant that there are dark regions of the spirit world that correspond directly to our dark regions on Earth. If you think of any current 'dark' regions on Earth, (the places you would not necessarily visit as a tourist), some of the people who live in these places are good, and they are spirits who have sacrificed their spiritual growth to help those who inhabit these areas to become more spiritually aware. These are like gems among the rough. For these good spirits help those of a lower spiritual nature and their rewards come from helping these spirits move up the ladder of spiritual progression.

However many people who inhabit dark areas of the earth are not necessarily good spiritual people and they are not ready to learn. Those who commit mass genocide, for example, are hardly going to rub shoulders with angels. They are materialistic in nature and like power over individuals, greed, lust, and material items. When a spirit dies from a dark region on earth and they have a lower spiritual existence, they will gravitate to these regions of 'hell'. Again this is assuming that they have spiritually grown very little. You get what you deserve, or like attracts like. The regions of hell are areas of lower spiritual growth, and are not as described in religious terms such as 'full fire and brimstone', but they can be repugnant places in which to live. The dimension to which one goes is dictated by your spiritual growth, not by your location on earth. We gravitate to like-minded places, and people. The natural Law of Attraction, or 'like attracts like' operates no matter how much we hide our thoughts and feelings on Earth - we can't even hide them from ourselves!

When we change our attitudes and move onto a spiritual path, or when we collectively raise our spiritual and mental awareness these regions will disappear because there will be no one to inhabit them. Unfortunately if we look around today it appears that it is unlikely this will happen anytime soon, but as I have indicated all spirits turn to a spiritual path eventually even if it takes a thousand years or more.

Unfolding other cards wrapped inside the wallet I came across another postcard with writing on the back. It was a picture of a steam ship called the 'Windsor Castle' from the Union-Castle Line to South and East Africa. As I turned the card over I read a very odd quote with the heading '*Hell*':

> ***Do you still hold the doctrine of eternal punishment?***
> –
> ***It was an error. All will have opportunity and in time all will progress.***

Later I was able to ask Sir Arthur about this message. He told me clairvoyantly that it was an answer to a question asked in a psychic circle to a priest, in a trance session, about being punished in hell regions for eternity if one does wrong; an error perpetrated though current religious views. The priest replied from spirit that "it was an error" and that all of us will be able to progress from the hell regions. Sir Arthur told me that the question was put to the priest of whether he still believed in 'the doctrine of eternal punishment', but the priest replied with the truth that all spirit guides profess: "Nobody is beyond redemption".

As mentioned earlier there is no Heaven or Hell as written in the Bible, but there are regions that could easily be described as heavens or hells. We can and eventually will progress to the lighter regions no matter what we have done on Earth. Eternal progress is open to all of us and there are spirits ready to help those who want to change and move out of the dark regions.

However the spark or realisation that attracts these guides must come from the spirit itself.

Inside the steamship postcard was a personalised plain one from SIR ARTHUR CONAN DOYLE - 15, Buckingham Palace Mansions, with a quote on the back. It read:

> *Time after time I have thought, it is all a beautiful wonderful dream from which I will wake up shortly*
>
> —
>
> *but that feeling has passed away completely and left behind it a feeling of calm restful happiness.*

I asked Sir Arthur to what he was referring and he replied "The quote was taken from a spirit guide who spoke to me in a sitting trance, whereby he was asked what it felt like on his spirit after he died, to which he gave a description of how he felt before and the feeling he has now." It was so touching that he wrote it down on a spare card so he would remember it after the trance session.

The last folded piece of paper was stationary from another of Sir Arthur's addresses - he certainly seemed to have moved around! This time the address was Bignall Wood, Minstead, Lyndhurst. The typed and unsigned letter is shown below:

> *This world offers everyone a chance to fulfill his or her heart's desire; whatever that may be so long as it is good. They generally take up what was their talent on earth, so that no effort here is lost. Every branch of study can be reached; sculpture, art, science, music, literature, all are at hand and it is the desire of all awakened souls to advance in knowledge and goodness.*
>
> *Love, not money is the ruling power. For gods sake! Sir Arthur strike hard at these people, these dolts who will not believe. The world so needs this knowledge. If I had known this on earth, it would have so altered my life. The sun would have shone on my grey path had I known what lay before me.*

It was quite obvious to me that the message was to Conan Doyle from someone in spirit describing the wonderful conditions that exist in 'his' spirit world. They are quite emphatic that Sir Arthur should promote this knowledge to as many people as possible that would listen. For if he had known the truth while on Earth it would have made such a huge difference to his life that he would have taken a better path. Instead he took a less spiritual path - "my grey path" as he called it. His world, the spirit world, is dominated by love, not money and materialism.

When you open up to spiritual truths you set out on a path that is more fulfilling, rewarding, and meaningful than anything else. It is not necessarily easier because you feel a greater sense of responsibility for all your actions. More care is needed in your thoughts and actions. The materialist's path which can be described as a 'grey path' is usually dominated by the pursuit of money and material goods without a thought about what one's actions may cause. Once you have material items you must be careful that they do not in the end control you, or your life. If you worry about your possessions being stolen, broken, or losing value you should consider this. They should be enjoyed, of course, as many beautiful material objects are treasures to have, like I enjoy my Conan Doyle wallet, but if you know that we live forever and that spiritual growth is more important these material objects become less important. This is the responsibility that you start to learn when you tread a spiritual path. I am not proposing that you have to give up your material possessions and join a hippy commune, far from it. Material possessions need to be regarded in their true perspective. They are temporary items that we can get pleasure from, use, and maybe leave behind for another generation to enjoy.

In the last pocket of the wallet I found two cards with cut-out shapes that looked like masks, and which were described as such in the Christies sales catalogue. The cards were both the same size - 5 inches long by 2 ½ inches wide. I couldn't figure out what they were or why Sir Arthur kept them so I put them aside. In the pocket I also found a newspaper clipping from the classified ad. I looked at it, and thinking it was a little strange wondered why he kept it. Looking at the back of the ad I tried to figure out if there was something relevant on that side, but it was just a split paragraph about some government loans. It was quite tedious so I figured that the classified section was what he was after. There were seven small ads that could have some relevance and I thought that maybe he cut this out as an idea for a new novel. The first ad read:

> **Accountant. Retiring from responsible position, SEEKS part-time POST (day or evening) as Business adviser or confidential secretary to lady or gentleman – D.A.R 6557...**

Perhaps Sir Arthur was looking for a new accountant or personal business advisor. I decided that it was unlikely, however, because as he was a very successful author in his own right he would not be interested in business advice. He may have had a need of a secretary. He was a busy man. I looked at the next ad:

> AUTOMOBILE ENGINEERING TRAINING COLLEGE CHELSEA – S.W.3 (day and residential) Founded specially to train boys of good education for the Automobile industry. Probationary Term. Appointments for qualified students. Syllabus from principal.

Sir Arthur would have been very unlikely to be interested in this. His sons may have needed a career on leaving school but I feel sure that he would have had some academic profession in mind for them. So I disregarded it.

> BATCHELOR. 32 Public School man, staying in London for short time, offers his services as COMPANION in return for hospitality. – B.P.S 6596 …..

What can I say about this? A young, educated bachelor wants to stay in London for a short time and offers his services as a 'companion'! I think it is fairly obvious what this ad is for but did this mean Sir Arthur was looking for a 'companion'? I moved on to the next ad.

> HOSTESS REQUIRED. Hotel North. Trained Ballroom dancer; experienced entertainer; age 25-35; height 5ft 6in – Box 523, Harrods Advt Agency, S.W.1

It is almost certain that Sir Arthur was not interested in this ad, although from what I heard, he was a good ballroom dancer. His height, however, was greater than 5 feet 6 inches so there goes that ad did not work.

LADY, slightly crippled. Rheumatism, interested in history and art would be glad to find another lady who in return for home would run small country cottage. 25 miles from London; three rooms, bath, hot and cold. – C.M.K 6625 "Morning Post", E.C.4

This was certainly not of interest to Sir Arthur. It does show that people are always lonely and in need of friendship. It's a big risk opening up your home to share with somebody through a small ad in a classified section.

REMEMBER TO GET your CHILDRENS PARTY ENTERTAINER. From KEITH PROWSE, 159, New Bond St, W.1

Sir Arthur did have a young daughter, Jean (A.K.A. Billy), who was probably in her early teens. Assuming this ad was placed in the wallet sometime in the late 1920s, and most of his children were beyond the stage of party entertainers at that point, I feel that this was unlikely to be of interest to ACD.

SALES PROMOTION – Opportunity for CAREER with great possibilities for young men of PUBLIC SCHOOL Education. – Details from Director Business Careers Association Ltd. Premier House. Southampton Row, W.C.1

These were the ads listed in the newspaper clipping in Sir Arthur's wallet. What was he searching for? Which ad was he interested in? Was there some kind of Sherlock Holmes mystery being thought out in his mind? A possible murder mystery played out through the classified ads? One can speculate and wonder what it was all about and admit we will never know the answers. However, when you have mediumistic abilities things take on another dimension. I concentrated to see if Sir Arthur was around and he entered my thoughts. I could see his spirit standing next to me. I greeted him as I connected with him and asked him why he kept the newspaper clipping? I was hoping for some interesting revelation, a new book, or maybe some dark mystery about his sexuality.

No, the simple answer was the fact that he was so busy that he needed some help organizing various things in his life, and the paper clipping advert was kept because he actually was in need of a secretary!

I had thought that there was going to be more of an interesting story and felt a little let down. Little did I know that there was more to come later a revelation that would shock and fill me with wonder and awe.

Chapter Twenty Eight

The Revelation

In the second leather pocket on the folding strap side there were five items, three of which were folded together. The first piece that caught my eye was a scrap of paper with writing on it in ink. The top corner had the word **_messages_** underlined. The message seemed to describe how knowing about the afterlife before passing over helps to speedily adapt to that world. Those on earth who have unfortunately not thought, in advance, about the afterlife live in a 'confused' state of mind. Here is the text:

Messages

Some having a comprehension of this truth (of the afterlife) before passing over come full of understanding and [are] easily able to adapt themselves to their new environment. Others, who have not been taught, wander round aimlessly, dazed and stupefied, finding none of those things, which their earthly teachers had led them to expect.

As you can see Sir Arthur wrote this down because it can so easily apply to any person who 'dies' and knows nothing of an afterlife. The majority of Religious teaching tells us to expect that there is some kind of Heaven and Hell beyond death and they give all various (conflicting) ideas of what it would be like.

The usual description of Heaven is something similar 'to angels sitting on clouds and playing harps in a warm, loving atmosphere', and Hell is 'a place of fire, heat, and devils with pitchforks'. Most Christian sects also talk of purgatory, a waiting area between Heaven and Hell; therefore a lot of people envision all three places. I have often heard of many Christians waiting for Judgment Day when their souls will be raised into Heaven. I can see them as those spirits who *"wander round aimlessly, dazed and stupefied"*. This quote easily describes those religious followers who have taken the word of their religious teaching as the complete truth, so have no idea that they are dead and await some form of judgment day and resurrection.

Additionally I found among the other pieces of folded papers a receipt from '**African Theatres, Limited'**, Empire buildings, Johannesburg, dated January 10, 1929, *"Received from A Conan Doyle the sum of fifty five pounds, eight shillings and nine pence"* - a considerable sum in those days. The last document was a letter from a Danish man named J. S. Jensen, dated May 14, 1930:

Dear Sir Arthur,

The meeting was not a success. The public protested against the aggressive ways of the speaker by stopping at home, and the concert palace was not half full. Financially we lost considerably, although the press helped us wonderfully. It gave us great publicity all over the country, but it did not move the public like your visit did.

I think the speaker has the best intentions, but the Danes no doubt know that spiritualism should be approached in a somewhat humbler spirit. Hope that you will soon recover and that we shall have the pleasure to meet you again healthy and fighting.

Yours Sincerely,
J S Jensen

It must have been one of the last letters Sir Arthur received before he died the following July. It describes a spiritualist church service that didn't go well. He was always promoting spiritualism to any individual or country that was interested. He was known, and is still acknowledged today, as the 'St Paul of Spiritualism' for his evangelical approach to what he considered the most important aspect in his life. For me Sir Arthur is more like a messenger who brings a message of truth that is just as strong now as it was in his day. Today people are spiritually lost and have a greater need for spiritual knowledge. Unlike the great religions of the present day that promote spiritual qualities, and life after death, the spiritual truths promoted by Arthur Conan Doyle can be proven with demonstrations of mediumship, and scientific investigation. It is my hope that mediumship will be investigated with a sympathetic and positive approach.

The two paper cards with cut-outs, which I had put aside earlier, were the least interesting as far as I could then see, but in the end proved to be the most fascinating. Looking at them I did not really pay much attention. They are on plain white paper card, both, slightly folded on one corner's edge to hold them together. Why were these cards kept in the wallet? I didn't think any more about it until we later opened the wallet to take some photos. We discussed the items Sir Arthur kept there and agreed that he was a great family man, very much devoted to his wife and children. He was also passionate about his promotion of the afterlife as there was so much material communicated to him from different mediums. I am sure he kept these messages to use them at times for inspiration, and to always remind him in any low periods of his 'mission'.

As we sat there Sir Arthur appeared to me and said *"it was amazing how things that one would normally discard and think unimportant can have such an effect in ways one cannot imagine"*. I told him that I was delighted to have received the wallet, and couldn't believe it when the hammer finally went down. He said *"it was meant to be."* Karl then asked if I could ask Sir Arthur about the paper cards with the cuts-out. Doyle told him to write the answer down as it was important.

The reply from Sir Arthur was as follows:

ACD: You will see two paper cards; the first card with the small ink stain was given to me (Sir Arthur) from a medium in psychic circle. I was talking to a spirit who had taken over the medium who was in trance. The subject of the master spirit guide was discussed and I asked the spirit in trance what the master spirit [guide who controls the circle] looked like. The spirit replied, "I will show you, can I have one of your cards?" [Sir Arthur had some blank paper cards that he used for taking notes.] The medium who was still in trance proceeded to cut out a shape in virtual darkness from the card and handed it back to Sir Arthur saying that "if you shine a light through the card and project it onto the wall you will see the face of the Master."

After this came through it took a moment for me to register what had been said. We were both shocked and excited. I was not expecting such an amazing reply. It was certainly exhilarating. Karl then said, "Can you ask him what the second paper card is, the one without the ink stain which looks very similar. Is it a copy?"

Sir Arthur said, *"You could say it is a copy. I showed the original card to Harry Houdini later and he said 'It was a trick, I could do the same. Do you have another card?' I gave him a blank card and he copied the cut-out from the one I had. I said that didn't prove anything except that you can copy my card. Try doing it in virtual darkness as I saw it done, and not from my template."*

One could not convince Houdini as he was an arch-sceptic. I must add that he is not a sceptic anymore.

He really was a fantastic magician, one of the best ever, and I was thrilled that not only did I have this wonderful picture of a master spirit guide I also had a cut-out made by the great Houdini. There were so many wonderful surprises in such a small item.

I wanted to see what the master spirit actually looked like so I took Conan Doyle's card and looked for a flashlight in the cupboard. I turned down the lights and shone the light onto the card to see the image it projected onto the wall. The effect is quite startling especially in the dark. You can easily see a face, eyes, beard, and long hair with a parting down the middle. It is a wonderful portrayal of what the 'master' looks like in spirit.

("The Revelation" card with light showing The Master spirits face.)

We must remember the card itself was cut out with scissors by a medium in trance in front of Conan Doyle, in darkness. So there were two cards, as I said, and the other card was Houdini's attempt which is a good attempt, but again he did it in light, and I'm sure looked at the original template for guidance.

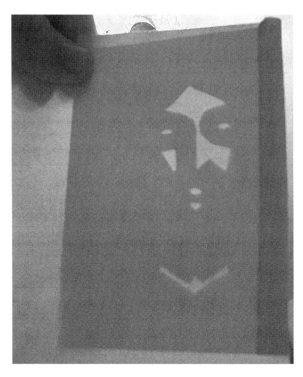

("The Revelation" card cutout with Master spirits face.)

It is quite evident to me why Sir Arthur kept both cards in his wallet. When he travelled, and he travelled a lot, he had all the things that could remind him of why he was doing this. With these cards he could readily see those who believe on one hand, and who are in denial on the other. This was a secret he kept with him for many years and I believe that he waited over seventy-five years to find the right time to reveal the contents of his wallet. I am quite certain that before he died Doyle never realised the importance of his wallet and its contents. Most people finally realise what is important to them when someone else points it out or it is lost.

Sir Arthur was not a 'flashy' or egotistical person. He didn't have to prove anything to anybody, let alone himself. His belief in the afterlife was absolute, and his message was always a simple one: love one another and do unto others as you would have them do unto you; treat everyone in your thoughts and actions as you would like them to treat you. The picture card of the master is a wonderful item, but for Sir Arthur it was only there to remind him that the message is what is truly important, not necessarily the person that brings it.

The same concept of thought that inspired Sir Arthur is stronger now than it was in the twentieth century. There is new inspiration, regained strength, and more guidance to help us through the experiences and instability of the twenty-first century. People are lost and looking for answers. They are walking away from the old traditions that collectively held society together. As never before in history, orthodox religions, beliefs and social structures are being questioned.

This is why the spirit and message of Sir Arthur is needed more than at any other time. There is a vast army of spiritual beings from all the realms of the afterlife who are trying to impress, shape, change, and restructure the spiritual path of mankind. Orthodox religion is beginning to crumble. It is now time for science, logic, love, and understanding to come together ready for this new dawn. We are surrounded by a present wave of people searching for answers.

More and more people are joining psychic circles, expanding their minds in new directions, and reading books about spiritual growth. The early mediums and spiritualists who expounded these truths had to fight the enormously powerful structures of the establishment that wanted to maintain a heavy hand on the belief structures of ordinary people. In the past we have been blocked from learning the truths of our world, and the next, which are now so obviously evident. It only took a few journalists to discredit certain mediums and people soon lost interest. However the truth is really out there and you have to go look for it.

For example you could investigate all the evidence gathered by the Society for Psychical Research (SPR) in their library over one hundred and twenty years of knowledge. Or hear the stories on YouTube and some of the entertainment channels of people who survived death or have seen ghosts. All across the world people experience apparitions, clairvoyance, clairaudience, and prophecy, you can see that this is not paranormal, but in fact, very normal. Have you seen the number of stories in newspapers, magazines, or on television and radio concerning the afterlife? Can it really be disregarded as 'things that go bump in the night'?

If you compare the evidence for the continuation of the soul given by priests, rabbis and mullahs, you will find they all say that you must believe in it because the truth has been provided in some books written over millennia. Why not ask them "Can you prove it?" They will say you must believe, or have faith. Why should you believe them or me? Although I am a medium who has on countless occasions provided evidential proof of life after death I will not ask you to take my word for it; find the truth for yourself!

We must open our minds to this new wave of knowledge. We must search within ourselves through meditation, looking within our minds, allowing the knowledge of the Great Spirit to permeate our beings in the quietness of our lives, and let the wonderful influences of our spirit guides enter our lives. As we open you will see that, while far from perfect, we can overcome barriers and problems that have been obstructing growth and understanding of spirit. It is not easy; we have to confront many of our own prejudices and weaknesses such as greed, lust, power, and misunderstanding that create so many of the hideous problems we have on Earth.

Sir Arthur has said "Only by Love can we find the way". He and many others who suffered bigotry, and were belittled for their beliefs and knowledge are aware of the problems on Earth. How many people were burned at the stake and how many psychics and clairvoyants were brought before judges or destroyed by the church to maintain a belief structure? As recently as the 1940s and 50s a famous medium called Helen Duncan was persecuted for telling the truth with an archaic witchcraft act dating from the 1700s. When she materialised the full form of a sailor with the name H.M.S. BARHAM on his cap - a ship which the English government denied had been sunk. Once the word spread back to the War Ministry that she knew top secret information she was arrested and charged with spying. She did not have a fair trial as her mediumship was too good, and she told the truth which was dangerous to the war propaganda. When she went to court she wanted to prove her mediumship was not fraudulent by giving a demonstration as evidence, but the judge was frightened and would not allow it. Helen was found guilty and gagged. It was said that Churchill visited her while in prison. He certainly heard about her because she announced the sinking of the ship the HMS Barham in a circle during the War before the allies announced it. Can you imagine the uproar today if that occurred? It shows how we have changed as a society; we no longer accept the status quo.

The Witchcraft Act is now seen for the prejudicial folly it was created for. The way is now clear for the work of many great psychics and philosophers who were suppressed. They can now bring forward their knowledge, understanding, and truth. This band of brothers and sisters who have come together in great company are now trying to influence politicians, scientists, musicians, writers, and artists.

It will not be easy to sway those with influence as all the old forces are still there, still creating the same fears and keeping people controlled, but nothing can stop this new tide. The media and Internet are such strong influences today that people can now make up their own minds without being constrained by the current laws of society. The old control is breaking down and people will continue to ask "Who am I? What am I doing here? Is there a god? What is the purpose of my life? Is there an afterlife? Am I responsible for my actions? Can I help myself move forward?"

All these millions of voices can be freed from the ignorance that surrounds them. At long last we are finally beginning to understand that we are all spirits encased in bodily flesh. One of our greatest assets today is the advancements in science and technology. This will help make the proof and evidence of the spirit world possible. Digital cameras allow us to see light orbs and physical manifestations. Current video recording equipment will enable our friends in spirit to prove the continuous existence of our friends and loved ones. On my Ghostcircle website you can see manifestations from the spirit world.

It is very difficult to get full figures on infrared light. One tends to see the spirits as light anomalies or orbs. However if we film in a very low intensity light, in the right environment, we can record a spirit presence. Ordinarily the vast majority of people in a room with a psychic circle will see some spirit presence with the naked eye, but because white light tends to break up the energies it is very difficult, but not impossible, to capture them on film. With the help of Sir Arthur, and my spirit guides I hope to produce something more tangible on video.

This is a truly exciting time to be a medium as we are being empowered and helped by the enthusiasm and faith of new members joining our circles with their guides and helpers. New TV programs on mediumship and clairvoyance are bringing hope, help and love to all of us. It is capturing the imagination of many people and beginning to open the doors of understanding. I am grateful for the new army of wonderful mediums who are now joining those who fought through the dark periods of history, from the early pioneers to the present day advocates such as Michael Roll, Victor Zammit, Archie Roy, and the mediums Derek Acorah, Gordon Smith, John Edwards, and James Van Praagh. All of these wonderful mediums have had the courage to push forward the message of eternal life, and to give incredible evidence and proof that has uplifted and helped millions.

There is a global movement looking at the paranormal and thus the afterlife, and it is gathering momentum. The truth is out there and it is up to us to open the doors of understanding. However we must always be wary of fraudsters and tricksters who wrap themselves up in titles like 'parapsychologist', spuriously titled professors of so-called 'occult' studies, and certain members of society who have their own agenda to keep the status quo the way it is. They will fight in every conceivable way to stop the truth being told. The main tactic is not always to discredit good mediums, but generally go after bad ones thus tarring all mediums with the same brush. The sceptics try to discredit orb theory by saying it is always dust and moisture, but there is also intelligence and even faces and images within orbs that cannot be explained. They don't have an answer for this, but now their loud brass band is slowly being drowned by the sound of the spirit voices, common sense, and spiritual truth emanating from books, TV documentaries, and the thousands of mediums that have finally been given a voice.

The contents of the wallet show many aspects of what Sir Arthur Conan Doyle was trying to teach others. The family letters and photographs show his message to love one another like he did with his own family. All the written notes and transcripts from séances he had attended, and the two nondescript picture cards which are a treasure and of course his secret, show Sir Arthur's commitment to spreading the message about the spirit world. Once he communicated to me about the contents it became clear that all these items were the most important things in his life. Maybe he felt that in having the cards placed next to the letters and photos of those he loved the most the benign influence of the mask that pictures a master spirit would cast a shadow of protection and peace on them.

Sir Arthur's letter concerning the unsuccessful spiritualist demonstration in a Danish church showed that it was always going to be a struggle. From the postcard messages about life on the spirit side taken from trance sessions he attended, Doyle, could plainly see that personal responsibility for all thoughts and actions is key to the spiritual conditions that each individual earns in the next life. I am quite sure he pulled these fragments out on long journeys around the world to remind him of where he was going. He told me that he was quite ill in the last few years of his life something of which not many people were aware. Sir Arthur knew his time was near, but was trying to remove other people's fear of death, and bring comfort to those who had lost loved ones just like the loss of his first wife, Louisa, and his son Kinsley during the war. How can this message be wrong?

I recently read that the British Library bought over ten lots in the Christies sale, comprising of over 1,200 documents, and are now exhibiting them. The echo of Conan Doyle's message can still be heard after all this time; the truth is as valid today as it was at that time. Life is eternal.

Sometimes I feel the need to go into trance because some spirit feels the need to speak through me. On certain occasions when something needs to be said my spirit control makes his presence known. Soon after I bought Sir Arthur's wallet I was speaking with Karl who often assists me, and usually records conversations from spirit guides who speak through me, when I felt a spirit desiring to talk. I sat down and felt myself drift off. Sir

Arthur spoke through me and the following is what was recorded.

Unknown: Good Evening!

Karl: Good Evening. Who is speaking?

Arthur Conan Doyle (ACD): It is Arthur Conan Doyle.

Karl: Ah, welcome, Sir Arthur. What do you have to say?

ACD: I am so pleased you got my wallet. At least I know now that it is with somebody on Earth who really appreciates it and will use it in the right way. It's amazing how there are so many things we don't appreciate on Earth until it's too late.

Karl: Arthur, did you write that line in your wallet? Time after time I have thought... ["Time after time I have thought, it's all just a beautiful and wonderful dream from which I will wake up shortly – but that feeling has passed away completely and left behind it a feeling of a calm restful happiness."]

ACD: Yes. I wrote it down. It came from a trance session I attended, and the spirit said that since it had passed over from death it had been like a wonderful dream, but this had turned into calm restful happiness. I wrote the quote down to remind me of the struggle and where I was going. A lot of people didn't realise that I had bad health problems at different points in my life.

Karl: Are you friends with Houdini? [Harry Houdini and Sir Arthur had a mutual interest in mediums and the afterlife but their five-year relationship was more a professional rather than a personal friendship. Sir Arthur stopped associating with Houdini a few years before he passed on.]

ACD: I never fell out with Houdini, as such. He was a paranoid man who used me to further his career; there was no great friendship. He built his reputation out of destroying mediums, therefore, I had to have him on my

215

side otherwise he would have tried to turn me into a laughing stock. It's basically a case that he was more to be pitied than anything else. He really loved his mother. He wanted the evidence, but even when he got the evidence presented to him he wouldn't accept it because he was a con artist and illusionist himself, you understand. Because 'he knew' how these things could happen, or manipulate them he thought everybody was a liar and a cheat. But you know by your own mediumship that this reality is real. We are here, invisibles and etherians are here, and all the different dimensions. Even the fairy folk are here. They are not there to the degree that I thought they were. They come in a different form.

Karl: I have seen fairies myself; they appeared [in a vision in my mind] as cartoon-like pictures.

ACD: That is how they show themselves to you because that is how you would understand it. They appeared like cartoons to imitate the Cottingley fairy pictures published in the 1920s. This is how you would recognise them in your mind. It is the same for spirit guides and it is dependent on the energy and ability it has to show itself to you, but with a fairy how would you show yourself if you were a fairy? Perhaps as a blob of energy, or as a Cottingley fairy which you might be familiar with? It may be a cartoon to look at but it is what you would recognise as a fairy. This does not mean that they look like the Cottingley fairies as they have many different forms. But remember, as you think so shall it become. If you want to help the etherians or guides to appear in your circle then you must visualise them appearing; such as hands or faces or even whole bodies. These thoughts can make it possible. [Changing the subject] There are several items you will receive in the future, including a bulky item.

Karl: A bulky item?

ACD: I cannot say any more on that. Let it be a surprise.

Karl: Should I look at a particular lot in Christie's [sale] coming up next month?

ACD: It's entirely up to you. You will have lots of bits and pieces. I cannot influence you. I am being told off from my side now. [*This does happen quite a bit in trance sessions since some guides are not allowed to tell you certain things in case it brings about a change in the direction of your path or unduly causes an unforeseen effect elsewhere.*] I must not colour your perspective beyond helping you to develop your belief in spirit and how to also develop the functions of faith that create spiritual manifestations.

Karl: I understand. Do you still write on the other side?

ACD: I do, but it's a different form of writing. I also help inspire writers on Earth.

Karl: Do you influence writings in mystery, crime or historical novels?

ACD: Oh no I have gone far beyond that. Don't get me wrong; on Earth it was my bread and butter. It was very good and I used techniques that were ground-breaking in their own way that other people followed. It is a case of there is so much that you do not know what is going on. There are so many concepts just like the concept of Sherlock Holmes, or a murder mystery. All the concepts that could be put together are beyond your comprehension. So I write plays and stories now in a different concept for people who live in spirit.

Karl: Because people on Earth have thoughts about Sherlock Holmes have they created spirit forms of Sherlock Holmes in your world? [*When people think about different thoughts on Earth, if they believe strongly enough, they can actually create thought-forms which actually have a life of their own on the spirit side. Quite a few people believe Sherlock Holmes was a real person.*]

217

ACD: Ah! There are many thought-forms of Sherlock Holmes walking around. There are a couple of ghosts constructed of thoughts. The thing is that constructive thought is the most powerful thing in the universe, your universe. There are elements that go beyond that, but thought is a living thing. Everything that you think all your thoughts are collected around you. All the knowledge you could access around you is amazing if you could access it. Nothing is ever wasted. It just dissipates and changes. You always have your etheric double. The sad thing or unpleasant thing is that you also get the etheric double of the bad thoughts. The bad thoughts go out just like the good ones. Hence you have the constant battle [*between good and evil*]. If you surround the earth with bad thoughts then you get conflict and wars, famine and diseases. These thoughts have to be dissipated. Everything has its own life. Be careful what you think!

Karl: You were a spiritualist on Earth what is your view on religion now?

ACD: Life has nothing to do with religion. Some of my friends were Buddhists, Hindus, Jews, Catholics, and so on. The power of God encompasses everything. It's your attitude that is important. There are many so-called religious people who are not religious or spiritual at all, but use it to blind people, and bind themselves to dogma and ritual. That is their power base. When you come over to spirit you start to see things exactly as they really are, and some people feel very foolish when they look back. What really matters is the philosophy of love. Maybe love is the wrong word for you to understand. I mean the philosophy of love in tolerance, understanding, and patience of purpose. It is not the problem but how you deal with the problem. Some react to a problem in an angry way, some react with a practical solution, others cannot cope. I must go now.

Karl: Thank you.

218

With that the trance session ended.

Spirit guides can use a lot of energy in coming through thus leaving a medium shattered afterwards. Trance is a very strange feeling. When it starts I can feel the spirit guide coming in, but am not sure exactly who it is. When I go into a trance it is as though I am encased in a warm, comfortable light. I am placed somewhat behind myself so that I am aware of a genial, relaxing, communicating and talking presence. I can sometimes hear a little of the conversation, and can understand that there is more than one person in the vibration of my aura, along with the emotions of the communicator. As one guide speaks I will hear some of it, but it is forgotten almost instantly because it is absorbed through my brain and sent out of my vocal chords. So, while I may be hearing and thinking about what is being said I am a bystander and basically unaware of the totality of the message. When I come out of trance and control my body once again I might remember segments of the conversation, but it takes a while, if ever, for those memories to come back. I usually forget most of it when I return to my conscious state.

On a physical level I feel as though I cannot move. I am warm and comfortable, my arms and legs are heavy. It's like being in that blissful state between sleep and wakefulness, aware, but at ease. My spirit body feels like it is being pushed to one side, and in my mind I feel distant from the world. I can make out what is being said until the spirit guides have finished with what they wanted to achieve. Normally more than one spirit guide will speak through me. I believe that on one occasion nearly ten spoke through me for over seventy-five minutes.

There is an element of trust set up between the spirit control and the medium. The spirit control is very important, as he or she, is usually an appointed guide on the spirit side who allows each spirit to take over and speak through the medium. Although the spirit body is, as I said, moved to one side I believe that trance communication is a form of telepathic link to the mind, which can often result in a change of voice and personal characteristics alien to the medium. Some spirits speak slowly, some quickly, others with great passion, or even deep regret. One guide even spoke with a stutter a condition that he had on Earth. When a spirit speaks through a medium, or returns as a physical apparition they often take on the conditions that they had as a physical incarnate. They need to remember how they spoke on Earth because the spirit world is one of thought where speech is unnecessary. You have to think to communicate in their world as opposed to using speech to converse on Earth. It is quite striking to see the change of personality when you see a good trance medium. I know Sir Arthur saw quite a few in his time.

Chapter Twenty Nine

Conan Doyle and Houdini

It is important to look at the relationship between Sir Arthur Conan Doyle and Harry Houdini and the reason is quite simple. It puts Sir Arthur, the total believer in the afterlife, against Houdini, the non-believer arch-sceptic, and the man who aimed to expose "fraudulent mediums".

Both men were exceptionally successful in their own art. Doyle was a brilliantly successful writer while Houdini was, and still is, considered one of the greatest magicians of all time, and undoubtedly the most famous. They struck up a 'friendly' relationship which they both used for their own personal advantage. Doyle felt that having an 'ally' on board like Houdini would help him to expose fraudulent mediumship, and at the same time promote his spiritualist philosophy. Houdini loved the kudos of corresponding and being seen with one of the most famous writers of his time. The relationship was business like rather than personal.

Mediumship has been around since the beginning of time. It is older than what many consider to be 'the world's oldest profession' of prostitution. This is because mediumship inhabits a natural ability in all humans. We call it the 'paranormal', a 'sixth sense', or 'psychic ability', but the highest service is actually called '*mediumship*', or communication with the spirits.

It has been stated in the writings of all major religions that man has communicated with angels or the gods. The Greeks, Romans, Celts, Egyptians, and Native Americans all had mediums, oracles, or shamans. It has always been a part of every culture in the history of the Earth and there have been as many believers as there are disbelievers. For me this now comes down to whether you believe that there is a God, a life force or personality, and that your character is made up of a spirit body incarnated in a physical body, or whether you have the contrasting view that you have one life and must live it to the full 'burn the candle at both ends', and grab what you can.

It is easy to understand both sides. As the old expression goes "Nothing in this world is certain except death and taxes". Everything else needs to be analysed. We are neither saints nor sinners. Having faith in an afterlife is not enough; proof of some type is needed and you have to be sceptical of every message received. If you look for it there is always evidence to be found. Evidence can be disregarded for a while but every now and then something happens that will confuse even the greatest arch-sceptic. The arch-sceptic uses the usual get out clause of "I cannot explain it" even though the answer could be paranormal and a spirit contact. They don't follow things up just apply their get out clause. So if you are a sceptical observer looking for answers the question then needs to be asked: "Do I believe what has been presented to me? I have evidence here that does not fit with what I believe. Or do I construct a reason so the evidence fits with my current view that it is not real?"

Sometimes it's OK to sit on the fence on some evidence presented to you as a believer *and* a sceptic. But, if you jump onto one side, you must also be willing to look over to the other one so as to be open minded. Blind obedience to your belief is not good enough. This is what led to the downfall of the relationship between Sir Arthur and Houdini. They each believed that what they were saying and seeing was, as in doyles case for real; and for Houdini, no more than illusion and stagecraft therefore fraudulent. There are some even today that look upon Conan Doyle as gullible and foolish for believing too easily, and conversely, sceptics look at Houdini as a god and follow his lead with unquestioning loyalty. We have therefore two camps: the believer and sceptic, just as we have light and darkness, good and bad, balanced and unbalanced.

Due to the proof I have had in my life I can look from one side of the fence with a bit of smugness at the sceptics like Houdini, but I question everything I receive and continually evaluate the afterlife. What if I got it wrong? Am I deluding myself? Are these hallucinations that I am seeing? Am I mad? I ask all of these questions and the answers that come back reinforce my belief that there is an afterlife. I also ask the question of Houdini: Did he find any evidence or was he disregarding everything he received with an emotionless certainty to the point of obstinacy? I think Houdini should have looked over to the other side of the fence a little more, in the same way, I believe Conan Doyle should have examined Houdini's position.

To understand Doyle and Houdini's relationship we need to look back at the past to a time when modern spiritualism began. Spiritualism, as it is known today, had its beginning in Hydesville, New York in 1848. It centred around three young sisters, Kate, Maggie, and Leah, who are now known as the Fox Sisters. They moved to a small house in Hydesville on December 11, 1847, but it was March 31st of the following year that would change their lives forever and have far-reaching consequences. On that night the girls heard some strange knocks and raps around the wooden building in which they lived. They treated the noise like a game and clapped to each rap. With their mother joining in they made up codes for yes and no replies in answer to questions put to the entity making the raps. The entity was intelligent and would rap back in response. With some careful questioning using letters of the alphabet and raps they were quickly able to establish that the entity was a thirty-one-year-old male peddler who was murdered in the house by the previous owner, and that his body was buried down in the cellar. They dug up the cellar but due to a high water level, no body was found, although they did find some teeth, human hair and bone fragments.

But in Hydesville the news about the incident spread quickly, and neighbours from near and far came to the house to witness the developments. Word eventually reached the press, and subsequently the three sisters became celebrities going on tours with their 'act' and traveling all over the USA. Leah was the manager and on stage, Kate and Maggie were the medium performers. On many occasions they were hailed as frauds while the majority of performances were seen as sensational. Sceptics said that the noises produced came from clicking bones in their toes. The women's act was probed, they were even bound tightly around the ankles but the raps still occurred. Nothing fraudulent was ever proven. On a trip to England in 1871 in-depth enquiries about Kate were made by Nobel Prize winner, Sir William Crookes. He was astonished with the results of his investigations where he reportedly heard loud sounds produced on the floor and walls while Kate was sitting in a chair with her hands and feet tightly bound.

However Maggie, an alcoholic who had converted to Catholicism many years before, announced to a theatre in 1888 that she and Kate caused the raps by clicking bones in their toes and that spiritualism was all fraudulent. She later recanted her story and said the raps were paranormal. There were rumours that Maggie was paid by a newspaper to state the latter since she needed money to support her drinking habit. Many years previously Leah had disowned both Kate and Maggie, and both women died as penniless alcoholics. However the story doesn't end there. In 1904, during an excavation of the cellar walls of the Hydesville house, the skull and bones of a male person were found. So they were telling the truth.

If you had read this story, as Houdini did and many others since, you would have thought that it was totally fabricated. However I believe the Fox sisters did have mediumistic abilities. Unfortunately, due to the need to perform, they had to make things occur for their paying public. Our spirit friends are not in the business of performing by demand no matter how much we may want it. During the late Victorian period and following years there were blatant fraudsters who were exposed. However it didn't mean that all mediums were fraudulent since many of them were honestly making a living out of it.

Sir Arthur's interest in spiritualism started after he became disillusioned with Catholicism. This was due in part to the strict practice of Jesuit priests. He started learning about spiritualism in 1878, but publicly declared his belief in spiritualism in 1916. Sir Arthur studied it, weighed the evidence, and came to the conclusion that it was true; he was so convinced that he spent most of his fortune on promoting it.

Harry Houdini also spent years investigating mediums and spiritualism and even established one of the finest libraries on the subject. He gathered and assorted psychic books and recreated physical séances which he sometimes included in his act. However, after many years investigating the subject, he believed there was no such thing as spirits in séances, and mediumship was fraudulent. Houdini spent a lot of his time and money opposing spiritualism and psychic beliefs.

The relationship between Houdini and Sir Arthur began in 1920 when Houdini sent a book and a letter to Conan Doyle while he was doing a tour of Great Britain. The book was titled, *The Unmasking of Robert Houdin (1908, New York, The Publishers Printing Co.)* and made reference to the Davenport Brothers who were stage medium/magicians. They were famous for their performance of the Séance Cabinet in which they were bound tightly in pre-inspected ropes. Once the door closed the public would hear strange raps, bells and other noises while hands would appear out of the front and sides of the cabinet. At any time during the performance, or conclusion of this act the mediums could be seen tied as they had originally been secured.

Both Houdini and Conan Doyle corresponded frequently regarding the Davenports. Houdini believed that it was all stagecraft and illusion, while Doyle believed that they must have had genuine mediumship ability because they had never been exposed as frauds. With their opposing opinions a cordial relationship started between them. Although they were never going to be true friends they used the relationship to one another's advantage.

Houdini's interest in séances and spiritualism had started several years earlier when he attended a number of trials of famous medium fraudsters. His interest was more likely out of curiosity of learning how these tricks were performed. He went to Germany for Miss Anna Rothe's trial. While Conan Doyle despised fraudulent mediums more than Houdini he was aware that genuine mediums were falsely accused. Arresting mediums became commonplace and Houdini was delighted because it provided new material for his stage act. Although he admitted to Conan Doyle that he was a sceptic he told him that he was also "a seeker of the truth."

While on his tour of Great Britain Houdini met Sir Arthur and his family for lunch in Crowborough. As he had never been to one Houdini asked Conan Doyle if he could arrange attendance at a séance. Conan Doyle agreed to a sitting at the Society of Psychical Research in London with the famous French physical medium Marthe Béraud, also known as 'Eva C'. Houdini attended the séance and witnessed ectoplasmic phenomena protruding from Eva's mouth and nose. She took some of the substance and showed it to Houdini who shined a flashlight on it, and it immediately disappeared. This is a common problem with ectoplasm as it dissolves in white light. Houdini later wrote to Doyle that he saw nothing of interest and thought that Eva C did a sleight of hand trick with the ectoplasm.

This is, of course, the typical sceptic's attitude. They always assume it's a trick when presented with evidence that could be real phenomena. The actual number of magicians involved in trying to expose séances and mediumship as fraudulent is amazing. It's like a rite of passage for a magician these days. The question begs: Why aren't they doing magic for a living instead of so-called 'fake séances'? Physical mediumship requires many factors to produce actual phenomena. It requires a combination of a sympathetic mind(s), a harmonious group of sitters, a medium in good physical condition, and the correct atmospheric conditions.

It is possible that Houdini went into the séance with a positive mind, but when phenomena started to occur the magician within him took over and displayed inharmonious vibrations which affected the phenomena. To be successful good mediumship requires a lot of harmony. Most mediums can break the disharmony that people create by using will power and the help of their spirit guides. Houdini's scepticism always worked against him when experiencing physical phenomena. The relationship between a medium's reading and a sitter must be earned. Those who believe, at least to a certain extent, and have a positive attitude will have their evidence. Believers seem to always get results while unbelievers do not get any. Of course all the evidence received must be evaluated. Did Houdini really evaluate the evidence when he was not sure? Sir Arthur did. It took him thirty-eight years before he was ready to publicly say it.

One thing is certain. Houdini wanted to be successful at all costs and his reputation for exposing mediums diminished considerably during "The Margery Case". After which Sir Arthur and many other leading investigators lost their trust in Houdini's objectivity for psychic investigation. It really brings into question whether any of Houdini's endeavours can be counted as fair whenever he searched for the truth?

Mina Crandon, also known as 'Margery', was born in Ontario, Canada and moved to Boston in her teens where she later married a local shopkeeper's son. She was an extremely talented medium who had a large following. She met Dr Le Roi Goddard Crandon, a prominent surgeon at a time when she required an operation. He was immediately attracted to her. Margery subsequently divorced her husband in 1918 and married Dr Crandon. It was not until May 1923, when Dr Crandon organised a home circle, that Margery became interested in séances. During the séance the table tilted when the sitters asked questions. Dr Crandon suggested that if each of the participants would leave the room they would learn who was causing the phenomena. The tilting stopped after everyone left the room, including Margery. However once she came back into the room the table started tilting once again. It was clear to the group that Margery had some psychic ability. Interestingly a few days earlier a psychic had told her that she possessed mediumistic abilities in addition to Walter, her late brother who died in 1911 in a railway accident. The psychic advised Margery that her brother was trying to communicate with her. As Margery's fame spread worldwide, Walter was to become one of the most famous spirit guides of the time.

J. Malcolm Bird, the Associate Editor of the magazine *Scientific American,* offered a prize of $2,500 to any person who could show genuine psychic ability that gave notoriety to Margery. A committee of judges was established to oversee the investigative process. The judges were Hereward Carrington, a writer and psychic investigator, Daniel Comstock, physics lecturer from the Massachusetts Institute, William McDougall, Harvard professor, Harry Houdini, escapologist and magician, Franklin Prince, member of the American Society for Psychical Research, and J.Malcolm Bird, who acted as recorder and observer. Bird didn't trust Houdini's motives and wanted him excluded from the panel of judges. Houdini did not seem to be fully committed to the investigation and was rarely part of the committee. Apparently he told Carrington that he wanted to expose mediums.

The committee was discordant and they were fortunate if anything was achieved. Dr Prince and Dr McDougall were hostile to one another, while Bird, Carrington, and Margery were suspicious of Houdini. Margery was not involved for the money and had stated that if she won the prize it would be handed over to psychic research. It took nearly ninety sittings before the committee came to the conclusion that there were genuine psychic phenomena. Bird and Carrington were diligent sitters, while Prince and Houdini were notably absent. When it was announced that they should consider awarding the prize to Margery, Houdini decided to be present, mainly to expose her for the fraud that he believed she was committing. He went to Bird's office in New York to ask if he believed Margery was genuine. Bird told him that he did believe her. As a result Houdini announced that he would attend some of the séances in Boston, and expose her as a fraud. He explained to Bird that his reputation rested on it.

Houdini arrived in Boston and attended the séances on July 23rd and 24th. On the first day he bandaged up his leg just below the knee which made his lower leg swollen and tender. Margery sat to his right. He then rolled up the leg of his trouser to be able to feel any movement by Margery. Up until that time tests on the medium had proceeded along certain lines as Sir

229

Arthur explained in his paper published in the *Boston Herald* on January 26th:

"The chief tests, however, centred round an electric apparatus which consisted of two dry cells and a bell inside a padlocked box. On the box lid was a hinged piece of wood held up by a spring. If this flap were pressed down it established an electric contact and the bell rang."

Houdini was expecting Margery to stretch out her leg and make the bell ring with her foot. He would easily feel any movement from her direction since, at this point, his leg was very sensitive. During the séance Houdini did not report anything unusual although the bell did ring on a few occasions. It was only later that Houdini said that he felt Margery's leg move toward the box with the bell in it, which rang, and stopped ringing when he felt her leg move away.

Nobody else detected any movement and Houdini said nothing during the ringing of the bell. Houdini was tied to her left leg on one side, holding her hand, while J. Malcolm Bird was on her right side holding her other hand, pressing his feet against her foot to restrict any movement. If Margery was going to 'cheat', as Houdini suggested, why would she move her leg towards the box while sitting next to the man who wanted to expose her? One important fact about this is that when physical phenomena occur the medium sometimes needs to stretch. This happens as a result of the body being uncomfortable with all the energy. Sitting in a certain position in a séance would cause your legs to cramp as it would when sitting for long periods on an aeroplane. Houdini's published notes said that Margery told him to press hard against her legs.

"At times she would say: "Just press hard against my ankle so that you can see that my ankle is

there", as she pressed I could feel her gain another half inch". Harry Houdini

Margery knew that Houdini was looking for any excuse to expose her; therefore, she made certain that Houdini could feel that she was restricted and was not able to move. It was quite the opposite of what Houdini had said. Houdini's explanation that Margery had stretched out was a blatant lie because he had no other theory as to how the bell rang. He refused to believe this was psychic phenomena and felt that only human contact could make the bell ring. His predisposition did not let him accept what was obviously occurring in front of him. Sir Arthur wrote an analysis of the transcript notes written by the investigators:

"It is manifest that if the hands and feet of the medium were controlled and her husband was under equally strict supervision then the ringing of the bell would be a true psychic phenomena, and must be done by some supernormal force. When I say this was done, not once, nor a hundred times, but more likely a thousand times, that it was done when out of all possible reach of the medium, that it was done in the darkness, in the red light, and in subdued daylight, and finally it was done in Dr Prince's lab while, in defiance of the laws of ectoplasm, he waved his arms all around it, one realises how invincible was the prejudice which the Crandon's had to overcome. We must all applaud the scientific caution, but it may be pushed to the point where it becomes unscientific obstruction. Occasionally an ordinary common-sense citizen takes a hand in the business and then one gets a clear judgment. Hearing that Mr DeWycoff, who is known as a rather strict critic, was present I asked him for his impression. It was as follows: "In good effective light playing directly upon the contact box I have known the electric bell to ring to my order, long and short rings, when the medium was at a clear distance of several feet, and I controlled her

hands and feet, all the other sitters being at the time plainly visible. I am prepared to make a sworn affidavit to this effect, Joseph DeWycoff." That single paragraph utterly demolishes all the theories afterwards put forward by Houdini."

Margery went into trance and Walter, her spirit guide, asked Bird, sitting on her right, to bring the illuminated plaque and put it on top of the bell box. Suddenly Walter called for control as the circle was broken and Margery put her hands and feet together along with Houdini's. Then a cabinet fell over. As she was still under Walter's control he told Houdini that the speaking trumpet was in the air and asked him where he wanted it. He replied "towards me". The trumpet landed in front of him.

Houdini refuted what had happened. His explanation for this event was that Margery kicked over the cabinet and put the speaking trumpet on her head which was then flicked off in whatever direction she chose. We only have his theory on this as the movement of the speaking trumpet had happened many times before while Margery's hands were held. Everyone was holding hands, and Margery's hands were being held too by Houdini.

The second séance was held on July 24th in Dr Comstock's hotel suite. The process was similar to the first one, but with the exception that there was no speaking trumpet. The table moved while all the sitters sat away from it, and then the bell rang. Once again Houdini said that Margery had moved the table. According to him this time she had used her head and stretched out her leg to ring the bell. Again he did not say anything to expose her. He used the buckles from his sock garters as fasteners in order to stick them to Margery's leg. He later removed them as she complained this was uncomfortable. Why didn't he leave the garter off since he 'sensitised' his leg with the bandage the previous evening? Houdini was meticulous in his preparation. He knew that the garter was going to be pressing against the medium's leg. It's possible the reason he wore the buckle was to cause discomfort to the medium, or more likely to cause a distraction that allowed him to engineer a trick. Interestingly, there was a distraction as Margery asked him to remove the garter because of the buckle. Perhaps Margery would have moved her leg due to the discomfort, and he could have accused her of cheating. Remember this was a man who was out to expose her. Sitting next to Houdini for the first time was Mr Munn, owner of *Scientific American*. He stood to lose the prize money which his magazine provided, and therefore was not considered an impartial witness. During the séance Houdini intimated to Munn that Margery was cheating. But Munn just nodded his head and let the séance continue.

Houdini's deception was exposed when the committee met in August. He was extremely angry when he saw the newspaper headlines praising Margery, but he was most annoyed with the one about himself which headlined *"Houdini the magician stumped"*. Subsequently he decided to test Margery but it backfired. He created a box in which Margery could sit with only her head and arms allowed to be exposed through holes. He became worried, though, when he realised that if the bell rang while she was in the cabinet he would be doomed, and psychic phenomena would be proven real. A surprising event occurred two days before the first séance with 'Houdini's box'. Below are Sir Arthur's notes on the proceeding:

"On Aug. 25 Houdini arrived for a final test. Two days before Walter warned the circle that some trick would be attempted. "What I think he will do is to slip die into the contact box. If you search his pockets you may find the rest of the dice." With such anticipation it is remarkable that any psychic power could manifest. When Houdini arrived he brought with him a portentous box into which the lady was to be shut and fastened in with eight

padlocks. Her arms were to be extended at two side holes and her head at the top. This clumsy apparatus was put into use, and the forces present showed what they thought of it by at once bursting the front open, bending the metal staples."

Walter, Margery's spirit guide, knew Houdini was going to attempt some trickery so he advised her beforehand. Walter proved his feeling by smashing the box with such force that people were convinced this was an act of paranormal. The bell also rang during the séance and Houdini tried to explain it by saying Margery had rung it with muscular effort. Everybody laughed as both Houdini and Dr Prince were holding Margery's arms. They both admitted that they felt no excessive force from the   small-framed lady who managed to smash the solidly built cabinet locked with eight padlocks.

(Margery Bell Box)

234

The séance continued the next evening and Margery was placed back in the box which had now been strengthened on the lid with steel strips and new locks. She went into trance and Walter came through and asked, "Houdini, how much are they paying you to stop these phenomena?" Walter called out to Dr Comstock and asked him to take the box out into the light and examine it. Conan Doyle's notes described what occurred:

"The voice of Walter was suddenly heard calling out, "Comstock, take the box out in the white light and examine it." This was done by Dr Comstock and shocking to relate the rubber erasure from an ordinary pencil was found to have been inserted into the angle so as to prevent the upper board descending and ringing the bell. Who placed it there? It was there to prevent phenomena - that was obvious. Who was it that had declared against the phenomena and who had therefore an interest in stopping them? Does the point need elaborating? A cruel trick had clearly been played in order to discredit the medium. It took some deftness to fasten that rubber eraser into the right place. Who was there present who might have had this cleverness of touch? These questions answer themselves and it is suggestive that Houdini's pamphlet suppresses the whole incident."

The séance continued a short time later. As Margery entered the box Houdini told Dr Prince to ensure he held her tight. He insisted that Dr Prince was not to let go until the séance was over. This provoked Margery and she asked Houdini to search her. He declined saying that it was not necessary. He told her that if anything had been smuggled into the box it would not be concealable as she was under tight control. Soon Margery went into trance and Walter came through. He informed everyone that Houdini had placed a ruler in the box with the help of his assistant. As he fastened her into the cabinet, Houdini did something very odd. He palpated along her left arm with his right hand until it passed through the hole in the cabinet. There was no reason for him to do this. Once Margery went into trance again, Walter came through and blasted Houdini. "What did you do that for, Houdini? He cried. "There is a ruler in this cabinet you unspeakable cad!" Houdini then used some expletives. "Oh, this is terrible! I don't know anything about any ruler. Why should I do a thing like that?" Houdini cried. The lights were turned on and Houdini was seen with head in his hands saying "I am not well. I am not myself!"

They searched the cabinet, and sure enough they found two folded foot rulers with six-inch segments. "I am willing to forget this, if you are!" cried Houdini. Sir Arthur precisely summed up the situation in his paper on the events:

"It might have been a deadly discovery for the medium, but owing to Walter's care it was really deadly to the man who placed it there. For consider the facts. The next experiment was to be one in which the medium's arms were drawn inside the holes. Suppose the contact-bell had been rung, it would have been a final proof of psychic power. But this ruler was the one thing one could think of which, if held in the mouth, would extend nearly two feet and so possibly reach the board. It has been suggested that it had been left there by some careless carpenter, but can any man imagine such a coincidence as that he should leave, not a hammer or a brad awl, but the one implement that would discredit whatever the medium would do? Can one not see the tremendous triumph and world-wide advertisement of the investigator who, in the moment of the medium's success, should suddenly dive his hand into the cabinet produce the ruler and expose what all the world would have believed a fraud? Is not the whole transaction as clear as noontide, and has not the man fallen into the pit which he had dug? The facts have only to be clearly stated to carry absolute conviction."

Although Margery was above suspicion Houdini was determined to expose her. His first attempt to discredit her with the cabinet failed. He knew he was under suspicion when they found the eraser used to prevent the bell from ringing. Time was running out and he was getting desperate. The next day Houdini had to make sure that Margery was exposed. To cast suspicion before the séance he asked Margery if anything was wrong. He reminded Dr Prince to hold her tight until the circle was finished. The ruler was planted in the cabinet by somebody. It was not left by a carpenter as Houdini suggested. Years later, a writer, William Lindsay Gresham, was told that Jim Collins, Houdini's assistant had hidden the ruler: "I chucked it in the box myself. The Boss (Houdini) told me to do it. E ('Ehrich', Houdini's real name) wanted to fix her good".

If you see a pattern emerging here then it probably would have ended with a headline such as "*Houdini Ends the 'Rule' of Mystic Margery*" and a photo of Houdini with ruler in hand. He would then have his usual adulation for finding 'another' fraudulent medium. Houdini was being manipulative behind the committee's back as Sir Arthur revealed in the *Boston Herald*, and Houdini had actually secretly contacted the magazine *Light* to inform them that an exposure was looming:

"Thus, my friend Mr Gow, editor of "Light," received a letter to that effect, saying that an exposure was imminent. I cannot quote the letter, as it is marked private, but it is to the last degree defamatory, and winds up by the curious argument that the medium had nothing to gain in any way and that therefore her action was suspicious -a curious inversion of reason."

Houdini was a magnificent magician, but as a psychic investigator he was biased and deceitful. We need to question how many genuine mediums he 'exposed'. I don't doubt at all that there was fraud in his time, there has always been some element of it from early times, however the 'theories' that Houdini put forward cannot be trusted. He went to the séance that day to be certain that nothing would happen; he had planned his theories in advance. After all he was a perfectionist in the art of deception. The act was already worked out. He couldn't catch Margery being deceitful because there were actual psychic phenomena present. He wanted to make sure Margery was proven a fraudster and he had the credibility to back it up.

Houdini did not want to believe in the existence of psychic phenomena, or search for the 'truth' as he often said. Conan Doyle and Houdini once had a conversation about the Zancigs, a couple of vaudeville mind-readers, which eventually led to the discussion of telepathy being real phenomena. Houdini disagreed of course. However it has been scientifically proven that telepathy exists. Houdini later wrote in his notes that he asked Doyle "Why, every once in a while I see something that I cannot account for?" This showed that he found many things impossible to explain. What did he do when he found something that he couldn't explain? Invariably he disregarded the facts. You have to be *open minded*.

I know that communication between this world and the afterlife is very real; I can see it, hear it and give evidential proof. I cannot always explain how it works, but it does work. That's why it was ironic when Walter, Margery's spirit guide, predicted that Houdini would die within a year from the last day of the séance. He was short by two months as Houdini died in October, 1926, just over a year later.

"I cannot explain this" is the typical sceptic's answer when presented with evidence that most people would believe to be real. However they never say "I believe this to be true" or "I suppose I should accept this as being true". Where do the questions end, and beliefs begin for a sceptic? Like Houdini, and most sceptics, they will never accept that psychic phenomena exist or that we have a spirit body and survive death. Some sceptics will never accept the facts even if they are tangible.

Mediums need to present good evidential communication. Observers need to weigh and assimilate evidence. It should be noted by investigators that the process is very subtle and depends on various factors such as good harmony, and sympathetic, objective observers. Negative thoughts can affect communication. I believe scepticism is good to some extent, but not when a person is intransigent. Not everything should be believed but we should investigate everything thoroughly. Therefore I will emphasise that there must come a time when Conan Doyle's famous quote in Sherlock Homes must be used:

"When you have eliminated the impossible, whatever remains, *however improbable*, must be the truth."

Chapter Thirty

Houdini Communicates From The Spirit World

It is not well known these days that arch-sceptic Harry Houdini returned a spectacular coded message from the spirit world nearly five years after his death. The interesting aspect of this was that many people knew that Houdini had promised to come back and give a message when he died. The press and public as well as his peer group in the Magic circle were all eager to see or hear a message from Houdini. But there were two coded messages to be received, one from Houdini's mother, and the other from Houdini himself. Both secret codes were only known by his wife Beatrice.

Before Houdini died he and his wife Beatrice had created a coded response that he would use to communicate from the afterlife. This code was based on secret responses that he used to interact with Beatrice during his magical stage feats so that no one else could understand his suggestions. He pondered that if the spirit world existed he would persist in finding a medium who could convey the secret message that was agreed in advance with his wife. If she died first she would also do the same.

Arthur Ford was one of the best known mediums during the 1920s and 1930s[6]. The evidence he gave from his numerous sittings was extremely accurate, but it was the evidence he received from Houdini that made him stand out from other mediums in history. Before his death Houdini spent many years looking for evidential proof from his departed mother whom he absolutely adored. He consulted several mediums since a number of them offered their services to provide evidence. Unfortunately he either disregarded the proof or they

240

were not accurate. He was looking for one particular piece of evidence that he and his mother had agreed upon before her death but while alive this never came through. Probably the main reason for this is because he didn't deserve it as he exposed all mediums to criticism, the good and the bad.

[6]Arthur Ford's "Nothing So Strange" New York: Harper and Row, 1958

During a regular sitting by Arthur Ford with friends in 1928, Arthur Ford went into trance and Fletcher, his spirit guide, said there was a woman present whom he had not seen before. She had a message for 'Harry Weiss' Houdini was actually born Erik Weisz and when his family emigrated to the USA he changed his name to Erich Weiss. His friends called him 'Harry'. He used the stage name 'Harry Houdini' after being influenced by the French magician, Jean Eugène Robert-Houdin. His friend, Jack Hayman, told him that in French adding an "i" to Houdin would mean "like Houdin" the great magician.

The message during the circle for Harry Weiss was taken down by a journalist and was as follows:

"For many years, my son waited for one word which I was to send back. He always said that if he could get it he would believe. Conditions have now developed in the family which make it necessary for me to get my code word through before he can give his wife the code he arranged with her. If the family acts upon my code word he will be free and able to speak for himself. Mine is the word 'FORGIVE!' Capitalise that and put it in quotation marks. His wife knew the word and no one else in all the world knew it. Ask her if the word which I tried to get back all these years is not 'FORGIVE!' I tried innumerable times to say it to him. Now that he is here with me I am able to get it through. Tonight I give it to you, and Beatrice Houdini will declare it to be true."

241

When Mrs Houdini got the message she was absolutely amazed. She made a public statement and said that the message was indeed "the sole communication received among thousands up to this time that contained the one secret keyword known only to Houdini, his mother, and myself." She wrote a letter to confirm this.

> 67 Payson Avenue
> New York City
>
> My dear Mr. Ford,
>
> Today I received a special delivery letter signed by members of the First Spiritualist Church, who testify to a purported message from Houdini's mother, received through you. Strange that the word "forgive" is the word Houdini awaited in vain all his life. It was indeed the message for which he always secretly hoped, and if it had been given him while he was still alive, it would I know, have changed the entire course of his life - but it came too late. Aside from this there are one, or two trivial inaccuracies - Houdini's mother called him Erich - there was nothing in the message which could be contradicted. I might also say that this is the first message which I have received among thousands which has an appearance of truth.
>
> Sincerely yours,
>
> Beatrice Houdini

There was more evidence given by Arthur Ford but this was of a personal nature. There was also mention of a secret ten-word code that Beatrice and Harry had agreed between one another to prove that he had survived death. Houdini's mother's final words were that now that her message had come through it would open the channel for his message to do the same. Houdini had sworn to get a message through to Beatrice if life after death could be proven. The message was based upon a ten-word code that they had used in one of their early shows and which no one else knew about.

Months passed before anything related to the pre-agreed Houdini message came through. In November 1928 during a pre-arranged sitting with Houdini's wife, Arthur Ford's guide Fletcher came through with the first part of the message. The spelling of the entire message took eight separate sittings covering a period of two and a half months. He announced that the first word was "ROSABELLE", and from this word the rest of the message would be unlocked. Below is the ten-word code.

ROSABELLE ** ANSWER TELL ** PRAY ** ANSWER ** LOOK ** TELL ANSWER ** ANSWER ** TELL.

Ford allowed Houdini to speak through him, and he asked everyone present to attest and sign to this communication. Once the message was given to his wife Beatrice, she had to then announce it to the public. He said that he had never believed that life after death was possible but was now doing his best to change that opinion. Houdini explained through Fletcher that the code to be returned by Mrs Houdini was a supplement to this code and the two together will spell a word which summed it all up. That word would be the message he wanted to send back. He refused to give that word until she and Ford were present.

The following day two members of the group unknown to Beatrice delivered the message to her. Although she was incapacitated due to a fall the previous week she was elated as she read the report. Beatrice dropped the paper at her side and said "It is right! Did he say ROSABELLE?" She was assured that he had and exclaimed "My God! What else did he say?" They repeated all the information they were given.

Beatrice Houdini went for a sitting with Arthur Ford. As soon as Fletcher came through he told Beatrice that Houdini was present. *"Hello Bess, sweetheart"*, he said through Fletcher. "He wants to repeat the message and finish it for you. He says the code is one that you used to use in one of your secret mind-reading acts." Fletcher said. Fletcher then repeated the ten words exactly as Houdini provided them. Mrs Houdini confirmed that these were the correct words and that she was to take off her wedding ring to tell everyone present what ROSABELLE means. She took off the ring from her left hand and held it before her and sang in a soft voice:

> *Rosabelle, sweet Rosabelle,*
> *I love you more than I can tell,*
> *O'er me you cast a spell,*
> *I love you, my Rosabelle!*

"Then there is something he wants me to tell you that no one but his wife knows," Fletcher went on. "He smiles now and shows me a picture and draws the curtains so, or in this manner." Evidently that was the clue for the unfolding of the next part of the code to which Mrs Houdini responded in French;

"Je tire le rideau comme ça."

Speaking through Fletcher, Houdini went on, "And now the nine words besides ROSABELLE spell a word in our code." He then explained the code accurately "The second word in our code was ANSWER. B is the second letter in the alphabet so ANSWER stands for B. The fifth word in the code is TELL, and the fifth letter of the alphabet is E. The twelfth letter in the alphabet is L and to make up twelve we have to use the first and second words of the code. The message was spelt out in this obscure way to the end he said;

"The message I want to send back to my wife is: 'ROSABELLE, BELIEVE!'"

Fletcher then asked Beatrice Houdini, "Is this right?" "Yes!" answered Mrs Houdini.

Fletcher relayed Houdini's final words to those present. He said: "'Tell the whole world that Harry Houdini still lives and will prove it a thousand times and more". "He is pretty excited." Fletcher said, and went on "I was perfectly honest and sincere in trying to disprove survival, though I resorted to tricks to prove my point for the simple reason that I did not believe communication was true, but I did no more than seemed justifiable. I am now sincere in sending this through in my desire to undo. Tell all those who lost faith because of my mistake to lay hold again of hope and to live with the knowledge that life is continuous. That is my message to the world, through my wife and through this instrument".

The code was:

1. Pray	A	6. Please	F
2. Answer	B	7. Speak	G
3. Say	C	8. Quickly	H
4. Now	D	9. Look	I
5. Tell	E	10. Be quick	J

The message itself was:

Answer	B
Tell	E
Pray, answer (1 and 2 = 12 which is "L")	L
Look	I
Tell	E
Answer, answer (2 and 2 = 22 which is "V")	V
Tell	E

Below is copy of the letter written by Beatrice Houdini after she received the message from her beloved Ehrich (Harry) from Arthur Ford in 1929.

New York City
Jan 9th, 1929

Regardless of Any Statements made to the contrary, I wish to declare that the message, in its entirety, and in the agreed upon sequence, given to me by Arthur Ford, is the correct message pre-arranged between Mr. Houdini and myself.

Beatrice Houdini

Witnessed;
Harvey R. Zander
Minnie Chester
John W. Stanford

The three witnesses are; Mr H. R. Zander, representative of the United Press, Mrs Minnie Chester, lifelong friend of Beatrice Houdini, and Mr John W. Stafford, Associate Editor of the magazine, *Scientific American.*

There were some attempts to discredit Arthur Ford, even a blackmail attempt, and a hoaxer who impersonated him and fabricated an account which was published in a newspaper. Subsequently he retracted the account and confessed the hoax when he learned that he was going to be prosecuted. Arthur Ford received no money or reward for breaking the code although there were considerably large sums of money on offer to the successful code breaker.

Finally Joseph Dunninger, known as "Dunninger the Mentalist", who was a friend of Houdin's and a Magician to boot, was totally opposed to the whole paranormal and psychic movement and was Chairman of the "Board of Science and Invention Magazine". He tried to convince Houdini's wife, Beatrice, that a woman called little Daisy White had been told the secret code in confidence by Houdini to which his wife was totally disbelieving of this and denied that her husband would give the secret code to her, it was ridiculous. And when Little Daisy White was confronted about this allegation she totally denied it too.

Those around Houdini have for years been trying to discredit Arthur Ford's message with very flimsy evidence and innuendo with no proof to back up the allegations. The fact is he came through and gave the message. Houdini's wife agreed that it was correct, and some people with vested interests had no intention of believing or letting the truth be hailed as a fantastic piece of evidence so they put out stories to discredit it. It's a very well-known tactic used today by sceptics to discredit any real phenomena. The sitting with Ford was witnessed by three independent people, and his wife in her published letter that regardless to any statements to the contrary this was the message he agreed with her before he died.

NEW YORK CITY.
JAN. 9TH, 1929.

REGARDLESS OF ANY STATE-
MENTS MADE TO THE CONTRARY,
I WISH TO DECLARE THAT THE
MESSAGE, IN ITS ENTIRETY, AND IN
THE AGREED UPON SEQUENCE,
GIVEN TO ME BY ARTHUR FORD,
IS THE CORRECT MESSAGE PRE-
ARRANGED BETWEEN MR. HOUDINI
AND MYSELF.

Beatrice Houdini

WITNESSED;
Harry R. Zander.
Minnie Chester
John W. Stafford —

Facsimile of statement made by Mrs. Houdini the day after
receipt of the message. Witnesses: Mr. H. R. Zander, Representative of the United Press; Mrs. Minnie Chester, life-long
friend of Mrs. Houdini and Mr. John W. Stafford, Associate
Editor of *Scientific American*.

Chapter Thirty One

Arthur Conan Doyle's Revelation

Arthur started his spiritual quest in 1878 with a similar type of observation made by Napoleon as he voyaged on a ship to Egypt. He questioned his atheistic professors about starry nights: "Who was it, gentlemen, who made these stars?"

In the 21st century we know so much more about stars since Napoleon pondered this question. Of course stars are actually made up of hot molten gases like our sun without which life on our planet would not exist, but we still don't know who actually created the universe, or what happened one minute before the 'big bang', and what existed before that time.

Sir Arthur started out like most people wondering about life. In his book, *The New Revelation*, he talked about being a "convinced materialist" just like many young men of medicine in his day. He was far from believing in the theory of an all-powerful, omniscient God, but he did believe in "an intelligent force behind all the operations of nature – "*a force so infinitely complex and great that my finite brain could get no further than its existence*".

Sir Arthur's materialist thinking needed no explanation with regard to survival of the personality after death. As far as he was concerned people were deluded if this was the case. He felt that survival after death was about as likely to occur as the survival of the light from a candle once it burned out.

Sir Arthur's frame of mind with regard to spiritualist phenomena is quite clear as he said *"I had always regarded the subject as the greatest nonsense upon earth, and I had read of the conviction of fraudulent mediums and wondered how any sane man could believe such things."*

You might believe that we have a spirit body that ghosts haunt premises and mediums communicate with spirit beings in the afterlife, or perhaps you are looking for someone to prove to you that the personality does survive death. Many sceptics have tried to prove that people are deluded like Sir Arthur himself felt at one time in 1882. *"However, do believers turn into sceptics? It is more likely that sceptics turn into believers."* For me we have ample proof of life after death with stories from millions of people all over the world claiming to have seen spirits, or having evidence of survival of some form or another. Many people believe there is a God in some powerful form.

Conan Doyle's initial interest began in 1886 when he read a book called *The Reminiscences of Judge Edmunds*. The book showed an account of an eminent U.S. High Court Judge describing how his wife had died, and how he had been able for many years to keep in touch with her. Although he was absolutely sceptical of the information he did find it interesting. There were nagging questions for Doyle. What had caused this man who was a respected personality to have this reaction? What made him believe that he was communicating with 'a spirit'? Sir Arthur was perplexed with the situation. Thinking as a doctor he proposed that it could be compared to someone cracking their skull and causing their basic character to change. He knew from his experience that alcohol and drugs could change a man's personality, but he now realised that the spirit body is dependent upon physical matter: *"I did not realise that it was not the spirit that was changed in such cases, but the body through which the spirit worked."* He analogised tampering with a violin, as an example, from which a musician would produce discordant notes.

Sir Arthur continued his interest in any psychic investigative literature with men of noteworthy reputations. He looked down on the spiritualist philosophy, treating it as something that was attractive to the deluded and uneducated but he found that a few eminent people believed that the spirit was independent of the physical body. The theory was endorsed by distinguished Victorians such as Sir William Crookes, who discovered the element 'thallium', and also cathode rays used in television sets. Sir Oliver Lodge, a pioneer of radio, also proclaimed spirituality to be true. The famous French Astronomer, Camille Flammarion, was a believer and so was Alfred Russell Wallace, the naturalist, geographer and biologist, who was Charles Darwin's rival. Even John Logie Baird, the inventor of Television, believed in the afterlife, and he subsequently worked on inventing a device that could communicate with spirits.

Conan Doyle wondered whether these men had a 'weak spot' in their brain which made them receptive to this knowledge, or had they actually been on to something? For some time his scepticism was sustained by the declarations from other famous men such as philosophers Charles Darwin, Thomas Huxley and Irish natural philosopher, John Tyndall. Looking further into the sceptic's mind he found that they would not even examine the subject, were disinterested in it or treated the subject matter with contempt. He was forced to say that "*I was bound to admit that, however great they were in science, their action in this respect was most unscientific and dogmatic,*" while he praised those who took the position of at least observing the phenomena following "*the true path which has given us all human advance and knowledge*". At last he felt that his sceptical position was not as solid as before.

Although Conan Doyle was interested in exploring more of the phenomena he needed a medium; someone who could muster the magnetic force and make things happen. At times he felt like an astronomer without a telescope because he had no psychic ability himself. The opportunity came his way, one night. He attended a psychic circle and the results were promising with a detailed message received from a commercial traveller who had lost his life in a fire at a theatre in Exeter. This all seemed accurate but the address provided by the spirit did not seem to exist. When they wrote to his family, as he had wished, the letter was returned with an unknown address called 'Slattenmere' in Cumberland. Doyle's interest in the subject waned because of that end result.

However in Southsea he knew a spiritualist named General Drayton, described as pioneer of spiritualism. Drayton addressed the inaccuracies concerning the evidence he had received in the psychic circles. Most of it was false and inaccurate. He shared an important lesson with Conan Doyle describing how we all meet the same people on the other side and just as a person is foolish on Earth they do not become a well-informed genius on the other side. That is the reason we must question all evidence we get. It seemed to the General that the psychic circle Conan Doyle went to, had encountered communication with some mischievous communicators. They received poor evidence because either Conan Doyle or the circle members had not properly protected the group, or they were aimless in their directions. In order for it to work properly the group needed to concentrate on receiving the finer knowledge from the spirits, thereby attracting the right spirit entities from the spirit side.

Conan Doyle was not really satisfied with Drayton's explanation and still felt sceptical. At least this time he began inquiring, whereas other critics around him lambasted spiritualism without presenting any real evidence.

Thirty-eight years after ACD first read about spiritualism and with evidential proof under his belt, his interest would go as far as to speak out in support of spiritualism and the afterlife. He agreed that his own evidence in those days had not been enough to convince him, but his continuous reading of the subject from men who had deeply researched the philosophy made him sure that "the testimony was so strong, that no other religious movement in the world could put forward anything to compare with it".

To prove his point Doyle used a famous incident by Alfred Russell Wallace [7], considered a modern miracle. Daniel Dunglas Home, famous medium and nephew of the Earl of Home, floated out of one window and into another one at a height of seventy feet above the ground. This feat was witnessed and attested to at the time by Lord Adare (Thomas Wyndham-Quin, Later the 4th Earl of Dunraven), Lord Lindsay (James Ludovic Lindsay, 26th Earl of Crawford and 9th Earl of Balcarres) and Captain Charles Wynne, who were, as Conan Doyle said "all men of honour and repute, who were willing afterwards to take their oath upon it." The medium, D.D. Home is considered to be one of the greatest in the spiritualist movement.

As the years passed, Sir Arthur continued to attend different psychic circles, which gave, as he believed, intermittent results. During this period he received relevant evidence where details matched those of respected books about the afterlife, such as Sir Oliver Lodge's book, *Raymond.* (Raymond; or, Life and Death. London: Methuen, 1916). In his publication, Sir Oliver explains how he communicated with his dead son, a World War I soldier. Conan Doyle received evidence from two specific communications during these circles.

The first one concerned Dorothy Postlethwaite, a name unknown to Sir Arthur and his group. She had attended the same school as some sitters in the group. Dorothy correctly identified the name of the headmistress from a random group of names. This impressed Sir Arthur, as he described the communicator:

She went on to say that the sphere she inhabited was all round the earth; that she knew about the planets; that Mars was [once] inhabited by a race more advanced than us, and that the canals were artificial; there was no bodily pain in her sphere, but there could be mental anxiety; they were governed; they took nourishment; she had been a Catholic and was still a Catholic, but had not fared better than the Protestants; there were Buddhists and Mohammedans in her sphere, but all fared alike; she had never seen Christ and knew no more about him than on earth, but believed in his influence; spirits prayed and they died in their new sphere before entering another; they had pleasures - music was among them. It was a place of light and of laughter. She added that they had no rich or poor and that the general conditions were far happier than on earth.

Although the information provided was not through a medium, but from table tilting and a Ouija board (definitely not recommended), it was interesting that she seemed to live in her own dimension of thought with like-minded people from Catholics to Protestants, Buddhists and Muslims, "but all fared alike". In other words, everyone was the same, even though they came from different cultures and religious backgrounds. She lived in a spiritual dimension where tolerance and happiness existed. For the short sixteen years that she lived on earth, she had earned a kind of heavenly dimension.

The second psychic circle which Sir Arthur described in his book occurred in 1896. It refers to the communication between Dodd (He never gave his first name), a famous cricket player he once met in Cairo, and himself. Conan Doyle questioned the gentleman, as if he was sitting opposite him. He explained that Dodd was not known by the two ladies in the circle, indicating that they seem to be involved in the communication. His answers came back with *"great speed and decision"* and *"were often opposed to what I expected, so that I could not believe that I was influencing them."* You can see that Sir Arthur was being careful about conducting his questions. It must be remembered that Sir Arthur was still very sceptical of the whole communication method, but at least he was still willing to investigate the subject, something that closed-minded people are not prepared to do.

Conan Doyle relayed a brief synopsis of the conversation between Dodd and himself. *"His death was painless. He remembered the death of Polwhele, a young officer who died before him. When he (Dodd) died he had found people to welcome him, but Polwhele had not been among them."* There was some talk about the war in Sudan, after which he told Sir Arthur that *"He knew more than he did in life. He remembered our conversation in Cairo. Duration of life in the next sphere was shorter than on earth. He had not seen General Gordon, or any other famous spirit. Spirits lived in families and in communities. Married people did not necessarily meet again but those who loved each other did meet again."*

For Sir Arthur the statements given did not substantiate proof of life after death, although they were interesting and seemed coherent. I personally agree with this because all the expressed facts need to be substantiated. If someone related to Dodd had been there and accepted evidence of his survival to be accurate, perhaps Sir Arthur would have gone away with a different opinion. But he also said, *"that these words should not be termed 'folly' either"*, as some critics at the time had often suggested. He stated that, *"There was no folly here unless we call everything folly which does not agree with preconceived ideas."*

ACD's conclusion was that while he was left bewildered, looking back as he did over two decades later in 1918 with so much evidence and experience behind him, he found that so many people had been given independent evidential proof in areas around the world, that it "*must constitute some argument for their truth*". Evidence from independent witnesses is the key. Can you really disregard the weight of personal evidence presented, no matter whether or not you believe it?

Sir Arthur's interest in the subject was not just related to séances but also included a wider theme. One book that sparked his interest further was written by the Chief Justice of the French Colony of Crandenagur, called Jacolliot. He was rather biased against spiritualism, but not the native fakirs where he resided. He conducted a series of experiments with native fakirs, who gave him their confidence because he was a sympathetic man and spoke their language. However, he investigated these people and the mediums with a series of experiments. Doyle was intrigued by the incredible phenomena Jacolliot found (his repeated experiments under test conditions could be compared to those of the great D.D Home's results). "*He got levitation of the body, the handling of fire, movement of articles at a distance, rapid growth of plants, raising of tables* [8]". The native fakirs claimed that the powers were handed down from time immemorial, which traced its roots back to the Chaldees, a race once noted for their psychic abilities.

ACD was further influenced by a report from the Dialectical Society, formed by reliable people with an enquiring and open-mind into the Physical Phenomena of Spiritualism. They gave a full account of their precautions against fraud and their many elaborate experiences. Conan Doyle pointed out that "*After reading the evidence, one fails to see how they could have come to any other conclusion than the one attained, namely, that the phenomena were undoubtedly genuine, and that they pointed to laws and forces which had not been explored by Science.*"

Slowly Doyle was turning from a complete sceptic, into an enthusiastic supporter who thought there was something that could not yet be explained by science. He argued that if the Dialectical Society's report concluded that it was nonsense, it could be the death knell for spiritualism. Unfortunately the endorsement of the phenomena was met with ridicule, a similar fate that has since occurred to many worthy investigations.

Stimulated by the endorsement, in 1891 Doyle joined the Society for Psychical Research (SPR). The SPR is a highly respected society dedicated to investigation of Psychic Phenomena by scientific means. They are methodical, practical in their approach and greatly influenced Conan Doyle. Around the same time Doyle read the classic book *Human Personality* by F.H. Myers (Human Personality and its Survival of Bodily Death. 2 vols. London: Longmans, Green, 1903). Myers proved quite convincingly that telepathy existed where mind influenced mind. His work was so thorough, with many examples, that it became scientific fact. Sir Arthur could see now that "*If mind could act upon mind at a distance, then there were some human powers which were quite different to matter as we had always understood it.*"

Conan Doyle's position as a materialist after reading Myer's book was destroyed. He revealed that "*If the mind, the spirit, the intelligence of man could operate at a distance from the body, then it was a thing to that extent separate from the body. Why then should it not exist on its own when the body was destroyed?*"

Today the spiritualist's philosophy accepts as fact that mind and body are separate. Sir Arthur could see that if thoughts could be transmitted between individuals, from mind to mind, they could quite easily be transferred from a mind separated from a physical body, that is, one who has died.

If we do not listen to our thoughts, or at least believe them all to be ours, how can we hear those who have passed on as they try to communicate with us? It

257

brings to mind the case of a haunting that Conan Doyle investigated with the SPR. The case concerned poltergeist (literally translated as 'Noisy Ghost') activity where strange noises and movement of objects occurred. So, if we do not 'listen' to our thoughts while spirits are trying to communicate, they find an alternative. This might be by using a medium, or creating poltergeist activity. A Poltergeist is usually an unsettled spirit that may want to attract someone's attention or perhaps even want to frighten people.

The SPR staked out the house, setting controlled conditions as much as possible. On the first night nothing occurred. The following night the investigators heard loud noises and sounds, like beating on a table. The investigation ended without any conclusion. However, a few years later Conan Doyle heard from the owner of the house that bones of a child were found in the backyard. Since people could not hear his cry for help, was the child trying to make contact by other means? A haunting somehow manages to create physical phenomena with a kind of ectoplasmic physical energy, usually drawn from the environment or living residents. These spirits are living in what is sometimes called 'an earthly vibration', because they are staying close to earth. In spirit this is usually a state of mind within the spirit that is 'haunting' a place.

One can compare Conan Doyle's poltergeist with the Fox sisters' poltergeist in Hydesville, also commencing with raps and knocks. Similarly bones of a murdered male were found buried in a cellar wall many years later. The man was a peddler and had tried to communicate the facts of his murder to the residents of the premises. Most likely, he was able to draw energy from the young Fox sisters because young teenage girls give off these natural energies during hormonal changes. Because of the delicate nature of poltergeists it is often intermittent and cannot always be controlled at will.

With regard to Physical Mediumship, Conan Doyle defended it as being a gift that should be treated carefully. He praised one of the greatest physical mediums, D.D. Home, and told how he was able to produce his phenomena in broad daylight, submitted to tests and in the presence of kings, queens, and statesmen.

Sometimes the smallest pieces of evidence were a revelation. Mediumship is very hard; do not be fooled when someone makes it appear easy. On occasions the evidence can be irrelevant or mundane. Sir Arthur experienced this in the same way it occurs today to most people. But every now and then, some piece of evidence comes through and hits its target.

Sir Arthur described two cases that made him take notice. The first concerned some mediumship using automatic writing that he received. Most of it was incorrect or written in generalisations, but when the huge ship Lusitania went down at sea, the early morning newspapers reported that there was no loss of life. However, the automatic writing medium said that "*it was going to be terrible, and would have a great influence on the war*". The ship lost 1198 passengers and this incident, of course, also helped bring America into the war. The medium also "*foretold the arrival of an important Telegram on a certain day, revealed the name of the deliverer, a most unlikely person*". The second piece of evidence was even more shocking to Sir Arthur. A lady died whom he had known in a provincial town. She was a chronic invalid and Morphia (morphine) was found next to her bed. He sat with Mr Vout Peters, a medium, who gave evidence to Sir Arthur that was vague or irrelevant. Suddenly however he said: "*There is a lady here. She is leaning upon an older woman. She keeps saying 'Morphia.' Three times she has said it. Her mind was clouded. She did not mean it. Morphia!*" The lady had accidentally killed herself with an overdose of morphine. Sometimes it's the little things that mean the most!

In 1918 Sir Arthur felt he should tell the world about his belief in the afterlife. The death and destruction from World War I provoked him to reveal the knowledge he had gained over many years. But it was upon *"hearing every day of the deaths of the flowers of our race in the first promise of their unfulfilled youth, seeing around one the wives and mothers who had no clear conception whither their loved ones had gone to"* that he knew this knowledge must be brought forward, to give some hope at least, and *"of guidance to the human race at the time of its deepest affliction"*.

Conan Doyle completed the first part of his book called *"The New Revelation"* in which he informed those people who considered the whole subject was the work of the devil. Doyle said, *"If this be the devil's work, one can only say that the devil seems to be a very bungling workman"*. To try and prove the existence of the afterlife is difficult. If mediumship is the 'work of the devil', he is making it look very difficult, especially in a world where the devil usually makes temptation effortless. A person should not be deterred from investigating because somebody says that it is forbidden or taboo. The same argument was used to persecute men of science, such as Galileo, Kepler, and Copernicus.

Conan Doyle was not Sherlock Holmes but he applied his methodology to come to the conclusion that life after death made perfect sense. I believe Sir Arthur was thinking like Sherlock Holmes when he investigated spiritualism. Although his character is fictional, Sherlock Holmes' investigative methods are entirely rational. Each case needs to be investigated thoroughly, and a logical conclusion should result from it, whether the answer is true or false. It was not one or two incidents that convinced him; just as I have not had one or two proofs either, but many proofs, coincidences, evidence, and physical materialisations. Little by little the evidence will 'materialise'. Be a seeker, not a doubter. For some, a lot of evidence is required, for others, a few evidential messages is sufficient. The rest of us are quite willing to believe that death is not the end but want the knowledge and philosophy. If we really want to find the truth our spirit guides will prepare the ground for us. Do not simply take my word for it or Sir Arthur's, or anyone else's word. The evidence really will come your way if you look for it.

[7] *Experiences in Spiritualism with D. D. Home*, by Lord Adare (Windham Thomas Wyndham-Quin, 4th Earl of Dunraven) Private print 1869, 2nd print by the SPR 1925

[8] Louis Jacolliot – Occult Science in India 1884.

Chapter Thirty Two

What is there to Fear?

Most of us have heard about séances, stories about ghosts, guardian angels and presumably, the topic of heaven and hell. But has any proof of the afterlife been presented to you throughout your life? Did some religious figure ever say that we have proof from our teachings that we live on after death?

The word 'occult' is derived from the Latin word *occultus,* meaning 'hidden'. It is also referred to as 'knowledge of the hidden'. To investigate your spirituality this has nothing to do with the occult, although many religious figures would have you believe otherwise. This book is not about promoting spiritualism or religion but it does advocate the simple '*Spiritual Philosophy'* that we survive death. You can go to any reliable medium and they will earnestly try to give you evidence of life after death. The occult topic has always been promoted as a frightening work of the devil. Mediums are not occultists. Most mediums accept that this term is used more with the darker elements of witchcraft. Mediums are conveyers of light, not darkness. They are not witches and they do not involve themselves in sorcery. They are just ordinary people with an extraordinary gift. People who ridicule or scorn mediums probably have a vested interest in preventing knowledge of the afterlife, otherwise why would they do it?

Looking at the topic of heaven and hell, the evidence provided by some of the notes left in Conan Doyle's wallet show that there are many regions of hell. These are physical and mental dimensions that we earn through actions and thoughts while living on earth. For example, if deeds are considered bad or evil, the result is that the vibration around your spirit body will match an equivalent vibrational dimension of 'thought' in the afterlife. Likewise, if you try to be a good person and you are loved, then a lighter vibration will surround your spirit. Thus, you go to a 'heavenly' dimension of like-minded beings. How is this 'revelation' translated into our current thinking from a religious point of view? We have been taught, or we may understand that if we commit sins, forgiveness might be attained on Earth. This may be done through prayer or perhaps sought through confession. If we followed our religious beliefs when we go to the afterlife we are supposed to be forgiven by an omnipotent being we call 'God'.

However with this there are a few misconceptions. The reality is that in the afterlife we are not actually 'forgiven' for our sins by anyone. Therefore no one person sitting in a confessional box, for example, wearing a frock and mechanically reciting a prayer of forgiveness can grant forgiveness. It probably makes some of us feel better afterward but the reality is that the vibration or aura that surrounds us does not lie. Any spirit that meets you in the spirit world can easily read your 'vibration'. They know exactly what type of person you are but they try not to make judgments because they too may have had flaws when they were on Earth.

Every action, deed, and thought we have, is creating our own heaven and hell in the afterlife. On earth our thoughts and deeds can create our own happiness or unhappiness, correct? We cannot lie to ourselves for all our faults and good deeds are known to us. Only you can forgive your own sins, not a religious figure. By some chance maybe we have not always been good, but we can make progress right now by trying to truly forgive ourselves for any misdeeds we have committed. Progression is open to all, no matter how dark the region is or what one might have done on while on Earth.

Once we pass over there is a spiritual life review of the mind, a point where we go through all the events in our lives and learn from our mistakes. It is termed a 'life review'. Earth is considered a hell region, even though sometimes it seems like heaven. The balance tends to be darker rather than lighter, with its poverty, war, injustice, materialism, oppression, torture, and torment.

If the reality of the afterlife was presented to all those who rule through fear and pain and they realised what their actions were creating for themselves, would they look at or behave differently in their lives? For example, I am referring to members of 'society', such as dictators, bullies, gang members, business leaders, religious zealots, ruthless politicians, and so on. Would they trust the explanations provided from a book? It is more likely they would listen to a departed person they trusted, who provided them with evidential proof about their existence on earth. They would really listen if a medium told them what they were actually thinking or divulged secrets only they knew. They may seem trivial but sometimes these are the most convincing proofs. People would be more aware of their actions and they might ask themselves: Am I being watched by my colleague or a Guardian Angel? If I do this what price am I going to pay?

A materialist is one who believes that we live our lives and become dust when we die. This person also believes that anything we do throughout our lives, whether it is good or bad, will have no bearing because death only brings blackness or extinction. These people will be in for a big shock. Materialists cause most of the problems in this world because they do not take any responsibility for their actions. Therefore they cheat, lie, abuse their positions, or destroy the environment by polluting our land and the oceans and worse. If they realised the harm they were causing to themselves and others perhaps life would be better for us all. We all need to make money, it runs our lives and the world, but should it be at any price?

Sir Arthur talked about Jesus Christ, his life and the message he left behind. Most of the messages we hear have to do with his death and resurrection, and not His wonderful life. Sir Arthur explained what the true reality of Christ's life was, as told by the spirit guides. He said, *"He came down upon it (earth) at a time of great earthly depravity - a time when the world was almost as wicked as it is now, in order to give the people the lesson of an ideal life. Then he returned to his own high station, having left an example which is still occasionally followed. That is the story of Christ, as spirits have described it. There is nothing here of Atonement or Redemption".* In addition to the message, Christ was also an exceptional medium. Did he not speak to his 'Father' or guides? Was he not a healer? Did he not have psychic abilities? I am referring to the evidential proof that Christ produced of life after death in his time. However, he is not the only one.

This is not an argument against religion; I am simply presenting the facts as told by Conan Doyle. Religion can be a great comfort for many people. Everything should be questioned. All I have written in this publication should also be questioned. Faith is not enough. What was relevant five hundred, a thousand or two thousand years ago, might not be relevant today. From where did the information in all these religious books come? Man or spiritual guides? If we received messages from the 'dead' over two thousand years ago, why can't we receive them today? The information received over many decades could have easily been clouded with prejudices. One should not forget that when a person dies it does not mean they become a sage or a saint. This is why we must question every message we get from spirit world. There are so many people in these spiritual dimensions who do not know the conditions of those in the spheres above, below, or adjacent to them.

We are more sophisticated and advanced as a race than previous generations. However, we still need to truly look at ourselves. In the current century there is a lot going on, a kind of 'catching-up'. I mean that we have progressed so quickly since the Industrial Revolution that we have neglected to develop our spiritual values. That is why we are searching for answers about life, God, the universe, and more. Perhaps technology will help us one day but at this moment, mediums can really help us to communicate with our loved ones on the other side. People should strive to develop their mediumistic abilities. Some people probably have natural abilities already but are frightened of them. Others will need to develop with the aid of their spirit guides. Mediumship requires an increase in sensitivity in your body. This can have quite disconcerting effects on your daily life such as emotional highs and lows resulting in mood changes. You might start picking up on people's feelings as well as their illnesses. As you start to develop this ability and subsequently produce evidence, you might at first feel a little frustrated. However, when you begin to give evidential proof to receivers and they can readily relate, it is the greatest feeling.

As you grow in sensitivity your guides will come closer and surround you with a feeling of love and warmth that is indescribable. You will experience a real sense of purpose in life and everything becomes much more interesting. The world will no longer be one dimensional because you are living within two dimensions, and possibly more. On occasion you will see cause and effect occurring. It is like having secret knowledge and at times you will be moulding events, rather than being swept along by them. While you may not feel that life is always under your control, at least you will know there are spirit friends who will never desert you, no matter how bad things might seem. For those who have suicidal thoughts this is not an escape, as they will still have the same conditions and feelings if they go through with it. Those who do succumb will still have to live through a purgatorial existence until their intended time on earth has been completed. However, it is best to confront all the challenges laid upon our path of life, no matter how difficult. Remember,

*"The Great Spirit will not give you a burden that your spirit cannot bear." - **Patrick McNamara.***

Epilogue

It is my hope that after reading *Conan Doyle's Wallet*, the reader will have a better understanding and acceptance that death is not the end of our life but a continuation in another form, a spirit body rather than a physical body. If you are not quite convinced perhaps you will at least consider that we can survive death in some way. Whether you agree or not with what Sir Arthur has imparted through me, the truth is that we have a spirit body that progresses into another world beyond our five senses.

The greatest thing about mediumship is that there will always be answers for those who are searching for proof. What Sir Arthur Conan Doyle has revealed through me is valid now and will remain in years to come. The best proof is the evidential proof from our spirit guides and loved ones that have crossed to the other side. Mediumship can provide this evidence now, something no other religious faiths have been able to do. Mediums simply ask you to believe and have faith. They should not be asking you questions during a reading, only if the evidence makes sense. Yes or no.

I would like to give personal advice to those people who have lost their loved ones. Sometimes it can take months, even years, before finding a medium who would provide them with the proof they need. I know some people may have travelled and spent a great deal of time and money trying to receive messages from loved ones in the spirit world. Our loved ones look down on us and feel our thoughts and emotions, they miss us, of course, but time moves differently for them and they know it won't be long before we are reunited forever. Time, progression and spirit are infinite.

And for those people who criticise mediums and psychics, or brand the paranormal as garbage, sometimes accusing us of making money from the grief of others, I would like to ask, "What is the price you would put on a message from your husband, wife, son, or daughter?"

I am not defending overpriced mediums to the rich and famous but if people want to pay them, it is their choice. I am not against high-profile international mediums that make a lot of money because generally they have earned their position. But, I do rally against the gross commercialism that some people use to establish mediumship as a business. Quite a few of these businesses are out for profit and not evidential proof of life after death. So I urge you to be wary of the evidence you get from them. Don't accept generalities, you need good evidential proof from those you are seeking. If you don't get your evidence, try a different approach, such as a recommendation or one-on-one contact, which is always better and usually less expensive.

While there are always a few con-artists, I will always defend dedicated mediums. Like those who may go out on a cold winter's night who may drive hundreds of miles to give evidence to someone anxiously awaiting an answer, and those who sometimes charge just enough to cover their travel expenses.

Don't give up if your message does not come through right away, as your loved ones will always be ready to contact you. Don't forget that your attitude also plays an important role. Negative or overwhelming grief in the presence of a medium can block the communication. It is not always the medium's fault. Relax, be positive, and let the evidence flow. Sometimes the evidence can be general; however, you might suddenly get some triumphant proof that makes everything worthwhile.

For people like Sir Arthur Conan Doyle, Sir William Crookes and Sir Oliver Lodge, it took the death of a loved one before they openly admitted their belief in the afterlife, or fully investigated the reality of the spirit world. We should not wait for the passing of someone special to search for the truth. Death is not the end and neither is birth the beginning. We are constantly developing our spirit, but we all move at different rates of progression.

The knowledge that we have now might be right for us at this moment but may not be applicable to another person. No one should despair for those who will not listen, as everyone will get there in the end. Nobody will be left behind and the philosophy for leading a spiritual life will reach everyone eventually, even if they are not willing to listen today.

Finally I leave you with the amusing words of Oscar Wilde on his deathbed when he said, "Either that wallpaper goes, or I go." But the last words will be Sir Arthur Conan Doyle's. He passed into sprit on July 7th 1930. In his final moments on earth, he lay there surrounded by his family, and just before he passed to spirit he whispered to his wife Jean, "You are wonderful".

"When you have eliminated the impossible, whatever remains, *however improbable*, must be the truth."

Appendix A

Famous People who believed in Spirits and the Afterlife.

Scientists

Sir Oliver Lodge: British physicist and pioneer of radio. He was one of the greatest scientists of the Victorian period. He sent the first radio signal before Marconi, from his college in Oxford. He wrote the book *Raymond* where he described his communication with his son, who died in World War I.

Sir William Crookes: British scientist, chemist and investigator of psychic phenomena. He was President of the Royal Society of Chemists. He discovered no less than six chemical elements including Thallium, and was the inventor of the cathode ray tube. He did repeated physical mediumship experiments with Florence Cook. He was a fellow founder of the Society for Psychical Research.

Dr Charles Richet: French scientist and Nobel Prize winner for the discovery of anaphylaxis. He was Professor of Physiology and Member of the Medicine and Academy of Science. He investigated a number of particular psychic phenomena including, psychokinesis, ectoplasm and telepathy.

Emmanuel Swedenborg: Swedish scientist and all-round hero, inventor, statesman, astronomer, and writer. He had prophetic visions and spiritual communications from the afterlife. He wrote many books about his experiences, as well as 150 works on seventeen sciences.

Thomas Edison: American Inventor. He invented the electric light bulb, and the phonograph. He believed in

271

the afterlife, and contemplated about how to invent a device for communication with those on the other side. He predicted that this would occur one day. In a deathbed vision his last words were, "It's very beautiful over there."

Sir J. J. Thompson: British scientist and Nobel Prize winner. He discovered the electron and gave credit to Sir William Crookes for his early work on sub-atomic investigations. He accepted that psychic phenomena existed.

John Logie Baird: British scientist and inventor of the television. He believed in the afterlife. He worked on a device to communicate with the afterlife through television.

Dr Alfred Russell Wallace: British Scientist and co-founder of the Theory of Evolution with Charles Darwin. He was an early pioneer in psychic research. He wrote about his psychic research and accepted that we survive death.

Professor Archie Roy: British Professor Emeritus of Astronomy in the University of Glasgow and Fellow of the Royal Society of Edinburgh, the Royal Astronomical Society and the British Interplanetary Society. He is a believer of life after death due to his many thorough investigations.

Sir William Barrett: Irish scientist and Professor of Physics at the Royal College of Science in Dublin. He was the founding member of both the British and American Societies for Psychical Research. He explored all aspects of the paranormal and the afterlife. His books and papers are classic works, standing the test of time as pillars for serious researchers of the paranormal.

Professor Brian David Josephson: British scientist and Nobel Prize winner for Physics. He is a retired professor at Cambridge University. He supports the objectivity of theoretical and the experimental evidence of the paranormal and life after death.

Professor William James: American scientist and Professor of Psychology at Harvard University. He was the founder member of the American Society for Psychical Research. He experimented with one of the great mediums, Lenora Piper. In Oxford 1909, he announced his firm conviction that "most of the phenomena of psychical research are rooted in reality."

Benjamin Franklin: American inventor, politician, author and statesman. He signed the American Declaration of Independence. He accepted the existence of the afterlife.

Dr Sigmund Freud: Czech psychiatrist. It was reputed that he saw "ghosts" during his childhood at the end of his bed. Although he suppressed his abilities he believed in telepathy and published the book *Psychoanalysis and Telepathy*.

Dr Carl Jung: Swiss psychologist and protégé of Dr Sigmund Freud, declared his belief in psychic phenomena, and attended séances with his cousin, who was a medium. He had a near-death experience which was "real and eternal" after which he declared, "The unconscious psyche believes in life after death."

Politicians

William Gladstone: British Prime Minister and member of Society for Psychical Research (SPR). Gladstone although a deeply religious man, he visited William Eglington, a famous medium, and posed questions of a confidential nature to him in Spanish, Greek, and French. Eglington, in turn, responded correctly to all of Gladstone's questions in these same languages and impressed Gladstone so much that he joined the SPR.

273

Lord Arthur Balfour: British Prime Minister and President of the Society for Psychical Research. He accepted Telepathy to be real and accepted the afterlife existed.

Sir Winston Churchill: British Prime Minister who believed and accepted the existence of the afterlife. It's known that he consulted a trance circle during World War II with other members of the establishment. He visited physical medium Helen Duncan in prison after she was arrested due over national security interests namely a warship sunk by the Nazi's. He also wrote about an encounter with a ghostly apparition in his library at Chartwell, his country retreat in England. During one of Winston Churchill's visits to the United States during World War II, he spent the night in the Lincoln Bedroom. Churchill retired late after relaxing in a long, hot bath while drinking a Scotch and smoking a cigar. He climbed out of the bath naked, except for his cigar, and walked into the adjoining bedroom. He couldn't believe his eyes when he saw Abraham Lincoln standing by the fireplace in the room, leaning on the mantle. The two men looked each other in the face, in seeming embarrassment, as Lincoln's apparition slowly faded away.

Abraham Lincoln: The 16th President of the U.S.A. He attended séances and believed in spiritualism. The spirit of Daniel Webster pleaded with Lincoln to follow through with his efforts to free the slaves. Medium J.B. Conklin conveyed a message to Lincoln from his close friend, Edward Baker, who had been killed at the battle of Ball's Bluff. He was reported to have received a trance communication with medium, Nettie Colburn Maynard at a very low point for the Union Army, which turned around the American Civil War. He was told to visit the battle front as a show of strength, which he did.

274

This result led to a huge morale boost and victory for the Union Army.

Ronald Reagan: The 40th President of the U.S.A. He and his wife Nancy consulted a psychic and astrologer on major decisions in the presidency. Joan Quigley became Nancy Reagan's astrologer after the two met on *The Merv Griffin Show.*

Hillary Clinton: Congresswoman and wife of former U.S.A. President Bill Clinton, consulted psychics and attended trance sessions purportedly with Eleanor Roosevelt. In 1995, during a séance with Jean Houston in the White House solarium, the spirits of Eleanor Roosevelt and Mahatma Gandhi reportedly spoke to her.

Woodrow Wilson: The 28th President of the U.S.A. was known to have sought the guidance of spirits for healing from famous trance medium, Edgar Cayce. Cayce reputedly advised Woodrow Wilson on the formation of the League of Nations.

George Washington: Wrote three prophetic visions he had for the United States including a prophetic vision of America's fate during the harsh winter of 1777 after retreating to Valley Forge. The prophecy was eventually written down by writer Wesley Bradshaw and is said to foretell of three great perils that would befall the republic, one was the Civil War.

Writers

Mark Twain: American writer and member of the Society for Psychical Research. He had premonitions as a young man and believed in telepathy. It was recorded that he witnessed apparitions on ghost investigations. He aggressively pursued those who fraudulently used the paranormal for financial gain.

Ernest Hemmingway: American writer and firm believer of the afterlife after describing his own near-death experience in his 1929 novel, *A Farewell to Arms*. "I felt myself rush bodily out of myself and out and out and out and all the time bodily in the wind. I went out swiftly, all of myself, and I knew I was dead and that it had all been a mistake to think you just died."

W B Yeats: Irish poet, playwright, and Nobel Prize winner. He deeply believed in life after death and the paranormal. He attended séances in Dublin and London. He investigated hauntings as a member of the Ghost Club in Britain. He advocated belief in the fairy kingdom, promoted Irish fairy mythology. His wife practiced automatic writing. Had a big interest in esoteric studies and mysticism and joined the Order of the Golden Dawn.

Dr Johnson: British poet, and writer. He spent an enormous amount of time investigating ghosts and the paranormal. His most famous investigation was the Cock Lane Ghost. He famously quoted "It is wonderful that six thousand years have now elapsed since the creation of the world, and still it is undecided whether or not there has been an instance of the spirit of any person appearing after death. All argument is against it, but all belief is for it."

Sir Walter Scott: British novelist and poet. He was deeply interested in the afterlife after having some paranormal experiences in his home, Abbotsford in Roxburghshire. Scott investigated reputed hauntings all over the Britain. His many novels include phantom encounters.

Arthur Koestler: British novelist, journalist and writer. He believed he had psychic abilities. He investigated hauntings and the paranormal. He founded the Chair of Parapsychology at Edinburgh University and established the Koestler Foundation to encourage the study of parapsychology.

Michael Bentine: British writer, comic, actor and Military Intelligence Officer. He enthusiastically wrote about his belief in the afterlife in many books. He was a Member of the Society for Psychical Research. He had psychic ability and saw many ghostly apparitions. He became an avid ghost hunter and paranormal investigator.

Lord Byron: British writer and poet, who was deeply interested in the paranormal and the afterlife. As a young man, he encountered a ghostly monk in Newstead Abbey, his family home. The monk was reputedly murdered by an ancestor, and when the spirit appeared, it heralded tragedy for the family. He called the presence "the Goblin Fryer."

Lewis Carroll: British novelist, poet, and mathematician, also known as Rev. Charles Lutwidge Dodson. He wrote *Alice in Wonderland*. He investigated the paranormal, especially ghostly hauntings, and telepathy. He was a Member of the Society of Psychical Research. In his poem "Phantasmagoria", he relates the amusing tale of a fledgling ghost assigned to haunt a house for the first time.

Daniel Defoe: British novelist, writer, and author of *Robinson Crusoe*. Extensively researched the afterlife and paranormal for his published work in 1720 "An Essay on the Reality of Apparitions". He anonymously wrote, due to witchcraft persecutions, a fictional pamphlet titled "The True Revelation of the Apparition of One Mrs Veal" in 1706.

Charles Dickens: British novelist and member of the Ghost Club of Britain. Although at times a sceptical person of the afterlife he exhaustively researched the paranormal and some of the more celebrated British hauntings, which inspired him to write some famous ghost stories, including his classic novel *A Christmas Carol*. Some of his other ghost stories included: *The Haunted Man, The Ghost in Master B.'s Room*, and *The Lawyer and the Ghost*. He was taught mesmerism by Dr Elliotson, practicing it on his wife, and famously tried to cure Madame La Rue of a nervous tic on a trip to Italy in 1884. He wrote about the phenomena of human combustion in *Bleak House*.

Edgar Allan Poe: American poet and author. He investigated spiritualism and mesmerism. His stories detailed communication with the afterlife. He attended the séances of the great medium Andrew Jackson Davis with Doctor Lyon, Bridgeport musician.

Other Notable People

Lord Dowding: Air Chief Marshall of Britain: masterminded the defeat of the Luftwaffe in World War II. He had no doubt about the continuation of the human personality. He wrote a book on his spiritualist beliefs titled *Many Mansions*. He left his London Mansion to the Spiritualist Association of Great Britain which is still used to promote mediumship today.

Arthur Findlay: The greatest writer on psychic research ever. His books *On the Edge of the Etheric* and *The Curse of Ignorance* are still ground-breaking and have never been rebutted by any sceptical observer. He donated his stately home and fortune to promoting his beliefs.

Dr Glen Hamilton: Physician and Member of Parliament (MP) in the Canadian government. Under strict laboratory conditions re-materialised people who had passed on. Observers present at his experiments included four other medical doctors, two lawyers and both an electrical and a civil engineer. Each of the witnesses stated strongly and unequivocally that, "time after time, I saw dead persons materialise."

Dr Edgar Mitchell: American Astronaut, Dr of Science. He was the sixth man to walk on the Moon with the Apollo 14 mission. He has spent thirty years investigating the paranormal. He established the Institute of Noetic Sciences.

General George Patton: American World War II General. He absolutely accepted reincarnation after having many personal reincarnation experience memories.

Joseph McMoneagle: American CIA Intelligence Officer. He was awarded the US Legion of Merit by the Military for his work on Psychic Intelligence remote viewing, proving that a person can detach their spirit body under certain conditions and travel to view locations anywhere in the world.

Laurence S. Rockefeller: American business magnate. He financially supported research into precognition, psycho kinesis, and the afterlife.

Henry Ford: American business magnate. He believed in reincarnation and financially supported investigations into the paranormal.

Dr Raymond Moody: American Doctor, Ph.D., MD. He was the foremost expert after spending twenty five-years investigating near-death experiences and out-of-body experiences. He wrote the classic book *Life after Life* where he describes his research. He is a convinced believer in life after death.

Professor Albert Einstein: German Scientist. He developed the Theory of Relativity and concept of space time. He wrote favourably about psychic process on telepathy research in the book *Mental Radio* by Upton Sinclair.

Plato: The great Greek philosopher. He revealed in his writings that the soul was separate from the body and survived death, where it continued in the spirit world. Plato understood that the actions of a person during his or her lifetime, and the way the soul interacts with the body, leave an impression on the soul, and affect what happens to the soul after it has left the body.

Bibliography

Arthur Ford's "Nothing So Strange" New York: Harper and Row, 1958

Borgia, Anthony, 'Life in the world unseen', Psychic Press, London 1954.

Boston Herald January 26th, 1925. Arthur Conan Doyle refutes Houdini.

Crookes, William, 'Experimental Investigation of a New Force' – Quarterly Journal of Science, July 1871.

Dr Carl A. Wickland – '30 Years Among the Dead', 1924

Desmond, Shaw, 'After Sudden Death', London, 1939.

Doyle, Arthur Conan, 'The New Revelation', London, 1918.

Edwards, Harry, 'The Mediumship of Jack Edwards', London 1978.

Findlay, Arthur, 'The Rock of Truth' London, 1933.

Findlay, Arthur, 'The Curse of Ignorance' Two Volumes, London. 1947.

Findlay, Arthur, 'The Psychic Stream' London, 1939.

Findlay, Arthur, 'On the Edge of the Etheric' London, 1931.

Gresham, William Lindsay, 'Houdini', 1961 p219 (Note about Jim Collins and ruler)

Houdini Harry, [Erich Weiss] 'The Unmasking of Robert-Houdin' 1908, New York, The Publishers Printing Co.

Lodge, Oliver, 'The Mode of Future Existence' Lecture paper presented in1933 at the Queens Hospital Annual, Birmingham.

Lodge, Oliver, 'Ether and Reality' Hodder and Stoughton, London, 1929.

Lodge, Oliver, 'The Survival of Man' London, 1909.

Lodge, Oliver, 'Raymond – Or Life and Death', New York, 1916.

Louis Jacolliot – Occult Science in India 1884

They Walked Among Us: by Louie Harris, Psychic Press, 1980.

Experiences in Spiritualism with D. D. Home, by Lord Adare Private print 1869, 2nd print by he SPR 1925

Maynard, Nettie Colburn – Was Abraham Lincoln a Spiritualist?

Moody, Raymond A, Jr, 'Life after Life', Mockingbird Press, 1975.

Polidoro, Massimo, 'Final Séance', New York, 2001.

Psychic Discoveries Behind the Iron Curtain, Sheila Ostrander & Lynn Schroeder, Bantam Books, U.S.A., p. 224; also read chapter on 'Healing with Thought', p. 293.)

Roll, Michael, 'The Scientific Proof of Survival After Death'.

http://www.cfpf.org.uk

Wickland, Carl A, 'Thirty Years amongst the Dead', Spiritualist Press, 1978.

Zammit, Victor, 'A Lawyer Presents the Case for the Afterlife'

http://www.victorzammit.com

Printed in Great Britain
by Amazon